DATE	BORROWER'S NAME
NOV 7 1983	

D1072226

© THE BAKER & TAYLOR CO.

Conceptual issues in psychology

Conceptual issues in psychology

Elizabeth R. Valentine

Lecturer in Psychology
Bedford College London

London
GEORGE ALLEN & UNWIN
Boston   Sydney

George Allen & Unwin (Publishers) Ltd,
40 Museum Street, London WC1A 1LU, UK

George Allen & Unwin (Publishers) Ltd,
Park Lane, Hemel Hempstead, Herts HP2 4TE, UK

Allen & Unwin Inc.,
9 Winchester Terrace, Winchester, Mass 01890, USA

George Allen & Unwin Australia Pty Ltd,
8 Napier Street, North Sydney, NSW 2060, Australia

First published in 1982
© E. R. Valentine

British Library Cataloguing in Publication Data

Valentine, Elizabeth R.
    Conceptual issues in psychology.
1. Psychology—Philosophy
I. Title
150'.1   BF121

ISBN 0-04-150079-2
ISBN 0-04-150080-6 Pbk

Library of Congress Cataloging in Publication Data

Valentine, Elizabeth R.
    Conceptual issues in psychology.
Includes index.
1. Psychology—Philosophy.   I. Title.
BF38.V34 1982   150'.1   82-8683
ISBN 0-04-150-079-2   AACR2
ISBN 0-04-150-080-6 (pbk.)

Set in 10 on 11 point Imprint by Alan Sutton Publishing Limited, Gloucester
and printed in Great Britain
by Biddles Ltd, Guildford, Surrey

To:

R.B., R.S.K., R.P. and J.D.V.,
from whom I have learned the things I value most.

'There is no escape from philosophy. The question is only whether a philosophy is conscious or not, whether it is good or bad, muddled or clear. Anyone who rejects philosophy is himself unconsciously practising a philosophy.' – Karl Jaspers

'In Russell's words, "All human knowledge is uncertain, inexact and partial." This conclusion is a sobering one, but no education is worth anything that does not impart it.' – D. J. O'Connor

Preface

The aim of this book is to provide a broad treatment of the main conceptual issues in psychology: to explain what the problems are, to outline the main approaches which have been taken to them and to indicate their relative merits and demerits, although my hope is that the reader will ultimately reach his own conclusions. The chief intention has been to provide a basic framework to guide further reading in an area which is often found difficult by students.

Chapter 1 provides an overview of most of the topics treated. The first part of the book is concerned with the more substantive philosophical questions such as free will and determinism, consciousness and the relation between body and mind, and includes a consideration of ways in which empirical work in psychology may be able to throw light on these perennial problems which have interested scholars and laymen alike. These lead on to the methodological problems of introspection and sources of artifact in experimentation. The second half of the book is concerned with different theoretical approaches and types of explanation within psychology such as behaviourism, reductionism, computer modelling and purposive explanation. These are overviewed in Chapter 8 and dealt with in more detail in the subsequent chapters.

The book is aimed primarily at the student of psychology who, it is to be hoped, will emerge with a more sophisticated understanding of the theoretical construction of his subject and in a position to give a balanced account of some of the controversies about its nature which have arisen both from within and from outside the discipline. Insofar as these raise fundamental issues about the nature of man and of conceptualisation, it is likely also to be of interest to non-psychologists.

Elizabeth R. Valentine
January 1982

Acknowledgements

I am indebted to my parents for financing my education and to members of staff in the departments of philosophy and psychology at University College London who first interested me in the philosophy of psychology. Since then generations of students at the North East London Polytechnic, the City of London Polytechnic and Bedford College London have pointed out errors in my thinking. Robert Bigio encouraged me to rely on my own judgment, without which this particular venture would have been given up long before it was half started. Many colleagues and friends have provided criticism, advice and encouragement. Some have commented on earlier proposals and/or read drafts of chapters: Mary Anne Coate, Larry Currie, Harry Fisher, Brian Foss (who read the whole manuscript), Don Houtman, Peter Kelvin (who acted as reviewer-in-chief), Susan Khin Zaw, Richard Kirby, Philip Levy, John Radford, John Valentine, Norman Wetherick and an anonymous reviewer. Others racked brains and searched bookshelves for elusive pieces of information. They include: Sheila Chown, Margaret Christie, Rob Farr, Ann Jarrett, Luke Kartsounis, Andrew Kirby, Monica Lawlor, Chris McManus, John Nicholson, Mary Pickersgill, Dave Swann, David Ward and John Wilding. Friends and relatives tolerated absences of body and/or mind, asked delicate questions and listened to interminable answers. At George Allen and Unwin, John Churchill, Roger Jones, Miles Jackson and Geoffrey Palmer have given friendly advice and shown remarkable patience. Valerie White typed and retyped chapters speedily and immaculately. I am grateful to them all.

I am also grateful to the following individuals and organisations for allowing the reproduction of material in this book:

Figure 2.1 adapted by permission of the publisher and author, copyright © 1970 by the American Psychological Association; Routledge and Kegan Paul (Figs 4.1, 4.2); Table 6.1 reprinted by permission of the publisher and author, copyright © 1969 by the American Psychological Association; Figure 8.1 reprinted from *Theories in contemporary psychology*, M. H. Marx and F. E. Goodson (eds) (Fig. 1, page 243. Direction of interaction between theory and data in four modes of theory construction), copyright © 1963, 1976 by Macmillan Publishing Co., Inc.; The Mental Health Research Institute (*Behavioral Science*) (Fig. 9.1); Professor E. Galanter (Fig. 9.2).

Contents

1

Psychology as a science

Is psychology different from other sciences? Many of its theoretical problems are based on such a belief. What particular problems does the nature of its subject matter raise and how may they be resolved? In this chapter we shall introduce a number of issues that will be dealt with in more detail later in the book and indicate the main approaches to be taken to them. Our first concern will be to consider psychology as science and what assumptions underlie such treatment. For convenience, these may be divided into: (a) metaphysical – fundamental views about the nature of the subject matter, (b) theoretical – relating to the nature of scientific theories, and (c) methodological – pertaining to observation and experimentation.

Metaphysical assumptions

The scientific treatment of psychology assumes that its subject matter, *the behaviour of Man and other animals, is similar in relevant respects to the subject matter of other sciences,* namely, other natural phenomena. This aspect of Man is indeed one of the most recently added areas of scientific investigation, partly due to theological objections: it was formerly considered sacred and not appropriate subject matter for science. (For the history of, and rationale for, the dichotomy between Man, as a possessor of a soul and reason, and subhuman animals, whose behaviour is guided by instinct, see Beach (1955).) This dichotomy was challenged by Darwin's assertion of continuity between Man and subhuman species, which led to the 'brutalisation of Man' and the 'humanisation of animals' (Peters 1953).

An important respect in which this similarity must be assumed is that of **determinism,** which implies that behaviour occurs in a regular, orderly manner which is predictable in principle. This appears to raise a difficulty for free will (how can a person be 'free' if his behaviour is completely determined?) and similarly for moral responsibility (how can people be held responsible for their actions or praise and blame be apportioned?). Possible resolutions of this dilemma will be discussed in Chapter 2, where it will be argued that the obverse of determinism is randomness, that free will may require rather than preclude determinism (the issue becoming one of the nature rather than the existence of determination) and that determinism does not imply compulsion, coercion or any mysterious force.

Determinism does imply *predictability,* at least in principle though not necessarily in practice. It is interesting to speculate as to whether our failures to predict are due to lack of skill on our part or the inherent nature of the subject matter. One successful prediction does not imply determinism (one might predict correctly by chance) but repeated successful prediction does imply an underlying regularity.

There are, however, a number of difficulties here, namely, areas of unpredictability. One of these is the possibility of the falsification of predictions (which has sometimes been used as an argument in favour of, or at least a test of, free will). The process of making a prediction may be subject to interfering effects which invalidate it. Attempts to take these into account lead to an infinite regress. A similar difficulty arises from Gödel's theorem, which demonstrates that within some consistent systems of logic there are propositions which can be seen to be true but which are not provable within the system. Neither of these, it will be argued, endanger determinism but both suggest that there are limits to the possible completeness of descriptions.

A discovery in quantum mechanics, namely, Heisenberg's uncertainty principle, threw doubt on the universality of determinism: according to this at the level of sub-atomic physics there are certain conjugate properties such as the position and momentum of a particle that cannot be simultaneously determined. Thus, there is some evidence for indeterminism in some aspects of the universe. The implications of this micro-level for the macro-level of human behaviour are, however, remote and obscure to say the least.

The possibility of prediction raises the possibility of *control,* and the consequent ethical problems of deciding who does the controlling, frequently held up against Skinner's Utopia (Skinner 1948, 1971). In a symposium with Rogers (1956) the latter points out that science, and Skinner, must presuppose values. Science can investigate the determinants and effects of values and hence may provide knowledge relevant to their selection and implementation (cf. Day 1976) but it cannot itself determine what they shall be (see also Heather 1976, who argues forcefully against the notion that psychology is value free).

A fundamental problem in the philosophy of psychology has

been whether laws of a different nature from those which apply to inorganic matter are required for the explanation of the behaviour of organic phenomena. It is unlikely that this can be solved until further advances have been made in the philosophy of biology. Generally, science has adopted a **mechanistic model** which enables the prediction of future events on the basis of antecedent conditions and assumes the universal applicability of causal laws. (It is worth noting in this connection, however, that modern physics has advanced beyond causal explanations. Psychology has frequently sought to ape outdated models from other sciences.) There are a number of features of the behaviour of organisms that have raised doubts about the appropriateness of the mechanistic model. One is purposiveness, essential to survival, which involves flexibility, sensitivity to consequences and the direction of behaviour towards goals; this has tempted explanation by reference to future events. On first sight it looks as though purposive and causal explanations are diametrically opposed and, indeed, many philosophers have taken the view that actions are intentional and fundamentally different from movements or happenings. Much heat has been generated on this question. We shall argue that the two types of explanation are compatible but different. Indeed, purposive phenomena depend on mechanistic ones. It can thus be argued that the truth of a mechanistic account is a necessary but not a sufficient condition for the truth of a purposive one. Purposive explanations are discussed in Chapter 12 and the use of cybernetic models in the explanation of behaviour in Chapter 10.

This intentionality of behaviour leads on to the issue of consciousness. What treatment it should be afforded in psychology and its relation to behaviour are considered in Chapter 4, and its relation to physiological processes as an aspect of the mind–body problem in Chapter 3. One particularly thorny issue is whether conscious processes should properly be assigned causal efficacy. This view, often labelled 'mentalism', has not found much favour amongst psychologists for a variety of reasons: (a) the difficulty of operationalisation (i.e. specifying observations that would be relevant to the truth of statements about a concept), (b) the difficulty of independent identification of mental states and resulting circularity of explanations in these terms, and (c) the successful prediction of behaviour without recourse to conscious states, though this does not preclude the possibility of alternative explanations in terms of mental states. Double aspect theory, according to which the mental and physical are two aspects of the same underlying reality, will be considered the most acceptable solution to the mind–body problem.

A general assumption held in varying degrees of strength by

scientists concerns the relation between different sciences. Many would agree that sciences can be arranged in a hierarchical order according to the size of unit or level of analysis, e.g. it might be crudely said that sociology deals at the level of groups, psychology at the level of individuals, physiology with parts of individuals, biochemistry at the intra-cellular level and physics at the molecular. Hence, what is relatively molecular for a higher level science is relatively molar for a lower level science (compare, for example, a muscle twitch for psychology and physiology). The question arises as to what the relation between these different level descriptions is or should be. **Reductionism** is the view that higher level descriptions can be reduced to lower level descriptions without loss of meaning. Thus, according to this, in due course psychology could be reduced to physiology, and the former dispensed with. There is a covert assumption that lower level descriptions are more fundamental and hence preferable. **Emergence** is the opposite view that higher level descriptions are not reducible to lower level ones. The assumptions underlying reduction and the whole issue of the relation of psychology to physiology are discussed in Chapter 11. It will be argued that, as in the case of the relation of purposive to mechanistic descriptions, psychology and physiology describe different aspects of phenomena and hence are complementary, that strict reduction entailing logical identity is untenable because psychological and physiological descriptions have different meanings, and that empirical reduction which requires the establishment of bridging laws seems unlikely.

Theoretical assumptions

Many of the characteristics of scientific laws raise potential problems for the subject matter of psychology.

A first requirement is that of *systematicity*. At the very least science must be a coherent body of knowledge. The complexity of psychological subject matter, notably the diversity and likely inter-active nature of relevant variables promises trouble for psychology, a promise that has been amply fulfilled. Grünbaum (1952), how-ever, has argued that the subject matter of other sciences such as physics is hardly simple, and may have seemed as complex as that of psychology at the time of its inauguration. It is unlikely that psychology can rely on youth to account for its lack of progress. Comparison with biochemistry is enough to suggest that the malaise goes deeper.

One such cause may be related to another characteristic of scientific laws, that of *generality*. It is generally accepted that scientific laws are unrestricted in space and time. A glance at typical psychological theoretical statements indicates that this ideal is seldom met with. Too often these statements refer to specific times and places. Of course this is a matter of degree: all statements are restricted to a greater or lesser extent, but the scientific ideal is that this should approach the latter rather than the former. The failure probably reflects a greater interest on the part of investigators in the content rather than what might be called the construction of behaviour. Many psychologists have failed to realise that, as scientists, their concern must be with the generalities of behaviour. As previously noted, a prime characteristic of behaviour is modifiability. From this it follows that psychological science can never be concerned with the content of behaviour (because this must necessarily vary) but only with the principles of adaptation. This puts it squarely in the realm of biological science. The sooner this is realised and attempts to ape either physical science on the one hand or so-called social science on the other, and the example of Aristotle and Piaget rather than say Newton or Hull followed, the better. There is room for social science – the empirical investigation of social phenomena – but it is claimed here that this is a pursuit of an entirely different kind.

Another possible challenge to generality comes from the conflicting demand to recognise the uniqueness of the individual. Since the movement of *Verstehen* psychology in 19th-century Germany, there have been cries to understand the individual rather than predict behaviour in general. It is frequently said that more is to be learned about human behaviour by studying literature rather than psychology. A comparison of idiographic and nomothetic approaches, which focus on the particular and the general respectively, and encompass differences in subject matter, methods and explanations, is the topic of Chapter 14. They probably largely reflect differences in aims: empathic understanding as against deductive, predictive explanation, and in application they may be complementary. As far as science goes, however, nomothesis must be the rule of the day. If a clinical method works it must be covertly nomothetic and if truly unique it could not be communicated (cf. Holt 1962). Nevertheless, there can be a scientific study of individuals.

Since, if not before, Popper's (1959) epoch-making work, the hallmark of scientific hypotheses has been testability, in this case falsifiability (further discussed in Ch. 7). This has raised problems for psychology because of the inherent difficulty in operationalising its concepts. Most of its area of interest is not directly observable. Indeed, Popper was led to formulate his demarcation principle largely as a result of noting the inadequacies in this respect of the psychological theories of Freud and Jung. The whole question of the relation of theoretical constructs to the evidence for them is thus a central one in psychology and discussed in Chapter 9.

Methodological assumptions

There may well be no definitive characteristics of science and, indeed, if there were they would probably change from one time to another. Strictly, 'science' means 'knowledge' but what it has come to mean in the modern western world is knowledge acquired as a result of employing empirical methods. If there is any one thing that characterises it more than anything else it is probably the empirical method. Other pursuits have been systematic, such as Greek cosmology, but we would not call them science. **Empiricism** involves checking things for oneself by appeal to sense experience as opposed to reliance on accepted authority or tradition or opinion; the criterion of truth becomes one of correspondence with the facts rather than logical coherence with the rest of the body of knowledge. Typically it involves observation, measurement and experimentation. In some sciences, such as astronomy and geology, only observation and measurement are possible but usually experimentation is regarded as the characteristic of science *par excellence*. There are some difficulties in the way of experimentation in psychology, as we shall see below, and it may be more akin to geology than has been generally recognised. The possibility of applying any of these three procedures to psychological subject matter has been doubted by many.

Observation presents problems for psychology on account of the previously mentioned fact that most of what is of interest, that which is essentially psychological: thoughts, feelings and the springs of action, is not open to direct observation. Hence, as indicated above, almost all psychological statements must be inferential. I would claim that this is true of all sciences but the gap between data and theory is probably greater and the connection looser in psychology than in other sciences. The issue of privacy will be taken up in Chapter 5, where it will be argued that all scientific statements are based on observations of private experiences, and that the distinction between subjective and objective is not as clear cut as at first supposed, and is ultimately a matter of degree.

Another factor which militates against objectivity results from the **reflexivity** of psychology. Not only is it the case that the observer and the observed are often members of the same species, but also that actually doing psychology constitutes part of its subject matter. This means at the very least that a psychologist's theories must be self-referring in the sense of explaining his own behaviour, as Oliver and Landfield (1963) point out. Bannister (1968) has used this as an argument for the non-reducibility of psychology to physiology (see Ch. 11). Apart from these theoretical considerations there are methodological implications. It has now become clear that neither the observer nor the observed are passive, non-interactive organisms in the experimental situation. The fact that observation necessarily interferes with what is observed, first discovered in physics, has now become the subject of experimentation in psychology with the recognition that the experiment is itself a social situation. This work is treated in Chapter 6.

Dualistic thought would suggest that quantifiability was the exclusive prerogative of the physical. Kant (1781) held that observation could be applied to psychological phenomena but that measurement and experimentation were impossible. However, since the latter part of the 19th century, advances in the *measurement* of psychological or mental characteristics have progressively been made and the grounds for such a belief gradually eroded. In 1861, Fechner published psychophysical methods, in the vain belief that they solved the mind–body problem. They did, however, provide methods for establishing functions relating psychological values or reported sensations to physical values of stimuli, though these have since been superseded. Ebbinghaus, coming on a copy of Fechner's *Elemente der Psychophysik,* was spurred to similar achievement in devising ways of measuring memorial associations. The turn of the century saw the beginning of attempts to measure intellectual ability, or at least performance, with the Binet–Simon intelligence scale, and Galton's predominantly physical measures and development of percentile ranks and correlation. From these sprang the whole field of psychometrics and factor analysis. Scaling focusses the difficulty of measurement in psychology. One of the central questions is the arbitrariness of the scale: to what extent can the values be said to reflect fundamental realities and relations and to what extent are they a function of theoretical constructs? For further discussion of this topic see, for example, Coombs, Dawes and Tversky (1970).

Herbart (1824) believed that observation and measurement could be applied to psychology but not experimentation; Wundt (1862), the first experimental psychologist proper, thought that experimental methods could only be applied to what he considered lower order processes: thinking, judgment and language were too socially conditioned to be similarly treated. Consistent with what was said above, it is probably the case that empirical investigation of social phenomena is possible, but that experimentation in the sense of isolating variables with the purpose of identifying causal factors is probably not because it is virtually impossible to implement sufficient *control*. There are a number of reasons why this is so: the number of variables, their interaction and the history of the organism.

One reason results from the adaptability of organisms. Behaviour is a function of the past history of the organism and can only be explained by reference to it. Only the blinkered would still fail to acknowledge that behaviour is not predictable on the basis of the observable, external physical stimuli but only on the basis of the meaning of these stimuli for the organism (cf. Underwood's (1963) distinction between the nominal and the functional stimulus). In addition, there are practical and ethical limitations to the amount of control that is possible. Despite transgressions in this direction, there are limits to noxious stimuli that can be inflicted on subjects. Deprived environments and brain damage have to be taken advantage of rather than created.

In conclusion, psychology does have particular problems but generally these represent differences in degree rather than kind from those of other sciences. Most are capable of resolution to a greater or lesser extent.

2

Determinism and free will

What is meant by free will?

It was noted in Chapter 1 that one of the presuppositions of
psychological science is determinism (the view that events occur in
an orderly manner: given a full description of the preceding situation the succeeding can in principle be predicted) and that this
appears to conflict with the notion of free will. How can responsibility for actions be maintained if they are determined by genetic
make-up and environmental experience? As psychology progresses,
knowledge of factors which determine behaviour increases.

But first it must be decided what is, or could be, meant by free
will. Part of the problem is that it is not at all easy to give a
coherent account. One possibility might be to suppose that what is
meant by an act of free will is that it is *uncaused*. But surely this
cannot be what is intended if it is assumed that the alternative to
determinism is randomness. Rather than *no* cause, what the libertarian, as the defender of free will is sometimes called, wants is
special causation. Support for a phenomenological distinction
between automatic, and willed or intentional motor responses
comes from the reports of Penfield's (1938) patients who described
cases where their arm seemed to be moved passively and cases
where they felt they were initiating the action themselves.

We must then ask what the nature of this special causation might
be. The gist of what is required is that the person is in some way an
active agent rather than merely a passive responder. Are cases of
free will those where the action is *preceded by a period of deliberation* and accompanied by a special feeling, an act of will or, as
William James (1890) called it, a 'fiat'? (James went on to analyse
this in terms of an effort of attention.) There are a number of
problems with this interpretation. One is that these cases may be
the exception rather than the rule: there may be others which we
would want to include as instances of free will but which are not
preceded by this special act of deliberation or will. More seriously,
there is no *a priori* reason why this act of deliberation should serve
a causal function. (Indeed, there are difficulties in supposing that
mental events can be the causes of non-mental events, see Ch. 3.)

There are some reasons for believing that subjective experiences may be deceptive. Perhaps they are best regarded as aspects of the process. They only appear more important because they are available to consciousness. The relations of experience to behaviour and physiology are problems central to the philosophy of psychology and discussed further in Chapters 3 and 4. As O'Connor (1971) points out, it seems that the libertarian cannot establish his view consistently with what is known about the working of the human nervous system. He can do so only by postulating a kind of cause with which we are totally unfamiliar and for whose existence we have no independent evidence. In the words of Karl Pearson (1892), 'Will as the first cause of a sequence of motions explains nothing at all; it is only a limit at which very often our power of describing a sequence abruptly terminates.'

One way of distinguishing how special causes supposedly typical of cases of free will differ from other causes might be along the lines of Spinoza's (1677) distinction, within a thoroughgoing determinist system, of two types of determination: internal and external. The latter type is inferior, the result of accidental contingencies and in modern terminology would be described in terms of conditioning (cf. Reeves 1965). The former is superior, logically determined, rational, acting in accordance with one's character or 'conatus' – the force according to which each individual persists in its own being or essence. This is in accord with much of what goes under the name of striving for authenticity in current psychotherapy, and with the view that acts we would call 'free' are moderately predictable: they lie somewhere between random (zero predictability) on the one hand and rigidity (perfect predictability) on the other. The 'free' person is not dictated to by the demands of the environment but acts consistently with his character.

This bears some similarity to the view known as **soft determinism** (see pp. 18–19), according to which all acts are determined but not all are constrained. Free acts on this view are those *free from coercion* or compulsion. For example, stepping out of a window at gun point might be said to be constrained and not free in the sense in which the same action in the absence of the gun might be said to be.

However, this is unlikely to satisfy the extreme, hard-liner libertarian, or the man in the street, who would probably maintain that what is required for free will is the possibility that the agent *could have done otherwise*, the situation remaining the same. The trouble with this interpretation, I think, is that it is untestable. It can never be known whether the person might have acted differently in the same circumstances, particularly as circumstances are never exactly repeated. What is known of the psychology of choice and decision-making leads to the surmise that it is unlikely.

As Seaborn Jones (1968) has pointed out, 'the only situations which are philosophically interesting for the student of the "will" are situations of conflict'. This suggests another interpretation of freedom, namely, *consistency between desire and action*. Presumably this is the meaning underlying the theological phrase 'whose service is perfect freedom' (*Book of common prayer*). We may note, extending Rogers (1951), that consistency may be attained by modification of either: if behaviour cannot be altered, perhaps attitude may be. I take this to be what is intended by oriental philosophy, which advocates acceptance (see, for example, Krishnamurti 1956).

Another possible criterion for distinguishing free from unfree acts would be to identify them as intentional or *voluntary* (coughs to attract someone's attention can be distinguished from those that result from a tickle in the throat). Such behaviour might be characterised as goal-directed, sensitive to consequences and involving some internal representation of the goal state inside the organism, which initiates, guides and terminates the sequence of behaviour in question. According to Kimble and Perlmuter (1970) the 'classical' theory of volition contains the following three notions:

(a) voluntary behaviour is always *learned,*
(b) a voluntary act begins with the *idea* of the response to be performed, and
(c) a *comparator mechanism* exists which monitors the response so that its present state can be related to the image that initiated it. It guides the response and also provides a stop mechanism or exit rule.

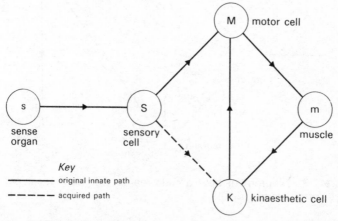

Figure 2.1 Diagram of voluntary behaviour (after James 1890, and Kimble & Perlmuter 1970).

James (1890) gave the following analysis of voluntary behaviour. 'When a particular movement, having once occurred in a random, reflex or involuntary way, has left an image of itself in the memory, then the movement can be desired again, proposed as an end, and deliberately willed.' Voluntary movements are secondary because they depend on knowledge of previous performance. According to James they depend on an anticipatory image of the movement's sensible effects, resident kinaesthetic and immediate, or remote (see Fig. 2.1). There is a tendency for these to become more remote with time. James' diagram of how a child learns voluntarily to avoid a flame is reproduced in Figure 2.2. James claimed that the anticipatory image is often sufficient and ideo-motor activity the norm, i.e. thoughts automatically become actions unless there is a conflicting thought or motor inertia. The classical theory was also expressed by Buchanan (1812) (who described a voluntary act as 'an acquirement, made at the expense of much labor', consisting in 'the association of a muscular action, with the energetic conception of that action and a predominating desire to perform it . . . In every process of volition then we discover three principal and essential parts: an idea of some action to be performed; a desire of performing it; and ultimately the action itself'), Ziehen (1898) and Sechenov (1935) (who believed that voluntary behaviour is made conscious through the mechanism of kinaesthetic feedback).

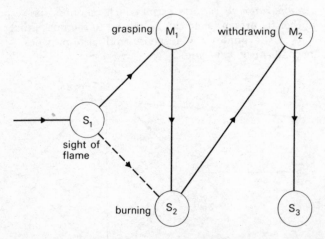

Figure 2.2 Diagram of how a child learns voluntarily to avoid a flame (after James 1890).

Kimble and Perlmuter criticise the classical theory on the grounds that it ignores motivation and attention and that feedback is not necessary. In their support they quote the deafferentation experiments by Taub *et al.* (1966), which demonstrate that voluntary acts can be acquired in the absence of sensory afference from the responding limb. This is not to say that feedback does not normally play an important role, as experiments on augmentation and distortion (e.g. delay) show. A similar line is taken by Bindra (1976) who argues that stimulus control provides a sufficient basis for explaining the development of voluntary acts. His view is that the basis of a voluntary act lies not, as William James thought, in the conditioned excitation of the central representation of that *act,* but in the conditioned excitation of the central representation of the *stimulus configuration* that is effective in activating the act assembly for the act.

Kimble and Perlmuter go on to distinguish voluntary behaviour as learned, inhibitable, preceded by an idea, and involving a comparator mechanism, from involuntary behaviour as automatic, unconscious, unintentional, susceptible to interference by attention, and independent of consequences. Voluntary and involuntary eyeblinks can be distinguished in terms of their form and latency (Kimble 1964, Grant 1968). The conditions suggested for involuntary behaviour to become voluntary are: the existence of supporting voluntary behaviour, exclusive attention to the desired response and ignorance of others which leads to increased differentiation, and verbalisation as an initial aid. Involuntary behaviour may develop from voluntary, becoming unconscious, unattended (attention actually interfering), not deliberately intended and free of direct motivational control. Studies of conditioned instrumental responding (eyeblink, finger press and vocalisation) serve as simple examples of automated behaviour, and are characterised by: (a) relative independence of consequences (as shown by relative resistance to extinction), (b) prompt occurrence without motivational and/or intentional intervention (as shown by short latencies), and (c) there is some evidence that circumstances which call attention to automatised responses inhibit them (Kimble & Perlmuter, 1970). (See also the discussion of teleological explanation in Ch. 12.)

Noble (personal communication) has suggested *ability to falsify a prediction about one's behaviour,* once informed of it, as a test of free will. Indeed, this possibility raises doubts about the feasibility of determinism (see pp. 16–17). My view is that this merely complicates the issue and requires that hypotheses be made both about what the person will do if informed of the prediction and about what he will do if not informed.

Mackay (1960 *et seq.*) has sought justification for the subjective conviction of freedom in the logical peculiarity of propositions which are not universally valid because their truth depends on who is believing them. A prediction that would be invalidated by informing the agent of it is a case in point. Mackay thinks that such propositions are logically indeterminate for the agent, in that no prior specification exists that has a well founded unconditional claim to everyone's assent. It is doubtful, however, whether this grants freedom in anything but a peculiar sense.

ARGUMENTS IN FAVOUR OF FREE WILL

'We know our will is free, and there's an end on't.' This statement, attributed to Dr Samuel Johnson by Boswell, expresses the argument for free will based on *subjective impression*. It is hard to deny but the trouble with it is that subjective certainty is no guarantee of truth, a point which has been clear since the time of Descartes. The phenomena of dreams and post-hypnotic suggestion are instances where convictions are invalidated by other evidence.

The subjective impression of free will is, however, a legitimate topic of investigation for psychology. Its determinants and effects can be studied. Mandler and Kessen (1974) suggest that belief in free will develops with age (it is a mark of maturity to delay decision) and is more common in cultures that demand explanations for action, responsibility and personal efficiency. In their view it is caused partly by the post-decision perception of choices. Bindra (1976) argues that conditioned sensation of the consequences of action is the basis of the subjective experience of volition, rather than being involved in its production as William James thought. Mandler and Kessen conclude that free will, though an illusion, is a beneficial one. Other areas of relevant empirical research include locus of control and self-esteem.

The other main argument in favour of free will is from *moral responsibility*. The apportioning of praise and blame, reward and punishment, appears to be premissed on the possession of free will. If we are not in control of our actions how can we be held responsible for them? Indeed, James (1890) opted in favour of belief in freedom of the will on ethical rather than psychological grounds. The notion of responsibility may require free will but administration of reward and punishment does not. As Skinner (1971) has pointed out, the latter is compatible with a deterministic system. The aim merely shifts from the evaluation to the modification of behaviour.

ARGUMENTS AGAINST FREE WILL

The first problem facing a proponent of free will is the *difficulty of giving a coherent account* of the concept, which is adequately attested by the length of the foregoing discussion.

The second problem is that of *inconsistency with science.* The progress of science, premissed on determinism, and all that is known about the world leads to a belief in the doctrine of determinism. However, it is not much easier to give a coherent account of determinism, a question to which we now turn.

What is meant by determinism?

O'Connor (1971) distinguishes metaphysical from scientific determinism, the former being independent of human knowledge, the latter dependent on it. The argument for metaphysical determinism he states as follows:

(a)   every macroscopic physical event has a cause;
(b)   every human action is a macroscopic physical event;
(c)   therefore, every human action is caused;
(d)   any event that is caused could not have happened otherwise than it did;
(e)   therefore, no human action could have happened otherwise than it did.

Metaphysical determinism allows the possibility that the human will is not free but that we could never know this.

As a statement of scientific determinism, Laplace (1820) is quoted:

> We ought then to regard the present state of the universe as the effect of its antecedent state and the cause of the state that is to follow: An intelligence, knowing at a given instant of time, all things of which the universe consists, would be able to comprehend the actions of the largest bodies of the world and those of the lightest atoms in one single formula, provided his intellect were sufficiently powerful to subject all data to analysis; to him, nothing would be uncertain, both past and future would be present to his eyes. The human mind in the perfection it has been able to give astronomy affords a feeble outline of such an intelligence.

Other definitions are:

> By determinism, we understand the belief that the future of the whole universe, or of an isolated part of it, is determined in

terms of a complete description of its present condition (Bridgman 1928)

and

According to determinism, the future can be completely predicted from the past (Schlick 1925).

Thus scientific determinism requires (a) a complete description of the present state of the system, and (b) knowledge of the laws governing it, which together enable prediction of a future condition of the system.

ARGUMENTS IN FAVOUR OF DETERMINISM

The *success of science* to date is usually given as the main argument in favour of determinism, though some might claim that an optimistic extrapolation from the success of physical science is implied. However, there are a number of problems with which any proponent of determinism must deal.

ARGUMENTS AGAINST DETERMINISM

There are certain difficulties in the way of giving a coherent account of determinism. Popper (1950) has demonstrated that indeterminism extends to the realm of classical physics. If the concept of the predictability of an event is made explicit, it can be proved that not all macroscopic events can be predicted. There are limits to the extent to which a machine (which can be considered an instantiation of a formal system) can predict its own future states. The Laplacean view of *universal predictability is incoherent*. Thus if determinism is accounted for in terms of predictability, determinism cannot be a defensible theory.

First, a difficulty arises from the fact that the description of the system's current state takes time to complete, so that it may be out of date by the time it is made and hence the prediction based on it invalidated.

The second argument involves an application of Gödel's theorem in mathematical logic which shows that, in any formal system of logic sufficiently complex to formulate the arithmetic of integers, there will always be propositions which are true but unprovable. A corollary is that this proposition itself is also undemonstrable within the system, and thus the system cannot be shown to be consistent within itself.

Popper's third argument concerns the fact that to pass information to a machine about its own state 'is liable to interfere strongly with that state and thereby to destroy the predictive value of the information'. I conclude from these arguments that it is unlikely that complete predictability can be attained.

It has further been argued that determinism is not identifiable with predictability in principle owing to the *limited precision* with which predictions can be formulated. Although every event must be perfectly determinate, no prediction can identify such a determinate event unambiguously. A given state of the world at an instant determines not a given subsequent state but a class of possible states, and no explanation why one rather than another of these possibilities should actually be realised. No prediction can distinguish the predicted event in such a way as to discriminate it from any of the other possible events that could fall under the same set of measurements. We are concerned with variable classes of events rather than complete descriptions of uniquely designated events. 'If anyone claims that all events, including actions, are predictable he is saying something that is either false or empty of content' (O'Connor 1971).

Other limits to determinism have been suggested by *Heisenberg's uncertainty principle* (1927), according to which there is indeterminism at the level of sub-atomic physics. There are certain conjugate properties which cannot be simultaneously predicted, namely, position and momentum, and energy and time. Thus, if the position of a particle is specified, its momentum cannot be. Two classes of events occur without any assignable cause: (a) the emission of alpha particles, electrons and gamma rays by radioactive material, and (b) the jump of electrons from one orbit to another within the atom. Such unpredictability in principle has worried some including Einstein who exclaimed that 'God does not play dice with the world'. Others such as Eddington (1935) and Jeans (1933) sought here a defence of free will but they have been criticised by Stebbing (1937). Likewise Eccles' (1951) attempt to construct a neurophysiological account has also met with criticism (cf. Smart 1968). The implications for macroscopic phenomena are unclear. As O'Connor (1971) writes: 'The findings of quantum mechanics do not offer any clear and indisputable evidence in favour of free will.'

An objection commonly raised against determinism is that it *would make rational deliberation impossible,* an argument expressed (1927) though later repudiated (1954) by Haldane: 'If my mental processes are determined wholly by the motion of atoms in my brain, I have no reason to suppose that my beliefs are true . . . and hence I have no reason for supposing my brain to be composed of atoms.' Similar objections have been raised against Skinner by those who claim that his theory that all behaviour is a function of environmental history must apply to the production of his own theory, and hence there is no reason to suppose it true. But the argument does not follow. Equally there is no reason to suppose that the theory is not true. The question of truth value is independent of the question of determinism. If anything, determinism favours rather than jeopardises the truth of a theory. A theory that bears some relation to evidence is more likely to be true than one that has arisen by chance. (The question of the relation between reasons and causes has been much discussed in philosophy, for example Toulmin 1970.)

Finally, there is the charge concerning the logical nature of the theory of determinism, to the effect that it is *not falsifiable*. When causes are not forthcoming, it is assumed that they have not yet been discovered rather than that they do not exist. Neither is the determinist maxim integrated into a logically coherent system. Paradoxically, the uncertainty principle, by limiting its empirical scope, strengthens its logical status by showing that it can be falsified.

Are free will and determinism compatible?

Attempts to reconcile free will and determinism have been variously called the consistency hypothesis, the compatibility hypothesis or soft determinism (a term coined by William James), and date from the time of Hobbes who wrote in *Leviathan* (1651):

> 'Liberty and necessity are consistent' for a man's liberty 'consisteth in this that he finds no stop, in doing what he has the will, desire or inclination to doe' . . . 'Every act of man's will, and every desire and inclination proceedeth from some cause and that from another cause in a continual chain.'

Other philosophers who have taken this view include: Hume, J. S. Mill, Schlick and Nowell-Smith. It has tended to characterise those of a logical positivist persuasion, for example Ayer (1946), who argues that free will implies determinism on the grounds that the opposite of determinism is randomness, and surely that cannot be what is meant by free will. Most of the attempts depend on distinguishing freedom on the one hand from constraint or compulsion on the other. A regularity theory of causation is adopted, such that deterministic laws are seen as descriptive rather than prescriptive. Causation does not imply coercion, necessity nor any mysterious force. (There have been some objections to this view;

for example, O'Connor has argued that it is not clear how con-strained and unconstrained acts can be distinguished on the compatibility hypothesis.) It should be pointed out that the type of freedom that soft determinism reconciles with determinism is that of consistency between desire and action, and not that of the libertarian who demands that the agent could have done otherwise.

Conclusions

Few issues have been discussed so frequently or inconclusively as free will. One feature of the controversy is the extraordinary difficulty in putting forward an argument for or against free will without covertly begging the question against the other side. This is due to the fact that the libertarian and the determinist have world views so utterly opposed to each other and offering so little in the way of common ground that can serve as mutually acceptable premises for the controversy, that the very first premises of the arguments on one side will be unacceptable to the other. Neither can afford to make the smallest concession without rendering his own position covertly inconsistent.

The discussion may be summarised as follows: the main prob-lems for the libertarian are the inconsistency of free will with the premises of (successful) science, and the grave difficulty of giving a coherent account of the view in the first place. The notion that free acts are uncaused acts seems not to grant what the libertarian wants. The interpretation required, namely, that the agent could have done otherwise, all circumstances remaining the same, is untestable. It is possible to distinguish instances of free will phenomenologically but no causal efficacy is thereby guaranteed. It is also possible to provide behavioural criteria for distinguishing voluntary from involuntary responses. Soft determinists have sought to reconcile free will with determinism by arguing that the former implies the latter, the proper contrast being between freedom and coercion rather than freedom and causation. However, the interpretation of free will that is reconciled here is that of consistency between desire and action rather than that of 'could have done otherwise'.

Though determinism seems to have the edge in this difficult debate, it is not without problems either. There are difficulties in identifying it with predictability and a number of discoveries show there are distinct limitations to its completeness.

3

The mind–body problem

Introduction

It is often said (e.g. Kendler 1970) that psychology has three subject matters: conscious experience, behaviour and physiology. The mind–body problem is concerned with the relation between two of these, namely, consciousness and neurophysiological processes. Part of the puzzle is how the latter can give rise to the former when they appear to be so different in kind. Described by Schopenhauer as 'the world knot', the problem, like so many others treated in this book, is a tangle of conceptual and empirical issues; both factual discoveries and logical considerations may be relevant. One of the things we shall be considering in this chapter is whether modern scientific evidence can throw any light on it.

In one form or another, the problem has existed for a long time. The western world has found it difficult to escape the inheritance from Greek and Cartesian thought, and it must be considered as a possibility that the whole conceptual apparatus is incorrect or misleading. In the history of philosophy, the problem was phrased in terms of a general ontological question of being: what kinds of things can be said to exist? Are there essentially different kinds of stuff in the world? This might be called the 'furniture of the universe' question. Any account of the mind–body problem couched in these terms is likely to involve prior analysis of the notions of substance and cause, in particular whether cause can be between unlike things and whether there can be gaps in a causal chain. If it is concluded that there are two distinct realities (**dualism**), then the further question arises as to their relation. Possible answers are that they are: (a) unrelated, (b) correlated but causally independent (e.g. **psychophysical parallelism**), or (c) causally related. Causal relations may be claimed to hold in both directions (**interaction**), or only one (e.g. epiphenomenalism). Alternatively, it may be concluded that there is only one fundamental reality (**monism**) and that the duality is illusory. In this case it may be argued that (a) physical phenomena are reducible to mental (**idealism**), (b) mental phenomena are reducible to physical (**materialism**), or (c) both are really something else (e.g.

neutral monism). In more recent times, the problem has been phrased in terms of the relation between different languages or descriptions, namely, those that refer to mental and physical events.

What is meant by 'mind' and 'body'? As they stand, these concepts are probably too vague to be useful. Mental phenomena include things like sensations, images, feelings, thoughts, beliefs, intentions and decisions. I suspect that 'mind' is commonly used in two main senses: (a) conscious experience, and (b) the system or 'program' which governs behaviour. Strictly speaking, the mind–body problem is concerned with the former. It is, however, sometimes discussed in terms of the latter (e.g. Fodor 1981). In this sense, 'mind' refers to the software whereas 'body' refers to the hardware. A third approach stresses mentalistic explanations, i.e. the suggestion that mental states can be causes. 'Body' appears to be more straightforward and might be said to refer to the physical aspect of an organism, in this case particularly the brain.

Feigl (1958), in an important but difficult paper, discusses various criteria for distinguishing mental and physical. One is in terms of the mode of verification. The suggestion is that the mental world is private whereas the physical is public. Thus the sort of knowledge a person has of his own mental states is different from the sort of knowledge he has, or can have, of others' mental states. Globus (1973) draws the distinction in terms of what is proximal and what is distal to the transformation boundary of the sensory receptor–transducer system; or, put in more manageable terminology, one might say the distinction is between the subject's and the observer's perspective. Feigl defines this type of physical, which he calls physical$_1$, as intersubjectively confirmable. However, all knowledge is ultimately based on private experience. The line between private and public is less clear than appears at first sight and is a matter of degree rather than kind, in that it is merely easier to reach agreement in some cases than others (see Ch. 5 and Valentine 1978).

Descartes (1641) termed the mental realm *res cogitans* and the physical realm *res extensa*. This introduces two further possible criteria. The first is in terms of spatial extension. The suggestion is that physical phenomena are spatially extended whereas mental are not; they cannot be said to be located anywhere. However, some mental phenomena, e.g. images, might be said to have spatial properties, and it may be doubted whether some of the entities of modern physics, such as energy and forces, are inherently spatial. Such a division would also of course be rejected by identity theorists (see pp. 28–30). Shaffer (1965) suggests that the denial of spatial localisation to mental phenomena is a convention which might come to be abandoned in the future.

Descartes' second criterion is based on the idea of obedience to different laws. He believed that physical phenomena were subject to deterministic, mechanistic laws whereas mental phenomena were 'free' or undetermined. Psychologists must reject the latter part of this statement (see Ch. 2). Feigl (1958) defines physical$_2$ as subject matter which can be satisfactorily explained in terms of the concepts which are sufficient for the explanation of inorganic matter.

Another way of expressing the distinction might be in terms of the organisation of a system. Features that have been canvassed as criterial of the mental have included mnemic properties (Russell 1921), purposiveness (McDougall 1912) and intensionality (Brentano 1874). Formerly these were contrasted with mechanistic processes. However, according to current opinion (e.g. Boden 1972) these qualities are not incompatible with mechanism (see Ch. 12 for further discussion). **Functionalism** (cf. Fodor 1981) defines mental states in terms of their causal relations to other mental states. These can be functionally specified in the form of Turing machine operations. On this view, mental states are independent of a particular physical realisation.

Other suggestions are that mental phenomena are qualitative, holistic or emergent whereas physical phenomena are quantitative, atomistic or compositional. Different levels of description are possible and required but again it is unlikely that this will satisfactorily distinguish mental from physical.

Evaluation of the main proposed solutions to the mind–body problem

We shall now turn to a consideration of the main solutions to the mind–body problem which have been proposed in the past, and in each case will attempt both (a) a conceptual evaluation – are there any logical arguments in favour of or against the view – and (b) an empirical evaluation – is there any empirical evidence that supports or disconfirms the view?

Classical solutions may for convenience be divided into three categories (though it should be stressed that this is not the only possible classification): (a) dualist – those that accept the common-sense view that both mental and physical processes have reality and are then faced with the problem of their relation; (b) monist – those that claim that only one of the two supposed stuffs or substances have reality and that the other can in some way be reduced to the one; (c) other, more radical solutions that claim that the problem as traditionally stated is misconceived in some way.

DUALIST SOLUTIONS

Those who credit both types of process with real existence are faced with the questions of whether they are to be attributed equal importance (symmetrical versus asymmetrical views) and whether the relation between them is one of independence (correlation) or causal dependence (two way or one way, and if the latter, which way?).

The common-sense or lay answer to the problem is *interaction,* made famous (or perhaps infamous) by Descartes, who espoused a two-way causal interaction between what he conceived of as two distinct substances: mental and physical (see p. 21). (The place of interaction between these two realms was deemed to be the pineal gland, on the grounds that this was the only feature not known to be duplicated in each cerebral hemisphere.) He had, however, the 'peculiar merit of being so clearly and distinctly confused that the difficulties of this position became apparent' (Reeves 1958). Such a position has also been espoused by Eccles (see e.g. Popper & Eccles 1977). Psychophysiology might be thought to be premissed on such a view too if it is concerned with the effect of psychological states on physiological variables (cf. Johnson 1977).

Dualist interaction is in accord with common sense and ordinary language, which attribute causal efficacy to mental and physical events. However, serious objections have been levelled against it. Descartes' followers have found it difficult to see how there can be causal relations between two things defined as distinctively different, namely, spatial, mechanistic and deterministic as opposed to non-spatial, non-mechanistic and non-deterministic. How, in particular, could bodily causes produce mental effects if the latter are supposed to be non-determined? Those impressed by the success of science based on assumptions of the efficacy of solely physical explanations, and the principle of the conservation of energy, have found it difficult to see how there is room for mental causes. If physical causes are sufficient, mental causes can hardly be necessary. How could they break the circle and get in, as it were, to the self-contained physical system? It would involve a break in what Feigl calls physical$_2$ and it offends against parsimony. Ryle (1949) has described the error of dualism as involving a category mistake, as in 'she came home in a sedan chair and a flood of tears' (see p. 30).

However, there are many pieces of evidence which are, in practice, interpreted within this framework. Examples of supposed mental causes of physical effects are psychosomatic disorders and voluntary behaviour of all kinds. Examples of commonly supposed physical causes of mental effects are almost too numerous to mention, but brain damage and hallucinogens may be cited as examples.

If dualist interaction is in error the whole of psychophysiology may be metaphysical nonsense, or at least psychosomatics may be a logical howler. My own view is that it can only be salvaged by appeal to psychophysical parallelism or double aspect theory (see pp. 25–6 and p. 30 respectively). My argument would be that all descriptions are to some extent arbitrary. In cases of apparent interaction, we simply choose to focus attention on one aspect of the cause and the other aspect of the effect. This does not preclude the existence of the other correlated aspect. For example, we may choose to say that a psychological stress caused a physical ulcer; this does not preclude there being some unmentioned physiological state correlated with the stress (indeed, any conventional scientist must assume this). Shaffer (1965) discusses another possibility, dual causation theory, according to which mental and physical events could each be sufficient but not necessary causes.

Emergence, while crediting physical processes with reality, wishes to establish mental processes as not reducible to physical and as being on a higher level. A foremost exponent is Sperry (1969) who claims that consciousness is a dynamic, emergent property of cerebral activity; it is higher order and holistic, i.e. more than the sum of its neurological parts; it supervenes and exercises directive, causal control. This is reminiscent of William James, who described consciousness as just what would be expected in a nervous system grown too big to direct itself (see Ch. 4). Others who are similarly disposed are humanistic psychologists who wish to attribute a genuinely causal role to mental processes, a view commonly known as 'mentalism'.

Such a view may be good for morale (see Ch. 2) and is in accord with common sense. I would agree that descriptions of mental phenomena are different in meaning from, and hence cannot be reduced to, descriptions of physical phenomena, but the question of causal ascription is more problematical and the attendant difficulties of attributing physical effects to mental causes have already been discussed under 'interaction' (p. 23). A better way of conceiving of the relation may be to say, as Boden (1972) does, that thought guides, rather than causes, action.

Psychical research and psychokinesis, if established, might provide evidence in favour of emergence. Evidence consistent with, though not establishing, it is multiple and/or variable localisation of function and the relevant part of the interaction evidence. Militating against it are the successes of physiological psychology and aspects of psychophysiology which correlate psychological with physiological processes.

Epiphenomenalism, while attributing reality to mental states, refuses to allow them causal efficacy. On this view mental processes or experiences are non-causal by-products of physical processes; they are caused by but do not themselves cause physical events. A famous exponent was T. H. Huxley (1874) who wrote: 'The consciousness of brutes would appear to be related to the mechanism of their body simply as a collateral product of its working, and to be as completely without power of modifying that working as the steam whistle, which accompanies the working of a locomotive engine, is without influence upon its machinery.'

This view goes some way towards meeting the demands of the principle of the conservation of energy in that no 'extra' causes are postulated. It has the advantage of conceptual economy, but we do have 'extra' effects. However, it does seem to reflect the asymmetry in the intuition that some but not all physical events have correlated mental events.

The view has been adopted by many behaviouristically minded psychologists. Skinner treats experiences as phenomena which can be disregarded in the explanation of behaviour. More recently, Wason and Evans (1975) have postulated two processes: type I, inaccessible to consciousness, underlying behaviour, and type II, accessible to consciousness, underlying introspective reports. They provide evidence consistent with Freud's view that introspections are, at least in some cases, rationalisations determined by previous behaviour. (I suspect that this is, as yet, an incomplete story.) Similarly, Nisbett and Wilson (1977) have argued that subjects never have direct access to the process underlying behaviour; their introspections may nevertheless sometimes be correct but this is by dint of inspired guesswork. There has been evidence since demonstrations of post-hypnotic suggestion that behaviour is sometimes not the result of conscious processes; whether it never is, is more difficult to establish.

One way of escaping the objections to interaction is to accept that mental and physical processes both have reality, but to reject the notion that either is causally dependent on the other. This view of independent correlation known as *psychophysical parallelism* was held by Leibniz (1714) who proposed that there was a pre-established harmony established by God at the beginning of the universe such that mental and physical events occurred simultaneously like two synchronised clocks or orchestras. The view was satirised by Voltaire who raised the question of the need for a conductor. Malebranche (1675) introduced the amusing variation known as occasionalism which required God to leap into action every time an event of one type occurred in order to implement the appropriate event of the other type. Many early psychologists based their work on a parallelist framework, e.g. Fechner, Wundt, G. E. Müller and the Gestalt psychologists, who postulated an isomorphism between psychological and physiological processes.

Such a view certainly meets objections to the notion of cause in general (see Russell 1913) and causal relations between unlike substances in particular. However, postulating two distinct substances militates against parsimony and many have sought to avoid this solution (see pp. 26–31). Unless panpsychism is adopted, there is also the problem of accounting for the intuition that not all physical processes have mental counterparts.

As examples of empirical work based on the assumption of parallel correlated functions, much of physiological psychology may be cited but in particular perhaps the work of Funkenstein (1955) who sought, through a variety of means, to establish a correlation between fear and the secretion of adrenalin on the one hand, and anger and the secretion of noradrenalin on the other. Examples of empirical work which goes against such a view are the failures to obtain correlations in the cases of aphasia, emotion and experiments on the motor theory of thought. My ideas here are that, in the first case, the same psychological dysfunction may be associated with a number of different physiological locations or patterns and in the last two cases that a great variety at the psychological, experiential level seems to be represented by much cruder differentiation at the physiological level (but this may well be due to lack of physiological knowledge).

However, many such as phenomenologists have rejected dualism and opted for some type of monism.

MONIST SOLUTIONS

There are two main alternatives: (a) idealism, which claims that only mental phenomena are real, and (b) materialism, which makes the opposite claim that only physical phenomena are real.

Idealism is commonly associated with George Berkeley (1710) who put forward the doctrine of *esse* is *percipi*, to be is to be perceived, whereby the universe was considered to be occupied only by minds and ideas, physical objects being entirely dependent on these and existing merely as ideas in someone's mind. (The permanence of physical objects was explained by appeal to God's omnipresent perceptions, hence the limerick attributed by Bertrand Russell to Ronald Knox:

> There was a young man who said, 'God
> Must think it exceedingly odd
> If he finds that this tree
> Continues to be
> When there's no-one about in the quad'

To which the reply was:

> Dear Sir: Your astonishment's odd:
> I'm always about in the quad
> And that's why the tree
> Will continue to be
> Since observed by Yours faithfully, God.)

The doctrine was taken one step further by Hume (1740) who eliminated minds from the universe, these being reduced to bundles of ideas.

Indeed, there is something fundamental about experience and it can be plausibly argued that all our concepts are constructions of inferences from these (see, e.g. Pearson 1892). The belief that only mental phenomena have real existence and that everything outside our experience has none goes against common sense however, and it seems highly unlikely that our intersubjective agreement about the outside world would be as good as it is if the latter had no causal effect on our perceptions. However, the phenomenologists are right to stress the dependence of our knowledge of the external world on our conceptual apparatus.

Empirical traditions which perhaps have not gone as far as to deny the existence of physical objects but have stressed the importance of experience are those influenced by phenomenology, and those calling themselves cognitive psychologists, who argue that behaviour is determined by, and hence can only be explained by reference to, the meaning of the situation for the organism. Opposing them is the behaviourist tradition which claims to have been successful in predicting behaviour without reference to the experience of the organism.

Materialism claims that only physical phenomena have real existence. This view was held by Democritus (*c.* 400 BC), and rose to favour more recently towards the end of the last century and at the beginning of this century under the name of physicalism. Freud belonged to a group of physicalistic physiologists led by Brücke and du Bois-Reymond, who:

> pledged a solemn oath to put into power this truth: No other forces than the common physical–chemical ones are active within the organism. In those cases which cannot at the time be explained by these forces one has either to find the specific way or form of their action by means of the physical–mathematical method, or to assume new forces equal in dignity to the chemical–physical forces inherent in matter, reducible to the force of attraction and repulsion.

Carnap (1934), as leader of the logical positivists, had as an ideal the provision of a systematic survey of all knowledge, a unified science based on objective observations whose truth could be inter-subjectively confirmed and guaranteed by the recognised procedures of science. Materialism has tended to be favoured by those of a scientific turn of mind who have frequently favoured reductionism (q.v.), the view that all higher level descriptions of molar phenomena can ultimately be reduced to equivalent lower level descriptions in terms of more molecular phenomena. Amongst psychologists, those who come closest are the behaviourists. Watson's classical behaviourism attempted to reduce mental phenomena to the publicly observable evidence for them. Skinner's radical behaviourism merely asserts that behaviour can be accounted for without recourse to mentalistic terms.

Such approaches might be motivated by parsimony and the desire for a unified science. It is true that the only knowledge we can have of other's experience is through that which is publicly observable, i.e. their behaviour and physiology, and the materialist might argue that science has achieved considerable success by relying on these sources. On the other hand, common sense does attribute reality to our experiences and one of the weaknesses of materialism is how to account adequately for them: especially those of other people, which on a materialist account are identical with their underlying physical processes. Watsonian behaviourism is false; radical behaviourism has had a measure of success.

Empirical evidence which might be said to militate against materialism is non-organic psychological disorder. Freud, for example, did find that there were cases which could not be explained in terms of the common physical chemical forces and felt obliged to assume 'new forces equal in dignity to the chemical–physical forces inherent in matter, reducible to the force of attraction and repulsion'.

A recently popular view amongst philosophers, namely, **identity theory,** might be said to constitute a special case of materialism. It claims that consciousness *is* a brain process, in the sense that 'a cloud is a mass of water droplets or other particles in suspension', 'heat is mean kinetic energy' or 'a gene is identical with a section of a DNA molecule'. Place (1956; see also Smart 1959, and Feigl 1958) makes it clear that what is claimed is **contingent identity.** It is weaker than logical identity (which is true by definition and does not require empirical verification) but stronger than correlation (where the two phenomena are independent). The two descriptions have independent means of verification (there are different ways of finding out about them), but one description gives a more adequate explanation of the phenomenon than the other. Feigl (1960) employs Frege's distinction between sense and reference: the two descriptions have different meanings but refer to the same thing.

Often advanced as an argument in favour of identity theory, by those who propose it, is that it eliminates 'nomological danglers'. By this are meant psychophysical laws which are irreducible and inexplicable on other views (such as psychophysical parallelism). Bridging laws no longer require explanation because we are dealing with cases of identity rather than correlation.

As with materialism, if such identities could be established this would certainly make for the simplification of science. (Indeed Horgan (1976) argues that grounds for deciding the mind–body question must be considerations of simplicity, whereas the criteria for deciding the reductionist question are empirical.)

The other argument in favour of identity theory is that, in accordance with common sense, mental states could be assigned a genuinely causal role. If conscious processes are identical with brain processes then the former as much as the latter can be said to be causes of behaviour (insofar as anything can be said to be a cause, see Russell 1913).

Identity theory has, however, not been well received by all. Ayer (1973) describes it as 'either not very interesting or not very plausible' and Joynson (1972) as 'a purely verbal solution which dissolves into what is effectively dualism, at any attempt to put it into practice'. There are certainly a number of difficulties in providing a coherent account. At best, identity is a misleading description and their provisos are well motivated. As Place (1956) rightly divines, the temptation is to think of logical identity. Further, the symmetry quickly dissolves: asymmetry is tacitly assumed. An identity theorist is unlikely to make the converse statement that brain processes are identical with conscious states. Descriptions in terms of brain processes are taken as more adequate than those in terms of conscious states. Functionalists (Fodor 1981) argue that mental states are independent of a particular physical realisation. The whole programme of course depends on the success of establishing the empirical truth of reduction, and the arguments are the same as those against it. It seems unlikely in view of the different meanings of psychological and physiological concepts, the lack of *a priori* reasons why they should correlate in a one-to-one fashion, and examples which suggest a one-to-many relation. *Maybe* we just do not know enough physiology yet but I do not myself think this is the answer. Borst (1970) argues that it is highly implausible that identity theory could apply to all mental concepts such as, for example, promising. Gray (1971) rejects the theory on the somewhat different grounds of not being very fruitful for science. If identity is assumed it precludes further investigation and prevents the possible discovery of non-identity.

Empirical work based on the assumption of the truth of empirical reduction or at least consistent with identity theory, is that on cortical localisation of function and perhaps the whole of physiological psychology. Evidence which would militate against it would be any which shows one-to-many relationships (see p. 26), as would extra-sensory perception, if established.

OTHER SOLUTIONS

A rather sophisticated variant of psychophysical parallelism is **double aspect theory,** which gives credence to the reality of mental and physical processes but claims that these are merely aspects of the same fundamental underlying reality. Such a view was held by Spinoza. An essentially similar position was adopted by Russell (1927) under the label of neutral monism. The philosophical objection to such a view is that the underlying reality remains basically metaphysical and unknowable. If such a pitfall can be avoided, double aspect theory is in my view highly attractive. The main objection to it is its vagueness. Variations on it have been accepted by many, perhaps most, modern writers until the advent of identity theory. It has frequently been formulated in linguistic terms.

Russell likened 'mind' and 'matter' to the lion and the unicorn fighting for the crown, considering them to be simply heraldic conventions or logical constructions. In similar vein, Ryle (1949) argued that the distinction is merely grammatical, matter usually being described in terms of nouns or pronouns, and mind in terms of verbs, adverbs or adjectives. Thus, properly, one should speak of 'behaving intelligently' rather than of 'intelligence'. Bannister (1968) refers to different semantic networks or modes of construing events and Kelvin (1956) to different level descriptions of the same event.

Conclusion

The mind–body problem may not at present be resolvable. In some cases conclusive tests cannot be carried out. For example, if certain physical processes are always accompanied by mental events, it is not possible to determine whether the former would be any different in the absence of the latter. In other cases it may be necessary to establish gaps in the causal chain, in order to decide between different views. It is possible, however, to consider the implications of holding a particular view, whether and what empirical evidence is relevant, which views are compatible with the empirical evidence and which are conceptually preferable.

At the beginning of this chapter we drew attention to the fact that there was a cluster of associated problems. Thus there may be no one answer. Epistemologically, there is an asymmetry between the subject's and the observer's perspective. Statements describing experiences are not identical in meaning to those describing physical phenomena, as can be seen from the example of a blind neurophysiologist who might have complete knowledge of the physiological basis of colour vision, and yet not know what it was like to see colour. Metaphysically, double aspect theory may be recommended. To the extent that descriptions have an element of arbitrariness, pragmatism may be appropriate. Thus, psychologists may adopt different frameworks to suit different purposes, given that the demands of conceptual coherence and consistency with the empirical evidence have been met.

4

Consciousness

Problems

It is perhaps even more the case with the topic of this chapter than with other issues discussed in this book that there is uncertainty about what the problems are. Gray (1971) has argued that psychology lacks a theory of consciousness. Hypothetical constructs should enable us to make deductions about relevant observations, in this case behavioural and physiological. Because consciousness has arisen as a datum from our own experience and has been generalised to others inductively by analogy, it lacks such properties. Thus we are unable to specify its nature or its relations to behavioural and physiological processes. Gray suggests that explanatory links are missing between conscious and other processes: there are no facts about behaviour, physiology or artificial intelligence, he claims, that would provide an explanation for, or be explained by, conscious events.

Some of the main questions which might be asked about consciousness are:

(a) What *status* should it be afforded in psychological theory? Can consciousness form part of the subject matter of psychological science? What particular methodological problems are raised by its private nature? How are they to be solved? What is the status of verbal reports and their relation to conscious processes?

(b) What is the *nature* of consciousness? What are its defining properties? Is there anything which distinguishes processes accompanied by consciousness? Is it an all-or-none process for which there is a cut-off point? Or does it represent a continuum: are there degrees of consciousness? Gray (1971) suggests that the criterial features might lie in the system, biological tissue, behaviour, the environment in which it occurs, or some combination of these. A satisfactory answer to these questions should enable us to decide whether consciousness is restricted to organic matter and whether computers could be said to be conscious. It is likely also to involve an analysis of the relation of consciousness to neuro-physiological and ultimately physical processes.

(c) What is the *function* of consciousness? What is its evolution-ary advantage? What is its relation to and role in behaviour? Are they unrelated? Or correlated? Are they aspects of the same or different processes? Is consciousness merely epi-phenomenal to behaviour? Or does it have causal efficacy in determining behaviour? Is it possible to provide a theory of consciousness?

The status of consciousness in psychology

Historically the fate of consciousness in psychology has followed a curious course. For the structuralist school, usually regarded as the first experimental psychologists, the subject matter of psychology was virtually coextensive with consciousness. The aim of psycho-logy was held to be the analysis of mental experience. For a variety of reasons, both theoretical and practical (see Ch. 5), the approach adopted by this school fell into disuse: large portions of the processes underlying behaviour are inaccessible to consciousness and there were methodological difficulties in investigating those that were. The rise of behaviourism demanded the removal of consciousness from the psychological arena. However, since the 1960s there has been a resurgence of interest in conscious pro-cesses, attributed by Holt (1964) to a variety of causes (substantive, e.g. contemporary political interest in subjective phenomena; theoretical, e.g. dissatisfaction with strict behaviourist formula-tions; methodological, e.g. improved techniques, both behavioural and physiological).

The confused state of consciousness in psychology is largely the result of misunderstandings of the behaviourists' methodological prescription which insisted on public data. Consciousness is private in the sense that each individual has immediate access to his own experience but that of other people can only be inferred by analogy. Consciousness is peculiar in that one has special access to one's own but this does not detract in any way from the possibility of studying it scientifically. Conscious processes of others, unconscious mental processes and the external world all have the same epistemological status, namely, that of inferred constructs. Conscious experience provides data of the observer's own consciousness immediately and directly, and of that of others mediately and indirectly through the observation of their behaviour, both in the form of what might be called performance responses as well as by means of verbal reports, and of their neurophysiology. These observations are themselves part of consciousness. Thus consciousness provides data for all sciences but its status as subject matter in psychological science is that of an inferred construct. So far as psychology is interested in the processes underlying behaviour, this is true of all its subject matter. The use of introspective reports is discussed in Chapter 5.

The nature of consciousness

WHAT IS CONSCIOUSNESS?

First we must attempt to delineate it and consider its characteristics. Consciousness has the paradoxical quality of being intuitively obvious, everyone having immediate knowledge of it, yet extremely difficult to *define*. Miller (1964) has drawn attention to the range of meanings it has had for different people: 'a state of being, a substance, a process, a place, an epiphenomenon, an emergent aspect of matter, or the only true reality'. Natsoulas (1978) discusses the seven meanings given in the *Oxford English dictionary*: (a) joint or mutual knowledge; (b) internal knowledge or conviction, first hand knowledge for which one has the testimony within oneself; (c) awareness, e.g. hearing a noise; (d) direct awareness, intuitive perception of one's own thoughts; (e) personal unity; (f) the normal waking state; (g) double consciousness.

The most basic sense of consciousness is in terms of experience or awareness. Many have emphasised this *phenomenal* aspect, for example Titchener (1899), for whom consciousness was 'the sum total of a person's experiences as they are at any given time'. It is highly probable that it is essentially sensory in nature, as was acknowledged by Freud (see below). Burt (1962) described consciousness as a 'generic term covering (i) certain specific relations (e.g. intuitive awareness), and (ii) certain specific contents (e.g. sense data, mental images, feelings, etc.)'. He considered it involved 'a specific relation between (a) someone or something who is said to be conscious and (b) something else which he, she, or it is said to be conscious *of*'.

An important distinction is that between consciousness in the sense of sensory experience and a higher order self-consciousness in which one is aware that one is aware. Thus, Boring (1937) distinguishes between discrimination and awareness, and Natsoulas (1970) between unintentional and intentional mental episodes, according to whether or not they possess contents. An example of the former would be being in pain, an example of the latter knowing one is in pain. The latter might be said to be propositional.

Others have emphasised the relation of consciousness to *physical*

processes. Freud (1895) saw it as 'a transient quality which attaches
to a psychical process only in passing', describing it as 'the subjective side of a *part* of physical processes in the neuronic system –
namely of the *perceptual* processes (ω-processes); . . . its absence
would *not* leave physical events unchanged but would imply the
absence of any contribution from the W (ω)-system.' Somewhat
more mystically, Deikman (1973) writes 'awareness *is* the organisation of the bio-system, that is awareness is the "complementary"
aspect of that organization, its psychological equivalent'.
Valentine's (1982) speculation that consciousness is the wave
function in a Pauli system (see p. 42) might be seen as an attempt
to specify this in more detail.

Yet others have emphasised the relation of consciousness to
behaviour. For the behaviourists, conscious awareness was merely a
matter of discrimination, i.e. they identified it with the behavioural
evidence for it. Thus for Skinner it is a matter of performing
discriminative responses, for Sperry (1952) 'implicit preparations
to respond' and for Lawrence (1963) 'the result of coding stimuli'.
Armstrong (1968) has given expression to the mentalist view which
attributes to consciousness a causal role; for him it is 'a mental state
of a person apt for bringing about a certain sort of behaviour'.

Shallice (1972, 1978), noting that consciousness is assumed by
many concepts in cognitive theory, such as attention and short-
term memory, has attempted an information processing account,
according to which consciousness is identified with aspects of the
operation of action systems. In his view it corresponds to an intermediate level of control, being isomorphic with strong inputs to the
dominant action system, having the properties of assisting in the
control of action, being retained in memory and being capable of
being spoken about. Mackay (1981) has suggested that the physical
correlate of conscious experience is the meta-organising activity of
the supervisory evaluative system of the central nervous system. He
distinguishes two functions of a supervisory nature which might be
expected to have correlates in conscious experience: (a) decision-
making, involving the determination of current goals and the
running assessment and ordering of priorities; (b) perception, the
evaluation of sensory input in terms of its implications for the
conditional organisation of actions.

A number of writers such as James (1890) have provided
intuitive accounts of the *characteristics* of consciousness. First, it is
a constantly *changing* sequence. In fact it is arguable that one could
not attend continuously to something unless it did change. Nevertheless, it is *sensibly continuous*. 'Consciousness, then, does not
appear to itself chopped up in bits,' wrote James, 'it flows. A
"river" or a "stream" are the metaphors by which it is most naturally

described.' Even when there are gaps, they are not felt as such. This may be related to a third characteristic, namely, its *personal* nature, the fact that it is confined to the individual. Items within one person's consciousness belong together and are separated from those of others. Fourthly, it is *holistic,* involving integration of information within and between modalities, perceived simultaneously. 'Whatsoever things are thought in relation are thought from the outset in a unity, in a single pulse of subjectivity' (James 1890). Fifthly, it is *selective* and limited in capacity. In James' words: 'The mind is at every stage a theatre of simultaneous possibilities. Consciousness consists in the comparison of these with each other, the selection of some, and the suppression of the rest by the reinforcing and inhibiting agency of attention.' James went on to distinguish the substantive parts (containing sensory images) from the transitive parts (concerned with the relations between these ideas in the margins of attention), using the simile of the perchings and flights of a bird. It is doubtful whether the flights can properly be said to be part of consciousness. What is clear is that there are degrees of clarity amongst conscious contents. Thus some items may be in the focus of attention, while others are more peripheral.

DESCRIPTIVE APPROACHES

There is a good deal of empirical evidence relevant to consciousness but little attempt has been made to integrate it into a coherent theory. There are a large number of phenomena which any adequate theory of consciousness would have to account for. In this section we shall consider evidence which comes from studies whose aim has been predominantly one of describing the basic facts. These rely mainly on verbal report but may also use behavioural and physiological measures. (As Stoyva and Kamiya (1968) have pointed out, the first provides primary, and the other two corroborative, validation.)

Much of the early work was concerned with the analysis of the *contents* and *dimensions* of consciousness. Using introspection, Wundt concluded that the elements of mental life consisted of sensations, images and feelings. Titchener later attempted to reduce images and feelings to sensations. As was previously mentioned, a good case could be made for the view that consciousness is essentially sensory. Titchener suggested quality, intensity, extensity and protensity (temporal duration) as dimensions of consciousness.

Studies in the areas of sensory and perceptual psychology and psychophysics are thus relevant to any consideration of consciousness. Much of the fundamental data on the modalities of vision, audition, touch, olfaction, kinaesthesis and proprioception were gathered in the early days of scientific psychology, where work was inspired by physiology.

The phenomenological tradition in the strict sense (i.e. that deriving from Husserl's philosophy, see Ch. 13), opposed to structuralist analysis which they considered artificial and misleading, attempted a more naïve description of what was immediately apparent in experience. Early studies were Stumpf's treatment of tones, Mach's on spatial and temporal sensations, Jaensch's on empty space, Rubin's on the distinguishing features of figure and ground, and D. Katz's on the phenomenal characteristics of what he termed surface (localised), volumic and film (not localised and without precise spatial relations) colour. This work influenced that of the Gestalt psychologists which, based on the theme of form qualities, implying the non-predictability of the psychological qualities of perception on the basis of an analysis of its physical determinants (e.g. the phi phenomenon where apparent perception of motion results from a particular spatial and temporal pattern of stationary stimuli), was aimed at demonstrating the principles governing the organisation of perceptual phenomena.

Imagery has been the subject of much recent work. The main dimensions of the subjective experience of imagery have been established as vividness (Sheehan 1967) and control (Gordon 1950). In its application to verbal learning it is now clear that there are a number of separable components involved, e.g. concreteness (a semantic feature of the material normally given preferential treatment) and imageability (a control process used in certain limited circumstances) (Richardson 1975, Baddeley et al. 1975).

With respect to feelings, Wundt suggested that these could be described by reference to three dimensions: pleasantness of quality, strength of intensity and suddenness of mode of occurrence. These bear a striking resemblance to Osgood's semantic differential dimensions, namely evaluation, potency and activity, of which it has been claimed that they measure affect rather than meaning. Other work has been concerned with the differentiation of positive and negative states in ontogenetic development, and the interrelation of experiential, behavioural and physiological measures.

Recently there has been a resurgence of interest in *altered states of consciousness* (cf. Tart 1969), for example dream, hypnagogic, hypnotic, meditational, trance and drug-induced states. Classic studies of hallucinations induced by drugs such as mescaline, LSD and those in peyote and datura include those by Huxley (1954) and Castaneda (e.g. 1968). Reported phenomena include distortions of space and time. James (1890) reports a case of loss of consciousness of self as a result of taking chloroform.

Physiological studies have distinguished different brain states associated with different meditational states. Thus normals show a blocking of alpha rhythm to stimulation; yogis, whose aim in meditation is to transcend the phenomenal world, show no response (Anand *et al.* 1961); whilst Zen monks, whose aim is to attend to the here-and-now of immediate experience, show a blocking of alpha which does not habituate (Kasamatsu & Hirai 1966).

A variety of evidence suggests it is reasonable to postulate a *continuum of consciousness–unconsciousness,* according to which there are degrees of consciousness. Medical practitioners distinguish the following states clinically on the basis of largely behavioural evidence, but relate them to levels of functioning in the central nervous system: (1) normal wakefulness, representing cortical activity; (2) drowsiness and confusion, characterised by responsivity to words, representing subcortical activity; (3) semi-coma, characterised by responsivity to pain, representing brain stem activity; (4) coma, characterised by a lack of responsivity, representing spinal activity.

Electroencephalographic (EEG) recordings generally enable the distinction of states of alertness, relaxation and four stages of increasingly deep sleep. Decreasing arousal is associated with increasing amplitude and synchrony, and decreasing frequency and voltage of brain waves. These states do not have sharp boundaries but rather represent points on a continuum, which is consistent with the behavioural evidence of decreasing sensitivity to environmental stimulation. One exception to this is the point at which consciousness is lost: a study by Dement (1972), in which subjects were asked to tap a key to a strobe, showed a sudden cessation of tapping when they fell asleep in the absence of any corresponding discrete change in the EEG. REM sleep, in which dreaming occurs, is considered to be qualitatively different from slow wave sleep. It is distinguished largely on the basis of rapid eye movements (hence 'REM') and is paradoxical in that cortical arousal is accompanied by loss of muscular tonus. Moreover, the two types of sleep are controlled by different neural structures, the raphe system in the lower brain stem in the case of slow wave sleep and the pons in the case of REM sleep.

Freud distinguished conscious, preconscious and unconscious processes. Preconscious material was that not presently in consciousness but to which conscious access could be gained without the use of special techniques, whereas unconscious material required the use of hypnosis, dream analysis or free association.

The facts of subliminal reception also suggest different levels of functioning. Here the organism responds to stimuli at a level which is insufficient to enable verbal report.

A number of people have distinguished different *modes of function-ing,* these sometimes being identified with hemispheric differences. Jackson (1878) distinguished two levels of speech production: (a) superior 'propositionising' where creative utterances are organised at the time of their production, which he believed to be dependent on a conscious voluntary system and associated with the left hemisphere; (b) inferior automatic speech consisting of well practised, already organised verbal habits, dependent on a subconscious system and associated with the right hemisphere. These levels might become dissociated in brain-damaged aphasic patients. Freud distinguished primary and secondary process thinking, the latter reality-oriented, the former characterised by the relinquishing of such restraints, or in neurological terms lateral disinhibition (the inhibition of inhibition). The relation of this to creative processes (especially the incubation phase) has been discussed by many (e.g. Koestler 1964). Ornstein (1972) has drawn a similar distinction between the analytic, linear mode favoured in the West, which stresses rational and reality-oriented adaptive functions, and the holistic mode favoured in the East which stresses intuitive processes, and like Bogen (1969), who distinguishes propositional from appositional thinking, has attempted to link these with left and right hemisphere functioning, respectively.

One of the few attempts to integrate evidence on mental states has been provided by Clark (1972) who has drawn on data from psychiatry (especially regarding manic depressive illnesses), studies of drug-induced states and mystical literature, as well as descriptions of more normal everyday experiences. He has produced a model of the mind, or 'map of inner space', in the form of a double cone (see Fig. 4.1) which possesses subjective dimensions of attention on the vertical axis ranging from waking to dreaming; certainty, an angular dimension in the horizontal plane, an intensity factor ranging from zero at Z to 100 at V; and things, a radial axis on the horizontal plane, the number of things attended to increasing with distance from the central origin O. The shaded half is negatively evaluated, the unshaded side positively evaluated. Arranged on it are the following states: A (average everyday slightly optimistic state), $\bar{A}$ (mild depression, as after influenza), P (euphoric states, as in peak experiences or mania), $\bar{P}$ (severe, clinical depression, as in manic depressive psychosis), M (mystical states proper), $\bar{M}$ (what is described in the mystical literature as 'the dark night of the soul'), Z (the Zen or zero state), and V (the ineffable void). Clark has also proposed a flow diagram to indicate possible transitions between the various states (see Fig. 4.2).

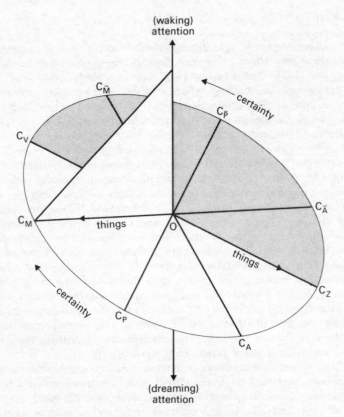

Figure 4.1 Map of inner space (from Clark 1972).

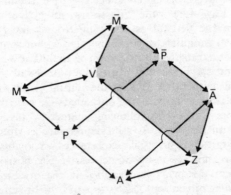

Figure 4.2 Diagram indicating possible transitions between mental states (from Clark 1972).

An interesting question is the relation between different states of consciousness and unconsciousness. They may interact, as in cases of creative writing (see, for example, Binet & Passy's study of dramatists (1895)), or they may appear independent and ignorant of each other, as in fugue states and hypnotic trances (see, for example, Erickson's study of Huxley (1965)).

Any theory of consciousness would have to account for such cases of *dissociated consciousness* as occur in multiple personality, hysteria and possession (see, for example, Prince 1905, Thigpen & Cleckley 1957). One relevant piece of empirical work is the study of split-brain patients. Sectioning of the corpus callosum results in structural and apparently functional independence of the two hemispheres. Sperry (1964) reports a patient who was unable to perform tasks requiring the processing of linguistic information (located in the left hemisphere) if either input or output involved the use of the right hemisphere. For example, he was unable to name objects presented to the left visual field, or to the left side of the body, when blindfolded. Similarly, he was unable to carry out verbal commands with his left arm or leg. If the dominant hemisphere was occupied with a task, it appeared not to register non-verbal activities going on in the left side of the body. Cases of potential rivalry were also reported, where the right hand grabbed the left correcting its false choice, or the left side of the body twitched at the mistakes of the right.

These findings have tempted conclusions such as 'two rather separate streams of conscious awareness' (Sperry 1974), 'double consciousness' (Gazzaniga & LeDoux 1978) and 'two free wills . . . inside the same cranial vault' (Sperry 1966). Mackay (1981), however, after a careful analysis of the work of Sperry, Gazzaniga and some of his own, concludes that:

> although the two half-systems in split-brain patients are clearly capable of grappling with one another in pursuit of conflicting low-level goals, and evaluating simultaneously-perceived situations according to conflicting criteria, we found no evidence of ability or inclination to engage in mutual conflict or criticism at the level of *criteria of evaluation*. Such 'twoness of will' as was suggested by the evidence seemed confined to the executive rather than the normative level . . . There is no evidence that . . . activities can coexist in parallel so as to provide 'two wills in one cranium'. The evidence suggests rather that the higher levels of the evaluative supervisory system have their neural basis in the undivided depths of the CNS, and that when functionally lower levels represented in the divided hemisphere are taken into the supervisory partnership this tends to be on an exclusive basis,

unless the left and right sides are prepared, so to say, to dance the same tune.

Other potentially relevant cases with implications for theories of consciousness would be the possibility of transplanting one person's brain into another's, or the possibility of one person receiving another's sensations; but these are perhaps more germane to questions of identity.

THE MECHANISM OF CONSCIOUSNESS

A few attempts have been made to produce theories of consciousness. One is simply to associate it with sensory processes. Potential problems for such a view are the phenomena of subliminal reception and responsivity to pain in states of semi-coma on the one hand, and the emptying of the mind in meditational states on the other. With regard to physiological conditions, perception involves the integration of primary and secondary projection areas, association areas and subcortical regions. Penfield (1969) suggested that consciousness resides in the thalamic nuclei of the higher brain stem since he observed that removal of the cortex does not produce loss of consciousness whereas removal of the higher brain stem does.

Valentine (1982) has produced a speculative, physical account. The etymology of consciousness suggests that its most striking feature is its oneness, which could have two meanings: (a) the fact that it is confined to the individual and does not spread out into the world (the privacy problem) and (b) the indivisibility or integration of different modalities and items within modalities (the unity problem). He suggests that both these problems can be solved if consciousness is identified with an electronic system within which Pauli's exclusion principle operates. The wave function describing such a system (and governing the probability of finding an electron at each point within it) comes to zero at the system's boundaries, so that no event proper to one system can be found in another: no two persons' wave functions overlap and their consciousnesses remain separate as required. On the other hand, within such a 'crowded' system of electrons, whose obedience to Fermi–Dirac statistics shows them to be fundamentally indistinguishable, it is more accurate to view the assembly as one unified and unlocalised entity than as a collection of countable particles. In this way, the events of consciousness are the changes of the state of the system induced by neural activity. These changes of state are quantised, and associated with each such change there is a characteristic evolution time during which the probability of observing the system to be in one or the other of the states changes continuously, even though any observation would show it to be in one state or the other and never between states. Given the spatially large size of the system, the difference between energy levels of neighbouring states is exceedingly small, so that mental events involve the uptake and omission of very closely defined quanta of energy. Through the operation of the time–energy uncertainty principle, it is impossible to locate quantal events involving very small amounts of energy closely in time. Indeed, such events (considered as *states* rather than *measurements* of states) must be thought of as *spread* in time. Haldane (1963) argued that the characteristic time of brain-sized events should be of the order of a second. Since neural events happen at a much higher rate than one per second, it can be seen that the system will usually be making a number of different transitions of state all at the same time. This corresponds with the paradoxical introspective fact that, for example, movement can actually be seen. Zeno's arrow paradox depends upon the divisibility of time into infinitesimal points. Mental time has moments that extend in time and overlap, and include each other just as the quantum theory would predict. Transitionality is, then, a feature of *each* psychological moment rather than a relation between separate moments.

The function of consciousness

What role does consciousness play in behaviour? Mandler (1975), in one of the relatively few treatments of the adaptive functions of consciousness, has argued that it serves to enable delay and reflection, thus increasing the likelihood of the selection of relevant behaviour patterns. He suggests it may play a role in the following:

(a) *The choice and selection of action systems.* Possible actions can be considered and their outcomes compared and evaluated covertly without the risk that overt testing would entail. This gives rise to the phenomenal experience of choice although the actual mechanisms are unconscious.

(b) *The modification and interrogation of long-range plans.* Subroutines may be retrieved and reconsidered.

(c) *Participation in retrieval programs from long-term memory.* Retrieval of information from long-term memory may be initiated by a command such as 'Where did I see this?'. This enables simple addressing of complex structures.

(d) *Commenting on current activity, enabling the storage of a representation of it,* as in images and labels. Once stored these can be retrieved.

(e) *Troubleshooting for structures not normally represented in consciousness,* e.g. automatised skills that have gone wrong.

Possible relations between consciousness and behaviour might be: that they are consistently correlated, that consciousness causes behaviour, that consciousness is the result of behaviour, behaviour causing consciousness, or that they are unrelated. These possibilities are considered below.

Mentalism, which asserts that *experience causes behaviour,* is the common lay view, the belief that ideas determine actions (cf. Ch. 2). Plato's ethics depended on such a view: knowledge automatically led to action; hence in order for people to behave well it was necessary merely to inform them of what was good. Right knowledge led to right action. Other traditions which attribute a dominant role to conscious experience are phenomenology and existentialism (discussed in Ch. 13) and certain approaches in social and clinical psychology. The most obvious way in which conscious experience affects behaviour is through perception. Behaviour is a function of the interpreted stimulus. It may also allow speedy and considered behaviour which would not otherwise be possible. It seems likely that its special role lies in the acquisition of behaviour, as Schrödinger (1958) suggested.

There are both conceptual difficulties in postulating causal relations between items from different universes of discourse (the currently most popular view being that mental states guide rather than cause behaviour, see Boden 1972), and also empirical *objections to the view that experience plays a causal role in behaviour.*

The accompaniment of behaviour by conscious experience is the exception rather than the norm. Much behaviour occurs without conscious awareness. Examples are discrimination (as shown by behavioural or autonomic responses) without reported awareness, as in subliminal reception and some pathological cases (e.g. Weiskrantz *et al.* 1974).

In other cases consciousness is relatively unimportant in the control of behaviour. Emotional experience may be felt after a behavioural adjustment to the situation has been made. One has taken one's hand out of the hot water by the time the pain is felt. Other examples come from studies of thinking and problem solving which show it is the products (the results or partial solutions) rather than the process which are available to consciousness (e.g. Hayes 1973, Maier 1931). Further evidence comes from skills where behaviour may become 'automatic' and performed without consciousness (indeed conscious attention may even be detrimental to performance), even though conscious verbalisation may have been necessary and beneficial in its acquisition. Kimble and Perlmuter's (1970) work, discussed in Chapter 2, illustrates the way in which the role of consciousness alters at different stages of the development of a skill. Penfield (1969) suggested, as a result of his work on neurological patients, that consciousness is required for starting and stopping automatic skills which are otherwise guided subcortically.

Consciousness may be correlated with, rather than causally related to, behaviour. There are cases where conscious experience exists but does not appear to influence behaviour. There is a great variety of evidence which indicates a *discrepancy between experience and behaviour*. A number of studies have shown a poor correlation between measures of the subjective experience of imagery such as vividness, and performance measures such as the recall of visualisable material (Sheehan & Neisser 1969, Neisser 1970). Other examples come from the study of attitudes, where there is frequently a lack of convergent validity. As Fishbein (1967) points out, failures to obtain correlations between attitude (as measured by reported affect) and behaviour may result from measuring attitudes and behaviours that are partially or totally unrelated: behaviour is also a function of cognitive, motivational and situational variables and these may be more important determinants in some cases.

Finally, there are other cases where experience occurs after behaviour and it may well be argued that *behaviour causes experience*. James (1890) argued that emotional experience was the result, not the cause of action: 'We feel sorry because we cry, angry because we strike, afraid because we tremble.' Recent experimental work by Laird (1974) tends to support this. He manipulated the facial expressions of subjects. Those who were made to 'smile' rated their mood as significantly more positive and laughed more at cartoons that did those subjects made to 'frown'. Much of the evidence on attitude change is consistent with such an interpretation, e.g. cognitive dissonance and role playing. Active participation (being forced to take the role of someone holding a view and to attempt to persuade others to favour it) leads to greater attitude change than does passive participation (merely being required to listen) (Janis & King 1954). Other evidence which suggests that consciousness may be epiphenomenal (i.e. a non-causal by-product of behaviour) is found in demonstrations of rationalisation of the kind described by Freud, who distinguished the subject's reason from *the* reason, and are exemplified in cases of post-hypnotic suggestion (where the reasons subjects give appear to be rationalisations of behaviour determined by suggestions made under hypnosis of which they are not conscious). Recently, a similar theme has been developed by Wason and Evans (1975), the results of whose experiments are consistent with their hypothesis that there are two types of process: type I underlying behaviour (better 'performance'), unavailable to consciousness, and type II underlying introspective reports, available to consciousness. They argue that subjects' verbal reports are sometimes rationalisations in that they appear inconsistent with the determinants of their performance responses, for which a theory exists on the basis of the examination of such responses in a range of other situations. (My own view is that an examination of a wider range of situations in which verbal reports are given might lead to a different theory, and one in which perhaps a common underlying process was shown to be responsible for both 'performance' and verbal responses.)

Much of the time, however, there is *consistency between experience and behaviour,* e.g. between so-called affective and conative aspects of attitudes; or there may be a complex interweaving, e.g. in emotion (cf. the work by Schachter and Singer (1962), on cognitive and physiological determinants of emotional behaviour) or biofeedback. Conflicting formulations may be more apparent than real, the result of incomplete observation and imperfect conceptualisation.

Conclusions

What answers, then, can be given to the questions posed at the beginning of this chapter?

The status of consciousness in psychology has had a chequered history. Consciousness is peculiar in that each individual has immediate experience of his own. But this privileged access neither provides a scientific hypothesis that would enable predictions about relevant observations to be made nor does it preclude the scientific study of it. Consciousness, as one of the phenomena which form the subject matter of psychology, is an inferred construct imperfectly indexed by observations of behaviour and physiology. Verbal reports provide primary validation and measures of performance and physiology provide corroborative validation particularly by the use of converging operations.

The nature of consciousness is still an unsolved problem. Relatively little progress has been made and most of the analysis is still at a fairly crude stage. Much work has been conducted on describing the contents of consciousness and the dimensions on which they may be categorised. There is both behavioural and physiological support for levels of consciousness, and it is clear that sensory discrimination must be distinguished from the ability to make verbal reports. There have also been a variety of studies on the independence and interdependence of different states. There is considerable agreement on the characteristics of consciousness, such as its holistic, personal and selective qualities, but little agreement on how to account for these. Most of the work on the physical basis of consciousness has been at the macroscopic level, in the form of gross anatomical localisation; only speculative accounts have been produced at a more molecular level. (If consciousness is indeed quantal, the appropriate investigations may be impossible, in that only the state of the system induced by the measurement can be known, not the prior state.)

With respect to the relation of consciousness to behaviour, it is clear that consciousness is not a necessary condition for behaviour: much behaviour occurs without it. In some cases it is likely that experience is the result of behaviour. Its role is in representing the environment, particularly in the learning of new response patterns.

5

Introspection

What is introspection?

William James saw no problem: 'The word introspection need hardly be defined – it means, of course, the looking into our own minds and reporting what we there discover' (James 1890). For Wundt, it was the observation of the contents of consciousness, self-observation (*Selbstbeobachtung*), as distinct from self-perception or inner perception (*innere Wahrnemung*). Natsoulas (1970) describes it as 'a relatively neutral term for the process(es) whereby one arrives on the spot at introspective awareness . . . process(es) whereby one acquires on-the-spot beliefs or convictions concerning his mental episodes'. Essentially, introspection is noting, and being in a position to report on, mental states and processes.

A number of attempts have been made to distinguish different types of introspection. McKellar (1962) notes the following sources of variance in the method: the circumstances in which the reports are obtained (e.g. laboratory, clinic or everyday life), and whether they are normal or special (as in the case of hypnosis, sensory deprivation or drug-taking); whether or not the procedure is systematic; the training of the subject and the experimenter; and the purpose for which the reports are required (e.g. for oneself or another). Radford and Burton (1974) distinguish self-observation (which might be called introspection proper), in which the subject aims to observe and report on his experiences; self-reports, in which the subject describes experiences perhaps of an unusual kind without trying to be particularly objective; and thinking aloud, in which the subject attempts to provide a running commentary on some on-going mental activity. Evans (1980) distinguishes reporting an experience and reporting a strategy.

Pilkington and Glasgow (1967) distinguish five kinds of verbal report in terms of the extent to which they can be checked by other methods. These range from descriptions of subjective experiences such as dreams and images, through reports about phenomena which have behavioural components, such as personality traits, to explanations of behaviour and experiences. These differences have important implications for the validity of introspection. In this connection it may be useful to distinguish reporting: the content of experience, the process of behaviour, and the determinants of behaviour.

History

A study of the use of introspection in the history of psychology highlights the different ways in which verbal reports can be treated. Introspection was the prime method used by the structuralists, other methods being considered supplementary. In their case, strictly controlled conditions were employed and subjects were highly trained. It is not quite clear in what the training consisted but one of its aims appears to have been avoidance of the 'stimulus error': subjects were instructed to exclude previous knowledge of the stimulus items, to eliminate meaning from their descriptions and to report only 'pure' sensations. These reports provided the data for a theory of the structure of the mind in which the contents of consciousness were analysed into sensory components.

The Würzburg psychologists attempted to extend this approach to the higher mental processes of thinking and judgment. Subjects, having completed tasks such as sensory judgment, constrained association and sentence evaluation, were asked to describe what had gone on in their minds. A relatively free technique was used, in which the experimenter might question the subject if his introspection was unclear. Two problems arose. The first was the discovery of imageless thought: the Würzburg subjects were frequently unable to give a coherent account of the contents of their consciousness while reaching their judgments. The conclusion was inescapable: mental processes could occur without conscious accompaniment. The second problem was the apparent disagreement between the results of the structuralist and Würzburg schools (the former challenging the existence of imageless thought), which contributed to the discrediting of introspection as a method. The inconsistency appeared to be at the level of data. Some thought that the privacy of introspection made it unclear how the argument could be resolved. With hindsight it seems likely that procedural differences were responsible for the discrepancies, and that the problem of inaccessibility has more serious implications for the method of introspection than has the problem of privacy. These are discussed below.

The immediate result, however, was that the behaviourists rejected introspection as unreliable. Watson, influenced by the positivist aim of basing all science on objective methods and public data, dismissed introspection as follows: 'Psychology as the behaviourist views it is a purely objective, experimental branch of natural science. Its theoretical goal is the prediction and control of behaviour. Introspection forms no essential part of its methods, nor is the scientific value of its data dependent upon the readiness with which they lend themselves to interpretation in terms of consciousness.' Later behaviourists were prepared to listen to what their subjects said, but not to take it at face value. Verbal reports were treated in exactly the same way as any other responses, as data which required interpretation.

The Gestalt psychologists, opposed to the structuralists' theoretical analysis, encouraged a more naïve attitude in their subjects who, in the phenomenological tradition, were instructed to report experience as it immediately appeared to them. Other traditions where introspective reports are taken at face value include those of Kelly (1955) who considered the person the best authority on himself, and Rogers (1965) for whom unconditional acceptance, empathy and positive regard are attitudes of the therapist towards the client necessary for successful therapy.

Psychoanalysis represents a paradoxical, interesting intermediate case, where the subject is instructed not to censor material (he is 'constrained' to be 'free') but an interpretation is then imposed by the analyst. In this sense psychoanalysis takes a behaviourist attitude to verbal reports. Thus constraint, and hence bias, can enter in either at the stage of production, as a result of the conditions imposed, or at the later stage of interpretation, in the form of the theoretical framework used. The increase in interest in conscious experience as part of the subject matter of psychology in recent years has led to a number of papers which have sought to reassess the role of introspection (e.g. Burt 1962, Joynson 1972, Pilkington & Glasgow 1967, Radford 1974).

Theoretical problems

Is introspection different in kind from other methods, and if so, in what way? Considerable debate has centred on the nature of introspection and the status of introspective reports. On the one hand, it has been suggested that it confers 'privileged access', and that it can supply unique data which could not be obtained in any other way; on the other hand, it has been rejected as a scientific method on the grounds of subjectivity. According to the mentalist, the subject observes inner states, to which he has direct access, as if on a private cinema screen. These determine, and are referred to in his reports. According to the behaviourist, the experimenter observes verbal responses, which are the product of, and provide indirect evidence for, underlying processes.

Ayer (1959) has distinguished a number of different senses of privacy. On the most stringent interpretation, introspective reports would provide the only possible evidence for the existence of a mental state. This is more plausible for images than for motives but is generally untrue. In most cases other behavioural and/or physiological observations can be made which are relevant to determining its existence.

On a second interpretation it might be held that the subject is the only person who has this particular type of evidence. This appears to be true of our current situation. People do have special knowledge of their sensations. Whether anyone in the future could have the same kind of evidence of another person's mental states would depend on technological advances and the conceptual analysis of personal identity.

Thirdly, is introspection distinguished on account of its subjectivity? The distinction between subjective and objective is less clear cut than at first appears. On the one hand, as we have seen, there are usually alternative public sources of evidence; private experiences can be made public by communicating them; and descriptions of private events are derivative from public ones. The impossibility of private languages has been demonstrated by Wittgenstein (1953) and the social origin of descriptions of inner states has been discussed by Skinner (1953). On the other hand, all so-called 'objective' observations depend on subjective experiences. 'Strictly speaking, every first hand observation is necessarily "private"' (Burt 1962). As Schrödinger (1958) pointed out of physics, 'All this information goes back ultimately to the sense perceptions of some living person or persons, however many ingenious devices may have been used to facilitate the labour . . . The most careful record, when not inspected, tells us nothing.' Observations are necessarily private and particular; the scientific statements inferred from them are necessarily public and general (Perkins 1953). Thus the distinction between subjective and objective is a matter of degree.

If verbal reports are allowable as scientific data, how are they to be treated? Can they be accepted at face value? Or do they have the same status as data from other methods, simply providing a basis from which inferences can be made? Some have argued that they carry special authority, perhaps even being incorrigible; others that they are particularly prone to artifact.

It might be claimed that the subject is the final authority on his mental states. This may be defensible with respect to experience but appears not to be so with regard to behaviour. The subject may be in a privileged position due to greater familiarity with his own biography. As Skinner (1953) observed: 'Because of his preferred position with respect to his own history he may have special information about his readiness to respond, about the relation of his behavior to controlling variables, and about the history of these variables. Although this information is sometimes erroneous and . . . may even be lacking, it is sometimes useful in a science of behavior'. The results of psychological experiments clearly show that introspective reports are not infallible. In many cases the subject may be in no better a position to make observations about his behaviour than another observer, and there is evidence that introspective reports are susceptible to various kinds of bias (e.g. Sheehan & Neisser 1969, Nisbett & Wilson 1977). But 'because one sometimes makes mistakes . . . it does not follow that one always makes them or even that one makes them frequently' (Kelvin 1956). Harré and Secord (1972) support a balanced view, espousing what they call an 'open souls doctrine', according to which introspective reports are authentic but revisable; a special case must be made out if they are to be rejected.

Introspection provides data like any other method, from which inferences are made. The behaviourist is incorrect in denying that subjects have privileged access to their experiences and in assimilating introspective reports to ejaculations such as 'ouch!' (Hebb 1968); they are conceptually different in that they make referential claims. The mentalist is incorrect in attributing to them superior validity.

Practical problems

Some have suggested that introspection is actually impossible. Kant claimed that introspective acts could not themselves be introspected. Comte (1842) argued the point explicitly: 'As for observing in the same way intellectual phenomena at the time of their actual presence, that is a manifest impossibility. The thinker cannot divide himself in two, of whom one reasons whilst the other observes him reason. The organ observed and the organ observing being, in this case, identical, how could observation take place? This pretended psychological method is then radically null and void.' That the thinker cannot divide himself in two, and that the organ observed and the organ observing are the same, are assumed rather than demonstrated. Parallel processing does occur, but to the extent that the processes involved are dependent on conscious attention there are likely to be severe capacity limitations. An extreme case of impairment would be attempting to make reports while in a state of heightened emotion.

J. S. Mill's (1882) reply was: 'It might have occurred to M. Comte that a fact may be studied through the medium of memory, not at the very moment of our perceiving it, but the moment after; and this is really the mode in which our best knowledge of our intellectual states is generally acquired.' The following dilemma arises as described by De Groot (1965), who has provided one of the most thorough discussions of the topic, having used the method of thinking aloud to study the making of moves in chess. If subjects delay their report until after they have completed the task, they may forget what happened and *memory errors* may creep in. If, on the other hand, they attempt to introspect at the same time as performing another intellectual task, there is likely to be mutual *interference* and alteration of processes. 'Verbalising one's thoughts unequivocally adds *an extra burden* to the subject's task. On the one hand, the added instruction to think aloud, necessarily influences the thought process to some degree; on the other, concentrated thinking on the problem itself must somewhat hamper its reporting . . . quite often thoughts move so quickly that the spoken word cannot keep up with them. The subject is then forced to skip steps or to deliberately slow down his thinking (if possible) which thereby disturbs the thought process' (De Groot 1965). Another effect his subjects reported was abnormal formalisation of thinking.

'With some subjects gaps and pauses in reporting are frequent and of such duration that they cannot be assumed to result from actual pauses in thinking. He may just temporarily forget his second task (to think aloud), or he may not be able to verbalise adequately what he is or has been doing mentally' (De Groot 1965). Thus the nature of the difficulty may lie in *communication*, in the translation of thoughts into words. Skinner has frequently remarked on the ambiguities associated with labelling private states. De Groot found that there were individual differences with respect to the ease with which subjects were able to describe their mental processes, intuitive thinkers finding the most difficulty. Introspective reports are likely to provide a distorted account.

Deception may be either *intentional* (some of De Groot's subjects suppressed strategies of which they were ashamed), or *unintentional*. A venerated case of the latter is rationalisation described by Freud, who distinguished the subject's reason from the reason, which might be an unconscious motive. A simple demonstration is post-hypnotic suggestion, where the subject constructs a reason for behaviour which is in fact determined by instructions of which he is unaware given under hypnosis. More recently, Wason and Evans (1975; see also Evans & Wason 1976) have argued that protocols given by subjects in reasoning tasks are sometimes rationalisations.

These appear to be determined by the situation and their behaviour in it, rather than being expressions of the causes of the behaviour, which are known from an analysis of performance in other experiments to be discrepant with the subjects' reports. (See also data from Nisbett & Wilson 1977, discussed on pp. 59–61.)

There is, in fact, evidence that introspective reports are particularly prone to experimental artifacts. For example, Sheehan and Neisser (1969), in a study which failed to demonstrate a relation between reported vividness of imagery and memory for patterns, found effects due to the experimenter (Sheehan obtaining higher vividness ratings than Neisser) and demand characteristics (vividness ratings increased after an enquiry which focussed attention on imagery). As Orne (1962) observed, the more ambiguous the situation for the subject the greater the likely resulting variability in interpretation. It is perhaps ironical that Orne recommends pre- and post-experimental enquiry as methods of attenuating the effect of demand characteristics.

The most serious objection to introspection as a method in psychology, however, is the fact that most of the relevant data are *unavailable* to consciousness. Conscious processes are the tip of the iceberg (Miller 1964). Most of mental life and behaviour proceeds unconsciously (as we saw in Ch. 4). Discrimination can occur without awareness, concepts can be formed and problems solved without subjects being able to report on the critical features. The Würburg psychologists made this discovery when they attempted to apply the structuralists' methods to thinking and judgment, and their findings were soon confirmed by Binet (1903) and Woodworth (1906). It is the perchings (the static images) rather than the flights (the relations in the margins of attention) (James 1890) that are in consciousness, the products rather than the processes of thinking. One example is the storing of running totals in mental arithmetic (Hayes 1973). Nisbett and Wilson's (1977) paper is devoted to showing that subjects are only able to give correct reports on the determinants of their behaviour when the stimuli are salient and plausibly related to the responses, these judgments resulting from *a priori* causal hypotheses rather than direct access to mental processes. Furthermore, introspection cannot be used with animal subjects and presents problems in developmental and abnormal psychology. Unfruitfulness rather than subjectivity was the reason for its decline.

At best, introspective reports are likely to lead to an account which is incomplete, at worst to one which is misleading. What is required is an analysis of the conditions which determine such reports so that their reliability and validity can be assessed.

The use of introspection in current psychology

An examination of the use of introspective reports in current psychology may illustrate some of its advantages and disadvantages, and ways in which the problems of reliability and validity can be tackled.

THE CONTENT OF EXPERIENCE

One of the most obvious areas for the use of introspection, and one in which systematic sources of error have been extensively investigated, is psychophysics. Fechner's methods may not have solved the mind–body problem as he had hoped but they enabled a start to be made on the investigation of sensory experience and an examination of the validity of sensory judgments. Few would hesitate to use verbal reports in the study of perception, but much has now been learned about their limitations (cf. Woodworth & Schlosberg 1954). One discovery that was made was that more accurate results were obtained if subjects were not allowed to use a 'don't know' category. In this case subjects may know more than they are aware of. Other systematic sources of bias such as time errors and series effects were also revealed.

The study of perception also illustrates one of the advantages of introspection. Although discriminative capacities can be studied by other means, for example by instructing subjects to adjust a comparison stimulus to match a standard or by operant conditioning (as must perforce be done in the case of animals, cf. Stretch 1966), verbal report may be a much more convenient method, avoiding the necessity of setting up elaborate apparatus and training schedules. Asking can save a great deal of time and trouble.

An extension of sensation and perception, posing even more challenging problems for experimental investigation, is imagery. A number of innovative techniques have been developed. Haber and Haber (1964) introduced the criteria for eidetic imagery of accuracy, scannability, positive colour and persistence, thereby increasing the stringency of claims for its existence. Accuracy can be objectively checked against the presented stimulus, scannability probably by observing the subject's eye movements, and positive colour perhaps by getting the subject to superimpose his image on different coloured backgrounds and observing the results. Persistence is more dependent on the subject's report but might be checked by observation of eye movements or a superimposition technique.

An extension of this last was used in an ingenious experiment by Stromeyer and Psotka (1970), employing identical Julesz random dot stereograms. On these a figure was superimposed, slightly displaced between the stimuli for the two eyes, such that it stood out in depth when viewed stereoscopically. The stimulus for one eye was presented to the subject, who was instructed to form an eidetic image of it. After an interval (of up to three days) the appropriate stimulus was presented to the other eye and the subject instructed to combine the two. Their eidetic subject was able to point to the corners of the figure. The likelihood of such a result occurring by chance is extremely remote.

A related case is the study of dream imagery, which is particularly interesting with respect to the use of multiple measures. Stoyva and Kamiya (1968) have documented the way in which the study of the subjective state of dreaming became respectable with the discovery of a correlation between rapid eye movements (REM) and dream reports (DR) by Aserinsky and Kleitman in 1953. This raises the question of whether the increase in respectability is justified. Is one measure superior to the other or is it the correlation that is important? In what way can a correlation strengthen an inference? They suggest that, in this case, verbal reports provide primary validation and behavioural and physiological measures corroborative evidence. REM by themselves tell us nothing about dreaming; their usefulness is dependent on their having first been validated against verbal reports. We take it on trust, arguing by analogy, that when other people report dream experiences these are similar to our own.

The corroborative value of the correlation between physiological measures and verbal reports was strengthened by establishing what might be described as gradations of correlation. Qualitative and quantitative improvements were made by making the correlation more fine grain. A nominal correlation (the co-occurrence of REM and DR) was raised to a quantified one by the following demonstrations: (a) a correlation between the time elapsed prior to awakening and the estimated length of dream (Dement & Kleitman 1957); (b) a correlation between the density of REM and the amount of physical activity reported in the dream (Berger & Oswald 1962); (c) a relation between the direction of REM and the visual activity reported in the dream, e.g. horizontal movements for watching tennis matches (Dement & Kleitman 1957), although this has not been confirmed by all subsequent work. These 'extensions of the empirical network' strengthen the corroborative validation.

Stoyva and Kamiya claim (rightly) that the mental state of dreaming is indexed imperfectly by both verbal report and physiological measures (i.e. DR and REM). This raises the very interesting question of what inferences are made when the measures conflict, and we may take this example as a case study.

Here we have two indices (DR and REM) of a hypothesised

mental state (dreaming). Logically there are four possible empirical situations: DR and REM, DR in the absence of REM, REM in the absence of DR, and neither DR nor REM. For each of these, logically, there are two possible conclusions: the existence or non-existence of the hypothesised state of dreaming. It is instructive to consider how the conclusion might be reached in each case.

Case 1: co-occurrence of DR and REM. This is represented by Aserinsky and Kleitman's (1953) original demonstration. Here workers seem to be in agreement that the appropriate conclusion is that dreaming took place. This inference is strengthened by the refined correlations with respect to duration, density and direction described above. However, it should be noted that it is logically possible that dreaming did not occur. Is the fact that this conclusion has been ignored an instance of verification bias?

Case 2: DR in the absence of REM. Here opinions differ. Those who take DR as the sole criterion of dreaming (e.g. Malcolm 1959) conclude that dreaming occurred; those who take REM as the ultimate criterion (e.g. Dement 1955, Wolpert 1960) deny that dreaming occurred and conclude that the DR was a fabrication. And indeed such reports might be considered suspect because of the lack of physiological corroboration; there is a sense in which they are less convincing than cases where both indices are present. There are a number of instances of this situation and they may perhaps warrant different conclusions. We shall consider them in turn. Foulkes (1962) obtained reports from non-REM periods. However, these were qualitatively different from reports from REM periods, being more thought-like. Distinctive verbal reports correlated with distinctive physiological measures might give credence to a conclusion of different mental states and hence non-existence of dreaming. Reports are sometimes also obtained from hypnagogic states (Foulkes & Vogel 1965). In the absence of further evidence, the choice is perhaps equally divided between a conclusion of dreaming on the basis of the similarity of verbal report, or not dreaming on the basis of a difference in physiological measure. Other cases of mental activity in non-REM periods, such as sleep talking and sleep walking, being so different from verbal reports of dreaming, might best be interpreted as indicative of non-dream states. And indeed this is confirmed by their occurrence in stage 4 rather than stage 1 sleep (where REM occur). Finally, subjects deprived of sleep often come to report dreams outside REM periods. As these might be thought to be abnormal and dream-deprived a conclusion of dreaming might be appropriate.

Case 3: REM in the absence of DR. In this case also opinions diverge and opposite conclusions may be reached. Those who define dreaming in terms of REM conclude that dreaming occurred; those who opt for DR as the sole criterion conclude that dreaming did not occur. There are a number of empirical instances of this situation: 15–20 per cent of times where subjects are awakened from REM periods they do not report dreams. Are these cases of recall failure or did dreaming not occur? Cases of nonreport where it may be plausible to argue that the subject has forgotten the dream are those where there is a delay before awakening (evidence for interference or decay theory could be brought in support), or where the subject is not awakened and reports the next day that he did not dream (here evidence for state-dependent learning could be adduced in support). In this latter case, the argument is supported by the knowledge that had he been awakened there is a high probability that a dream would have been reported. Here REM are preferred to DR as the criterion and, if this argument is accepted, it shows that DR are not always the sole or best indicator. Another difficult case is that of neonates, in whom REM periods form about 50 per cent of their sleep. Some have queried whether they dream. Here other theoretical ideas might help disambiguate the situation. For example, if dreams are thought to have the function of organising experience then a verdict of dreaming would be plausible. That DR are not the sole index of dreaming is shown somewhat trivially by an experiment of Antrobus *et al.* (1965), in which human subjects were taught to indicate dreams by pressing a switch, the frequency of such presses increasing during REM periods; and more intriguingly perhaps by one in which monkeys were taught, in an avoidance conditioning paradigm, to press a bar whenever a visual image appeared on a frosted screen (Vaughan 1964). High rates of bar pressing in REM periods were taken to indicate dreaming. This is noteworthy as an attempt to demonstrate dream imagery in animals but hinges on the verbal report validation in humans and the argument from analogy.

Case 4: neither DR nor REM. An example is the failure to give dream reports when awakened in non-REM periods. It would probably be concluded that dreaming did not occur, and indeed anyone who holds either index as the absolute criterion must conclude this. It might also be taken to confirm the correlation of DR and REM. However, it is logically possible that a dream experience did occur. If this were so then dreaming would not be a necessary condition of either DR or REM and neither would be an infallible index.

What can be concluded from this discussion? An examination of these situations has shown that a complex network of data and theory is involved. It appears that verbal reports are necessary for initial validation but that the physiological measure turns out to be slightly more reliable.

THE PROCESS OF BEHAVIOUR

Introspection is an obvious method for studying the content of experience. When it comes to the investigation of the processes underlying behaviour, however, its use is much more questionable. A number of classic studies have employed it, a popular technique being to ask subjects to think aloud. Duncker (1945) hoped to reveal the processes of problem-solving in this way. One of the most extensive investigations of this type in recent years has been De Groot's (1965) study, in which he aimed to infer the macroscopic structure of processes involved in chess playing, an activity he considered to be goal-directed and hierarchically organised. Shallice (1972) has argued that this work provides some of the best evidence for serial processing in thinking.

A particularly interesting case of the application of introspection to the study of thinking is that of Newell and Simon (1972), who used protocols both as an initial starting point from which to develop a theory and as final validation. They asked subjects to think aloud while solving symbolic logic and other problems and used the descriptions of the operations employed as a basis for the construction of computer programs to model the thought process. The resulting simulations were accepted as psychological theories if they generated behaviour which adequately matched that of the subjects. (See Valentine 1978, for a fuller discussion of the contribution of introspection to the study of thinking.)

As a final example, the case of personality questionnaires may be considered. These may be thought of as employing a type of introspection: the subject is asked to report on his feelings or behaviour. However, there is no necessity to take these reports at face value; a behaviourist approach is perfectly possible. It may merely be concluded that a particular pattern of responding (for example, 'neurotic introversion') is predictive of a particular pattern of behaviour in another situation (for example, taking fewer involuntary rest pauses in tapping tasks).

DETERMINANTS OF BEHAVIOUR

Nisbett and Wilson (1977) make it abundantly clear that subjects are often unreliable informants with respect to the determinants of their behaviour. Evidence is reviewed from subliminal perception, learning without awareness, problem-solving, complex decision-making, cognitive dissonance, attribution and helping behaviour, in addition to a number of experiments of their own, which demonstrates that subjects are, in general, unable to report accurately on the effects of stimuli influencing their behaviour. It is argued that subjects have little or no direct introspective access to higher order cognitive processes. They may be unaware of the stimuli (as in the case of subliminal perception or Maier's (1931) experiment, where the majority of subjects failed to report the usefulness of the hint which helped them solve the problem); they may be unaware of the responses (subjects in studies of attitude change may report their pre-experimental opinion inaccurately and thus be unaware that a change has occurred, as in experiments by Bem and McConnell (1970) and Goethals and Reckman (1973)); or they may be unaware of the relation between stimuli and responses.

On the one hand, subjects may fail to report influential stimuli. There is now an increasing body of evidence where an experimental manipulation is demonstrated to have an effect on behaviour but whose efficacy is denied by subjects. For example, in accordance with predictions, insomniac subjects given placebo pills said to produce arousal reported getting to sleep earlier, whereas those given pills said to produce relaxation reported getting to sleep later, than controls, but neither group attributed these effects to the pill, instead producing rationalisations for their behaviour (Storms & Nisbett 1970). In the bystander effect, subjects deny the influence of the number of other people present on the likelihood of their helping (Latané & Darley 1970), perhaps to avoid moral embarrassment. In one of Nisbett and Wilson's own experiments, evaluative judgments concerning the quality of articles of clothing showed a marked position effect, right-most objects being over-chosen; not surprisingly, subjects denied any such influence. These last two cases provide instances of phenomena which are dependent on subjects' ignorance for their existence. It seems unlikely that people would continue to behave in these ways if they were fully cognisant.

On the other hand, ineffective stimuli may be reported, as in Maier's (1931) experiment where some subjects reported the efficacy of a useless hint, or one of Nisbett and Wilson's experiments where subjects incorrectly reported that the inclusion of a 'reassurance' phrase in the instructions increased their willingness to take electric shocks. In this latter case, in common with many others, subjects' reports correlated very much more highly with the predictions of observers or control subjects not actually run in the experiment, but asked to say what they thought the effects would be, than with what actually happened. This led Nisbett and Wilson to argue that subjects' reports have the same basis as observers' reports, namely, *a priori* causal theories, which may have as their source cultural rules, implicit causal schemata, assumed covariation, or connotative similarity between stimuli and responses. (There is evidence that people's judgments of covariation are based on conceptual similarity rather than empirical observation, see, e.g. Shweder 1977.) Subjects' reports will sometimes be correct, but only incidentally and not as the result of direct introspective access. Conditions where they are likely to be correct are those where the influential stimuli are available, the connection between stimuli and responses plausible, and where there are few plausible non-influential factors available. One case where these conditions obtain is in learning without awareness paradigms (Dulany 1962). Another is where rules are overtly checked, as in the complex judgments made by stockbrokers and clinicians (Slovic & Lichtenstein 1971). Reports will be likely to be inaccurate when either the relevant stimuli are unavailable or non-salient, e.g. if they are contextual rather than in the focus of attention, non-verbal, removed in time, or where the non-occurrence of events is significant; or where the connection between stimuli and responses is implausible, as for example in the case of discrepant magnitudes between cause and effect. Other known factors which militate against the accuracy of verbal reports are what Nisbett and Wilson label the 'mechanics of judgment', such as order, anchoring, contrast and position effects.

It remains to explain the illusion of direct introspective access. People do have privileged knowledge of their sensations and personal biographies. Three factors which may help to maintain the illusion are the confusion of products or intermediate outputs with process; the fact that disconfirmations are relatively hard to come by, negative instances being easily explained away; and self-esteem, people preferring to feel they are in a position of superior knowledge and control.

Validation

Pilkington and Glasgow (1967) argue that the use of introspection may be more difficult than other methods but that it is not substantially different in kind. Conditions can be specified in which statements about subjective experiences can be intersubjectively confirmed and their truth checked. As they point out: 'Statements subjects may make about their subjective experiences are not unique in being difficult to confirm' and 'introspective reports are not unique in achieving only high probability'. Approaches to the validation of introspective reports have also been discussed by Natsoulas (1967).

Internal validity can be improved by ingenious experimental design as we saw in the case of Stromeyer and Psotka (1970) where the conditions devised left little room for doubt. Schoenfeld and Cumming (1963) are of the opinion that discrimination training might improve the control of perceptual responses over verbal responses.

External validity can be obtained by the application of a public criterion as a check on the accuracy of reports, as suggested by Natsoulas (1967), who comments that autonomic responses are often favoured. Behavioural measures can also be employed as was discussed in connection with the experiment on eidetic imagery by Haber and Haber (1964). That this is not a simple matter became clear from the examination of indexing the state of dreaming. Broadbent (1961) takes the view that 'amongst responses, it is perfectly legitimate to include the statements made by human beings, as long as the differences between such responses correspond to differences between other stimuli or other responses', implying that these other responses are somehow more respectable or reliable. This leads to the paradox that if verbal reports correlate with other measures then they are redundant; if they do not correlate, the problem arises of deciding which are valid. The example quoted by Natsoulas is an instance of a discrepancy between verbal and autonomic responses. In an experiment on the binocular fusion of colours by Gunter (1951) a galvanic skin response (GSR) was conditioned to binocular presentation of yellow spectral light. In one of the test conditions, red was presented to one eye and green to the other. The autonomic responses indicated fusion (a large GSR occurring) whereas the verbal responses indicated rivalry (subjects reporting that they experienced red and green rather than yellow). Our discussion of dreaming illustrated both the way in which the validity of verbal reports could be strengthened by corroboration from other measures, and how cases of conflict might be resolved by judicious theorising and experimentation.

Another possibility is to make *verbal reports the object of investigation* and examine their determinants. What is required is the discrimination of cases where they can be taken at face value from those where they cannot. Pilkington and Glasgow (1967) note, as general kinds of test, that it is possible to search for intra-subject consistency, and evidence of the subject's honesty and reliability in situations where these can be checked.

On the one hand it may be possible to distinguish different types of verbal report. For example, Carlson (1960 *et seq.*) tested the implications of hypotheses concerning subjects' errors in size constancy experiments. Empirical confirmation of these enabled conditions where phenomenal matches were obtained to be determined with some certainty. A possible technique is to obtain subjects' comments on their introspections. For example, Joynson (1958 *et seq.*) asked subjects, after participating in constancy experiments, to comment on the nature of their judgments, thus acquiring evidence, supplementary to that obtained by manipulating the instructions, on the distinction between judgments of apparent shape or size ('looking the same') and analytic judgments of 'real' shape or size ('being the same').

On the other hand it may be possible to uncover systematic sources of error. Pilkington and Glasgow refer to the elimination of motives for deception, artifacts such as suggestibility and demand characteristics. An experiment by Natsoulas and Levy (1956) suggests conscious monitoring of verbal reports: subjects who knew that tapes they heard were composed of repeated material were less likely to report transformations than subjects not so informed. Other examples are provided by the work on the 'mechanics of judgment' in psychophysics, and other evidence cited by Nisbett and Wilson (1977).

Most of these approaches involve *embedding reports in a theoretical network* (Dulany 1962) and testing the implications (Natsoulas 1967). Hypotheses may either be confirmed or disconfirmed. Platt (1964) and Garner *et al.* (1956) have argued that inferences can be considerably strengthened by systematic formulation and elimination of competing hypotheses. However, two points should be made: (a) The number of possible alternative hypotheses is unlimited. All scientific hypotheses are revisable. The possibility of a better one always exists. (b) There is no algorithm for formulating alternative hypotheses. The *elimination of alternative hypotheses* may be effected either statistically or experimentally (Natsoulas 1967). An example of the former is an experiment by Landauer and Rodger (1964) in which the hypothesis that apparent brightness judgments were composed of a combination of judgments made under 'reflectance' or 'luminance' instructions was disconfirmed by demonstrating that the variance for apparent judgments was lower than would be predicted on this basis, thus favouring the conclusion that distinct kinds of judgment were involved. Empirical elimination of alternative hypotheses is likely to involve the use of **convergent operations** (Garner *et al.* 1956). They write: 'Convergent operations are any set of experimental operations which eliminate alternative hypotheses and which can lead to a concept which is not uniquely identified with any one of the original operations, but is defined by the results of all operations performed. Thus converging operations can lead to concepts of processes which are not directly observable.' They illustrate the use of convergent operations to distinguish perceptual from response effects. For example, the demonstration that increasing the response set improves discrimination suggests that response factors may be involved in subception (Bricker & Chapanis 1953). Stoyva and Kamiya (1968) consider the use of dream reports and rapid eye movements to be another example of the use of convergent operations, enabling the rejection of the hypothesis that DR from REM periods reflect inaccurate recall and fabrications, and acceptance of the alternative hypothesis that they represent dream experiences reasonably accurately. Natsoulas gives as an example an experiment by Wallach *et al.* (1953) in which, in order to check that the three-dimensional perception of shadows cast by stationary wire figures was not due to knowledge that the shadows were of three-dimensional figures, a control condition was introduced in which subjects were not exposed to the wire figures rotating. Alternatively, competing hypotheses may be shown to be incapable of producing the effects, as in an experiment by Haber (1965), in which the hypothesis that experimental results were due to differential knowledge of the stimulus materials was eliminated by showing them to all subjects before the experiment.

All these methods involve the collecting of more data in a variety of theoretically linked situations, the progressive elimination and confirmation of hypotheses and the strengthening of inferences.

Evaluation

Introspection was first over-rated and then under-rated. The structuralists thought it provided a royal road to the contents of the mind. The behaviourists rejected it as unscientific on the grounds of subjectivity and privacy.

It has both advantages and disadvantages. Some of its advantages have been listed by Pilkington and Glasgow (1967). Introspection may provide important information on phenomena such as imagery, and in disciplines such as medicine, psychiatry and sociology. In clinical psychology it may additionally facilitate empathy. Reports by subjects or experimenters (perhaps themselves as subjects) may generate new hypotheses to test, or suggest modifications to experimental designs. They may aid in the interpretation, control and elimination of artifacts. Finally, it has the advantage of convenience, providing a method which is very much quicker and easier than most. Introspection as a method is not unique but it may be useful.

The disadvantages have already been discussed in detail. We

have seen that introspective reports are particularly prone to distortion but that the problems raised are not different in kind from those of other methods. No methods guarantee certainty and all can be validated in the same ways by theorising and experimentation.

Introspection has been under-rated because it was once over-rated. With hindsight we are in a better position to come to a more balanced view. With regard to the contents of experience introspection provides primary data, which can be supported by other measures. With respect to the process of behaviour, introspection is of relatively little use because most of the relevant data are unavailable to consciousness. Subjects have a reasonable chance of telling an experimenter what they experienced or did, but not how they did it. Products are available and these can be used as an aid in the reconstruction of the process. As to the reasons for behaviour, the evidence suggests that introspective reports are not generally a reliable guide on the stimuli influencing responses. Subjects may be able to report strategies and goals, and may sometimes be correct about the causes of their behaviour, but these judgments have the form of inferences and are not the result of privileged, direct access.

Finally, verbal reports are themselves behavioural responses. They provide data and are themselves in need of explanation. With the excesses of introspectionism and behaviourism in the past, a start can be made on their investigation. They can indeed be reinstated as part of the subject matter of psychology.

6

Sources of artifact

Most of the problems for psychological science dealt with in this book have arisen from fundamental philosophical objections. However, there is also a body of experimental evidence, namely, research on research, to be considered in this chapter, which has contributed to the debate about the appropriateness of the application of scientific methods as used in the physical sciences to psychology. Starting from the assumption of the experiment as itself a social situation, it has cast doubt on the traditional picture of an objective experimenter investigating an inert subject. Following similar discoveries in physics, it has demonstrated that non-interference and independence of observer and observed are scientific myths. (It is perhaps worth noting in passing that the models of the physical sciences which psychologists have studiedly aped have usually been outdated.)

Much of the work has been carried out and reviewed by Rosenthal (see Rosenthal 1966, Rosenthal 1967, Rosenthal & Rosnow 1969), using such methods as reports of experimenters' behaviour by subjects and films of experimenter–subject interactions. One task commonly used has been a person-perception one, in which subjects are presented with photographs of faces and asked to rate the persons depicted on a scale representing the degree of experienced success or failure. The work of Rosenthal has been criticised, e.g. by Barber and Silver (1968) on the grounds that many of his findings are based on the results of *post hoc* tests, without adjustment of critical values appropriate for multiple comparisons. Results are reported which do not reach conventionally accepted levels of significance. (I shall describe these as 'tendencies'.) Contradictory effects have been obtained and failures to replicate reported. Barber and Silver conclude that the experimenter expectancy effect is more difficult to demonstrate and less pervasive than is implied by Rosenthal. There is no guarantee that these experiments on experiments are themselves free from the kind of biases they seek to demonstrate. In some cases, for example, expectancy was confounded with desire: experimenters were told that they 'should' expect certain results or were paid more for obtaining them. We shall begin by considering some of the least plausible candidates for factors influencing the experimental situation.

The physical environment

Rosenthal (1967) cites evidence from Mintz that subjects judged others to be less happy when the judgments were made in an 'ugly' laboratory; and from Haley that experimenters took the experiment more seriously in disorderly, uncomfortable laboratories. Moreover, experimenters assigned to more professional appearing laboratories were perceived by their subjects as more expressive in voice, face and gesture.

Experimenter attributes

Perhaps Rosenthal's main contribution has been to demonstrate characteristics of the experimenter which may influence the outcome of an experiment.

There are effects due to *practice* and *fatigue*. Rosenthal's films showed that experimenters read the instructions faster and tended to read them more accurately to later than to earlier subjects. Their behaviour suggested that they tended to become more bored and less tense as the experiment progressed. That there are individual differences in these respects, and that these factors may have an effect on the experimental results, is suggested by the finding that subjects of experimenters who showed these changes rated stimulus persons as less successful.

Sarason (1965) and Rosenthal (1966) have argued that the *anxiety* of the experimenter may be a significant determinant of a subject's responses. Experimenters who had high scores on the Taylor Manifest Anxiety scale tended to show a greater degree of general body activity and a less dominant tone of voice.

Such personality characteristics have also been shown to extend to the principal investigator, even when he does not himself carry out the experiment. In one investigation when principal investigators collected their own data, their anxiety level correlated positively with the success ratings given by subjects of others pictured in photographs. When randomly selected research assistants ran the experiment for the principal investigators, the anxiety level of principal investigators, although not quite significant ($r = 0.40$, $p = 0.07$), was a much better predictor of the results than was the anxiety level of the research assistants ($r = 0.24$, not significant). These effects appear mystical but are presumably mediated through the research assistants. Experimenters who had been made more self-conscious by their principal investigators tended to behave less courteously towards subjects, as shown by film; those whose behaviour had been given more favourable evaluations by their principal investigators were described by their subjects as more casual and courteous, and obtained more positive results in a verbal conditioning experiment.

Similarly, experimenters who had high scores on the Marlowe–Crowne scale of *need for approval* spoke to their subjects in a more friendly tone of voice and tended to speak more enthusiastically, smile more often at their subjects and slant their bodies more towards them.

Rosenthal *et al.* have shown effects due to the *sex* of experimenter. Male experimenters were more friendly than female, as shown by their behaviour in films and by subjects' ratings. Most of the effects, as one might guess, are interactive between sex of experimenter and sex of subject. Female subjects evoked more smiling from their experimenters (data from Friedman cited in Rosenthal 1967). Rosenthal (1967) described the pattern of behaviour that female experimenters show towards male subjects as 'interested modesty'. Citing data from Katz, he reports that they took 13 per cent longer (not significant) to prepare stimuli for presentation to male than to female subjects, did not lean as close to male subjects, were friendly in the visual but not the auditory channel towards female subjects, whereas they were remarkably friendly in the auditory but not the visual mode towards male subjects. The pattern of behaviour shown by male experimenters towards female subjects, however, is described as just plain 'interested'. They took significantly longer in preparing stimulus material for presentation to female subjects, tended to be more friendly in movement than in tone of voice and to be somewhat unfriendly towards male subjects in the auditory channel. (Later work has suggested that such channel discrepancies may have some wider significance.)

In particular, Rosenthal's name has become associated with the phenomenon known as the **experimenter bias effect,** the way in which an experimenter's expectancy can determine the experimental outcome. Results have been obtained in the areas of animal learning, verbal conditioning, person perception and personality assessment. Experimenters who were told that their rats were bred for maze brightness on the one hand or maze dullness on the other obtained results in accordance with their expectations, i.e. 'maze bright' were perceived to perform significantly better than 'maze dull' rats despite being drawn randomly from the same population (Rosenthal & Fode 1963). In this experiment certain cases of cheating were observed (i.e. experimenters prodding subjects to run the maze) but whether such effects are sufficient to account for the results has not been demonstrated. In another study, children whose teachers were told (arbitrarily) that they would show unusual intellectual development within the next academic year showed significantly greater gains in I.Q. than children for whom such predictions were not made (though these children showed substantial improvements too), the effect being more marked in the youngest groups (Rosenthal & Jacobson 1966). Some of the technical defects of this study have been exposed by Thorndike (1968) and it has been subjected to detailed methodological criticism by Elashoff and Snow (1971).

Since Pfungst's (1911) study of Clever Hans, it has been known that experimenters can unintentionally communicate their expectations to their subjects. (Pfungst showed that Clever Hans' apparent ability to count was due to his responding to minimal movements the questioner made when the correct number had been tapped out, which cued the horse to stop.) Rosenthal (1967) has argued that unintended covert communication from the experimenter to the subject, which affects the subject's response, is the norm rather than the exception. He suggests that experimenters learn to communicate their hypotheses to their subjects covertly. It is obviously rewarding to have one's expectations confirmed, so experimenters are likely to be reinforced for, and repeat, behaviour which produces such results. That subjects' behaviour may affect experimenters' behaviour was suggested by one of Rosenthal et al.'s (1965) experiments, where confirmation or disconfirmation of the experimenter's hypothesis by initial stooge subjects differentially affected the responses in the experimental task and the personality test scores of subsequent subjects, these being predictable from a knowledge of the responses given by the initial, stooge subjects.

Analysis of films has led Rosenthal to claim that whether an experimenter will be successful in learning to influence his subjects to respond in accordance with his hypothesis can be predicted from his non-verbal behaviour during the first half minute of the experiment. Experimenters of whom this was true were more likeable, personal, relaxed, dominant and important-acting, and showed less leg movement. Later in the experiment, professionalism of manner became a predictor.

Some of these results, however, have been questioned by Barber and Silver (1968), who claim that even where the experimenter bias effect has been demonstrated, the mode of its operation is not clear. It may be mediated by subtle paralinguistic and kinesic cues which influence the subjects' responses, as Rosenthal suggests, but it is also possible that the mode of operation is independent of subjects' responses and may be intentional. Barber and Silver claim that, in the majority of experiments, misjudgment or misrecording of responses and fabrication of data have not been ruled out.

Such bias, if and when it does occur, becomes serious when it is differential rather than systematic. However, a thorough study of it may enable us to (a) correct for its effects, and (b) learn about communication in other dyadic relations.

Subject attributes

In a similar way, both long-term and short-term characteristics of the subject may influence the results of an experiment. We have already seen that sex is one of these.

Another factor is the amount of *experience* the subject has from past experiments. Holmes (1967) found that experienced subjects made more of an attempt to co-operate with the experimenter but showed less interest in what the experiment was about; they also tended to see the experiment as more scientific and more valuable than less experienced subjects (which of course might be the reason for their continuing to act as subjects).

Subjects also vary considerably with respect to their attitude towards an experiment. Gustav's (1962) investigation of attitudes of students towards compulsory participation revealed that 40 per cent expressed unfavourable attitudes ranging from irritation and apprehension; the remaining subjects reported positive attitudes including eagerness, curiosity and great interest. Of the group, 37 per cent said that they would not have participated voluntarily (but this is probably a good thing from the point of view of scientific methodology). Argyris (1968) reports that the majority of a large sample of American undergraduates were 'critical, mistrustful, and hostile' to the course requirement of research participation. Jackson and Pollard (1966) asked subjects to give their reasons for volunteering for an experiment on sensory deprivation. Curiosity was the reason given by 50 per cent, money by 21 per cent, and by 7 per cent a desire to help science. The motivations lying behind an attempt to discover the experimenter's hypothesis may be similarly various and aimed at validating it (Orne 1962), presenting oneself in the most favourable light (Riecken 1962), or fouling up the experimenter's research, termed the 'screw you effect' by Maslow (1966).

This active participation of the subject in the experiment has been particularly stressed by Orne, who has suggested that the reasons for the lack of reproducibility and ecological validity of psychological experiments may be due to failure to consider the role of **demand characteristics** in the experimental situation. These he defines as 'the totality of cues which convey an experimental hypothesis to the subjects'. They include 'the rumors or campus scuttlebut about the research, the information conveyed during the original situation, the person of the experimenter, and the setting of the laboratory, as well as all explicit and implicit communications during the experiment proper'. He goes on to point out that the experimental procedure itself may be a source of cues for the subject; for example, if a test is given twice with some intervening treatment, even the dullest college student is aware that some change is expected.

Demand characteristics will vary with the sophistication of the subject and the ambiguity of the experimental cues. It is likely that the demand characteristics which are most potent in determining subjects' behaviour are those which convey the purpose of the experiment effectively but not obviously.

The experiment, as has now been pointed out, is a special type of social situation with clearly defined rules and expectations. As Orne reports, people asked to do five push-ups as a favour will ask 'why?' but if the request appears in the guise of an experiment they will ask 'where?' Also reported is an experiment in which subjects, instructed to add numbers of sheets of random digits and then tear up the sheets, worked for several hours with relatively little sign of overt hostility, apparently imbuing the task with meaning, perhaps construing it as an endurance test. The experiment is a problem-solving situation in which the subject has to work out what the experimenter's hypothesis is (he has one clue: it will not be what the experimenter says it is because 'psychologists always lie'), so that he can act appropriately. Orne argues that the subjects in psychological experiments are active, unlike the passive inanimate objects of the physical sciences, and that this demands modifications in experimental methodology. Demand characteristics cannot be eliminated, because subjects are bound to impose meaning on tasks, but they can be studied. Attempts can be made to identify them so that their importance as determinants of behaviour in experiments can be assessed, by correlational means, for example: do subjects' perceived demand characteristics predict behaviour better than the experimental variables do?

Orne has suggested three experimental techniques for the study of demand characteristics, discussed below.

(a) *Post-experimental enquiry.* In this case it is necessary to proceed from general to specific questions, and difficult to get valid answers on account of the 'pact of ignorance' between subject and experimenter, by which the subject's naïveté is tacitly agreed. There are a number of difficulties, of which one is that the subject's perception of the experimenter's hypothesis may be determined in part by his own experimental behaviour rather than being a relevant determinant of it, a distinction which would be obscured by merely establishing a correlation between them. This problem may be dealt with by the second method.

(b) *Pre-experimental enquiry.* In this case the subject is interrogated after being given as much information as a real subject in the experiment would have but is not allowed actually to make any responses. Both these procedures, (a) and (b), are of course subject to their own demand characteristics, which may be mitigated somewhat by using independent experimenters.

(c) *Use of simulating subjects.* This is an attempt to keep demand characteristics constant while eliminating the experimental variable. The behaviour of subjects not exposed to the experimental variable but instructed to behave as if they had been is compared with that of normal subjects.

Orne (1959) first discussed demand characteristics in connection with his work on hypnosis, but he has also used the third technique mentioned above to demonstrate sensory deprivation effects without sensory deprivation. Significant differences in the expected direction were obtained between a group of subjects given all the accoutrements of a sensory deprivation experiment (e.g. careful screening, release forms and a panic button) but no actual sensory deprivation, and a group who were told that they were controls for a sensory deprivation experiment, and who had identical treatment except for the absence of the panic button (Orne & Scheibe 1964).

A considerable body of data is now available on the characteristics of an important subsection of our subject population, *volunteers.* Rosenthal (1965), reviewing a variety of studies, concluded that volunteers differ significantly from non-volunteers in the following respects: they tend to be more intelligent, younger, less conventional, less authoritarian, more sociable and show a greater need for social approval. The characteristics of volunteers may be subject to change over time. These matters would not be serious perhaps but for the fact that such a high proportion of subjects are in fact volunteers.

Samples

Lurking doubts about the representativeness of samples have now been amply documented. Smart (1966) examined the *Journal of*

Abnormal and Social Psychology between the years 1962 and 1964 and the *Journal of Experimental Psychology* between the years 1963 and 1964. Schultz (1969) examined the *Journal of Personality and Social Psychology* and the *Journal of Experimental Psychology* from 1966 to 1967. Their results are shown in Table 6.1, from which it can be seen that between 75 and 80 per cent of studies are conducted on students and that virtually none are carried out on a general adult population. Furthermore, Schultz found that, in 3.6 per cent of the papers in the *Journal of Experimental Psychology*, the nature of the subjects was not specified. The predominance of college students means that, in the United States, 80 per cent of research is performed on 3 per cent of the population, a group which is unrepresentatively young, intelligent, upper-middle class, literate, introspective and male. Any forlorn hopes that things are better in Britain are dashed by Cochrane and Duffy's (1974) survey of the *British Journal of Psychology* and the *British Journal of Social and Clinical Psychology* from 1969 to 1972, which showed that 76.4 per cent of non-clinical studies using adults were conducted on samples of students, in many cases introductory ones. Over half reported using volunteers; 28 per cent did not report how their subjects were obtained, some of which we may guess used volunteers. Less than 15 per cent clearly did not use volunteers and most of these used clinical or school groups.

Table 6.1 *Percentages of papers in American Psychological Association journals using given categories of subjects (from Schultz 1969).*

Subjects	Journal of Experimental Psychology		Journal of Abnormal and Social Psychology	Journal of Personality and Social Psychology
	Smart	Schultz	Smart	Schultz
introductory psychology	42.2	41.2	32.2	34.1
other college	43.5	42.5	40.9	36.1
pre-college	7.0	7.1	16.9	18.5
special adult	7.3	5.6	9.4	10.1
general adult	0	0	0.6	1.2
all male	22.3	19.3	33.6	26.7
all female	6.0	6.0	10.8	10.6

Of the papers, 75 per cent did not report information about response rate, i.e. what proportion of potential subjects approached actually agreed to participate. When it was reported, however, it was usually satisfactory.

Less than 15 per cent used a *sampling procedure* which was considered adequate, i.e. either a generally accepted method, or some demonstration that the sample was representative in appropriate respects. Most failed to provide information on this matter and it was concluded that 85 per cent probably used inadequate methods. Of these, only 5 per cent discussed these deficiencies and their possible implications.

Another cause for concern was the *size of sample*. One quarter of the studies were based on $n<25$. Cochrane and Duffy conclude: 'Only 1–2 per cent of all the studies reported in these two journals over the past four years based their findings on a true sample of the general adult population.'

Statistical analysis

Cochrane and Duffy scrutinised a random sample of 50 of these papers for various kinds of statistical error. Apart from random sampling, parametric tests assume a normal distribution and homogeneity of variance. One third of the 37 studies using significance tests made some basic error in the *application of the test*. None reported testing the assumptions nor discussed the implications of ignoring them. More than six, i.e. 26 per cent, seriously violated the assumptions of the test used. In most cases insufficient data were available for such an evaluation to be made.

Eight authors appeared to have *misinterpreted the results of their hypothesis testing*, usually by inferring that rejection of the null hypothesis implied acceptance of the experimental hypothesis.

No-one discussed the *strength of the relation* reported, as distinct from its statistical significance. Of the results for which it was possible to estimate this, 56 per cent showed a relatively weak relationship. In 25 per cent of cases, the results accounted for less than 10 per cent of the variance in the dependent variable.

It was estimated that 12 of the papers *confused psychological with statistical significance*, 16 were circumspect in discussing the results, and in 22 cases this distinction was not applicable. Their general conclusions detail a list of depressing deficiencies and they suggest that until these can be remedied 'it appears that most of our research efforts into human behaviour will be essentially trivial'.

Conclusions

The term **ecological validity** was introduced by Brunswik (1947) to refer to appropriate generalisations from the laboratory to non-experimental situations. The cry of lack of ecological validity in psychological research has been heard in a number of quarters both inside and outside the discipline. For example, Neisser (1976) has suggested that it applies to much of cognitive psychology, and Baddeley (1976) has discussed it in connection with specific research paradigms, such as Sternberg's high-speed memory search (see also Ch. 13). In this chapter we have discussed two factors in particular which contribute to a lack of ecological validity, namely, unrepresentativeness and smallness of samples, and ignoring demand characteristics. However, we have mainly been concerned with technical incompetence.

More alarming is the charge of irrelevancy and insignificance concerning the content of research. To some extent there is a conflict between the demands of science and those of the general public, though it is still true that some of the best theoretical advances come from applied research. What is scientifically important may not always be what is of greatest interest to the layman. The concern of the former is the establishment of funda-mental, general principles; the interest of the latter lies in the particulars of individuals. Thus the layman may wish to predict a specific piece of behaviour, whereas the scientist is only interested in the mechanisms governing the underlying processes. We shall consider some of these issues in Chapter 14.

The cause of significance is not helped by unrepresentative sampling nor by ignoring demand characteristics; much less is it served by tackling problems that are theoretically and/or practically unimportant in the first place. The execution of psychological research that is significant in all senses of the word is one of the most difficult but worthwhile challenges.

7

Determinants of scientific advance: theories and facts

In this chapter we shall consider some of the factors contributing to scientific advance. First we shall consider the relative contributions of cultural and personal factors. To what extent are discoveries the work of a great man and to what extent are they a product of the spirit of the times? In what ways do these factors interact?

Next we shall consider how far discoveries are dependent on conceptual frameworks and how far on the development of techniques. To what extent do they depend on asking the right questions and to what extent on the possession of appropriate equipment? What is the relation between these factors: is one dependent on the other?

Then we shall discuss the relations between data and theory. What is the role in science of induction (proceeding from particular observations to general laws) and of deduction (deriving specific predictions from generalised hypotheses)? To what extent are theories constrained by the data and to what extent are the data dictated by the theory? Does this vary from theory to theory and between theorists? What is the role of non-rational factors? How do logical and psychological factors interrelate? There are two aspects of the process to be considered: hypothesis formation (which Reichenbach 1938 termed the 'context of discovery'), and hypothesis testing (termed by Reichenbach the 'context of justification'), and two types of questions to be answered: (a) the psychological one of the way in which scientists actually proceed, and (b) the logical one of the valid inferences between theory and data, which specifies how they should proceed.

We shall also consider whether progress is typically cumulative or whether it is characterised by the occurrence of major shifts in orientation, and the extent to which the development of psychology is representative of other sciences in this respect.

Cultural and personal factors

The relation between cultural and personal factors in the determination of scientific development was the theme of much of Boring's work in the history of psychology. He formulated it in terms of the relative merits of the Great Man theory, according to which exceptional individuals direct the course of scientific advance, and the Zeitgeist theory, according to which men are merely the instruments of cultural influences. The former stresses psychological and the latter sociological factors. A similar theme of the transcendence of the will and decisions of men by greater natural forces occurs in literature in Tolstoy's *War and peace* and was common in classical Greek tragedy (e.g. Euripides' *Sophocles*). After discussion of the topic in a number of papers, Boring (see Watson & Campbell (eds) 1963) concluded in favour of a dialectical relation between them. Great men he saw as agents of progress, rather than simply cause or symptom, their ideas as events in the space–time field of history.

Evidence for the influence of cultural factors comes from a number of sources. One is case studies in the history of science. Hyman (1964) has discussed the variety of influences which led Pavlov to his work on the conditioned response. These include the intellectual climate of the time, particularly positivism (which stressed objectivity) and materialism (which espoused physiological reductionism). As is so often the case, the idea of the conditioned response was not new. It had been expressed by many before, for example Whytt's description (1751) of 'psychic secretion'. There were also more specific influences in the form of teachers and books. Pavlov acknowledges his debt to G. H. Lewes' *Physiology of common life,* which included a discussion of work by Bernard, who in 1855 had suggested an experiment to investigate psychic secretion in a horse using a salivary fistula exactly analogous to that Pavlov used on dogs. Pavlov was also influenced by Darwin's *Origin of species,* particularly with respect to the notion of adaptation, and Sechenov's *Reflexes of the brain* which gave central importance to the reflex and its cortical inhibition.

Another particularly well documented example is that of Freud (see Whyte 1960, Reeves 1965). In this case the idea of unconscious mental processes can be traced back to classical Greek times but was dominant in 19th-century German philosophy and literature. Freud claimed to have avoided reading Nietzsche for this very reason. More specific influences came from his clinical experience, especially with Charcot and Janet (with whom he studied hysterical patients) and Breuer (with whom he first tried out the 'talking cure' on Anna O.); from his attendance at Brentano's lectures on Aristotelian logic from which he may have gained the ideas of hierarchical levels and multiple causation); from his association with Brücke (a member of a group of 'physicalistic' physiologists committed to a reductionist programme, which also numbered Helmholtz among its members, who had recently revived the notion of the conservation of energy); and from reading von Schubert's *Die Symbolik der Traumes,* which described many of the ideas later adopted by Freud, including several of the defence mechanisms.

A second source of evidence is that of simultaneous, independent discoveries. Ogburn and Thomas (1922) list 148 such cases. Well known examples include the formulation of the calculus by Leibniz and Newton, the theory of evolution by Darwin and Wallace, and the conditioned response by Pavlov and Twitmyer. These suggest that discovery is not dependent on a particular individual.

A third possible source of evidence comes from anticipations or rediscoveries. Frequently discoveries are made but acceptance is delayed, so it appears, until the time is ripe, when they are rediscovered. Such cases have been discussed by Boring (1927), Idhe (1948) and Warren (1948). An example is that of the laws of inheritance, discovered in 1865 by Mendel and rediscovered in 1900 by de Vries. We have already noted similar phenomena in the cases of Pavlov and Freud, whose contributions seem to have lain predominantly in getting ideas accepted, perhaps in these instances by providing a sufficient amount of convincing evidence. The same was in fact true for Darwin's theory of evolution.

The contribution of the Great Man has been discussed by James (1880), Hook (1943) and Bentley (1947). How far the specific educational experiences discussed above should be taken as indicative of psychological rather than social factors is arguable. They are certainly events in personal biographies though symptomatic of social influences. Specifically personal factors have been argued for in the case of Freud (cf. Jones 1955, Galdston 1956).

Considering the relevance of the topic it is astonishing that more work has not been done on the psychology of psychologists. It has been discussed by James (1907), Boring (1942) and Stolorow and Atwood (1979); and Roe (1953) has carried out an exploratory empirical investigation. A literature on personal factors in creativity exists. For the application of these to scientists, see Taylor and Barron (1963).

Concepts and techniques

The dual importance of an adequate conceptual framework and

technology can be illustrated by reference to the history of work on cortical localisation of function. It was necessary both to have formulated appropriate questions and to have available appropriate techniques.

Theories of the soul had to give way to theories of the mind and these in turn to be made more precise in terms of faculties. Aristotle thought that the mind resided in the heart. The error of this was less serious than the correct assumption that mental qualities have a physical basis. The late-18th-century revolution in the treatment of the insane was consistent with such an assumption. It acknowledged that the mind might be subject to disease (rather than infiltration by demons) and hence possibly dependent on the body, the usual seat of disease. Similar remarks may be made about the phrenologists who were wrong in detail – development of traits or faculties is not mapped by corresponding development of part of the brain, nor do bumps on the skull reflect bumps on the cortex – but right in general principle: the brain is the organ of the mind and localisation of function is true to a large extent (cf. McFie 1972). The phrenologists borrowed the faculty theory of the Scottish philosophers, Reid and Stewart. Later attempts have leant on psychometric analyses. Progress is dependent on the belief that it makes sense to search for the physical basis of the mind and, in particular, the belief that different functions are differentially localised in the brain.

However, just as important was the development of techniques. These include: ablation (Flourens 1842), electrical stimulation in animals (Fritsch & Hitzig 1870) and of conscious humans (Bartholow 1874), improvements in the sophistication of behavioural measurements (Franz 1902), recording from single cells (Hubel & Wiesel 1962) and the use of a radioactive isotope (Lassen, Ingvar & Skinhøj 1978).

Theories and facts

It should be borne in mind that the contribution of the various factors discussed in this chapter are complementary rather than opposed. The true process is likely to be one of reciprocal interaction (cf. Carr 1961). Focussing attention on one or two merely represents selection for the purpose of discussion. In some cases the theory appears to dictate the method. An example from the history of psychology is structuralism which, taking the subject matter of psychology to be conscious experience, employed the introspective method. Conversely, functionalism, considering the behaviour of all animals to be the prime subject matter of psychology, preferred observations of performance responses to introspective reports. These effects are more obvious in the systems of classical psychology, which made methodological recommendations in addition to attempting to provide general theories of behaviour, but to some extent all theories delimit the methods used in their investigation.

Flourens (1842) claimed it was the other way about: that 'it is the method which gives the results'. Examples from the history of psychology where this seems to have been the case are the phenomenological study of what is immediately given in perception leading to the theoretical concept of form qualities, and the lack of methods for investigating heredity leading to an emphasis on the environmental determination of behaviour in behaviourism. Common jibes, which illustrate the point, are that intelligence is what the tests measure, that factor analysis gets out what it puts in, and that Skinner's results are specific to his experimental procedure (which depends on food deprivation).

In the philosophy of science, the traditional view of the way in which science proceeded was by means of induction, where conclusions go beyond the premises, or 'beyond the information given' (Bruner 1957). The argument is from particular observations to a general law. According to this view facts are prior to theories. A major exponent was Francis Bacon (1620) who proclaimed that 'the understanding must not . . . be supplied with wings, but rather hung with weights, to keep it from leaping and flying' on the grounds that nature is an open book. He who reads it with a pure mind cannot misread it. Only if his mind is poisoned by prejudice can he fall into error. Different types of induction were distinguished by Aristotle and James Mill. Adherents in more modern times include the positivists whose aim was to build a unified body of knowledge on the basis of observations guaranteed by the methods of science.

More recently, however, there has been a swing away from induction towards deduction, which gives priority to theories over facts. This latter view has emphasised the role of theoretical presuppositions in observation. It has had many supporters, as the following quotations show:

> He who does not expect the unexpected will not discover it (Gromshi).

> Hypotheses are nets, only he who casts will catch (Novalis).

> Luck only makes sense against a background of prior expectations (Pasteur).

How odd it is that anyone should not see that all observations must be for or against some view if it is to be of any service . . . I have an old belief that a good observer really means a good theorist (Darwin).

I have had my solutions for a long time but I do not yet know how I am to arrive at them (Gauss).

When you have satisfied yourself that the theory is true you start proving it (Polya).

Two of the foremost spokesmen have been Karl Popper and Thomas Kuhn, whose work is discussed on pages 82–5 and 85–7.

As we pointed out at the beginning of this chapter, there are in fact two questions intermingled here, a logical and a psychological, and there are two broad answers that might be given to them, namely, induction (which gives priority to facts) and deduction (which gives priority to theories).

The logical question concerns the inferences that can be made between observation statements and theoretical statements. Thus an inductive answer to the logical question would claim that it is valid to proceed from particular observations to the conclusion of a general theoretical statement. This is in fact constantly done in science with the tacit premiss that events in the future will resemble events in the past. Hume pointed out that such a procedure is a matter of psychological practice rather than logical necessity. Since then there have been a number of attempts to 'tighten up' induction to make it meet the standards of deductive logic (e.g. Hempel's logic of confirmation, Goodman's concept of entrenchment, Keynes' logic of probability, and perhaps Popper's notion of corroboration). However, these attempts are all in vain: induction can never be justified in terms of the standards of deduction, where the conclusion is entailed by the premisses. Scientific hypotheses are unrestricted in space and time; it is their essence to go beyond the information given, to extend from the known to the unknown, from past observed cases to future unobserved cases.

A deductive answer to the logical question would claim that the only valid inferences which can be made are from theoretical statements to observations. These are likely to occur as predictions from a hypothesis about future observations.

The psychological question is concerned with the way in which scientists actually behave. An inductive answer to this question would claim that scientists begin by making observations and on the basis of these formulate a general theory. Hume believed that people functioned in this way and it may be true to some extent.

However, there is also some truth in the deductive answer to the psychological question, which claims that people are unable to make observations unless they have some prior theoretical conception. Facts do not speak for themselves and observations cannot be made *in vacuo*. Certain traditions such as phenomenology and ethology have attempted preconception-free observation but it is probably impossible to achieve perfectly and leads to problems of interpretation (see Ch. 13). The quotations cited above indicate that many are persuaded of the contribution of theory to fact. Popper has used the example of the discovery of penicillin, a chance observation that could not have been interpreted but for prior expectations. Experimental confirmation comes from Rosenthal *et al.*'s demonstrations of experimenter effect (discussed in Ch. 6), which show that expectations influence results.

Popper

The work of Karl Popper in the philosophy of science has been so influential that it seems appropriate to devote a whole section to him.

One of his fundamental claims has been the provisional nature of knowledge. All that can be attained are approximations to doubtful truth. The truth may be attained but one can never know that it has been attained. Logical propositions are always dependent on premises: assumptions must be made before any programme can begin. Empirical propositions are always subject to falsification.

One of the problems with which Popper was concerned was the delineation of scientific from non-scientific statements. Testability was proposed as the *demarcation principle*: what distinguished scientific statements from non-scientific was the fact that their truth could be checked by reference to empirical evidence. The logical positivists adopted the verification principle as the criterion of meaningfulness. Thus in order for a statement to be meaningful it must be verifiable: there must be some way of deciding whether it is true or false. The universe of propositions was divided into logical propositions which were tautologous, i.e. true by definition according to the rules of the system (for example, 'two plus two is four' is true by virtue of the rules of mathematics), and empirical propositions which were verifiable, i.e. for which a decision procedure to determine their truth or falsity existed. Everything else, which included metaphysical, aesthetic and religious statements was mere nonsense. However, interpreting testability in terms of verifiability would rule out scientific hypotheses as meaningless. They refer to open (viz. all future cases) rather than closed (viz. all past observed cases) classes of events and hence are not conclusively verifiable. There is always the possibility that a negative instance will turn up.

The question of whether or not a statement is treated as a testable scientific hypothesis or not can be illustrated by reference to the example of the statement 'all swans are white'. In the event of a black swan being observed, two choices are open. One can either admit that one was wrong: that indeed it is not the case that all swans are white, in which case the statement is being regarded as having the status of a scientific hypothesis, i.e. it is falsifiable; or one can conclude that this black creature is not a swan – in this case the statement is being regarded as having the status of a tautology, true by definition, the assumption being that whiteness is an inherent quality of being a swan. It is therapeutic to apply this test to psychological theories, or perhaps better theorists, in the event of a negative instance: is it accepted as such and the hypothesis rejected or at least modified, or is the instance deemed not to disconfirm, in some way not to count, or be irrelevant? Popper was quick to point out that such theories, which are impervious to disconfirming evidence, are not scientific.

Noting the asymmetry between verification and falsification, that logically a scientific hypothesis cannot be verified by any number of confirming instances but can be refuted by only one disconfirming instance, Popper was led to an interpretation of testability in terms of *falsifiability* and proposed this as the demarcation principle. He defined the logical content of a scientific hypothesis as the class of non-tautological, derivable statements and the empirical content as the class of potential falsifiers. In his view the empirical content of a scientific hypothesis is directly proportional to its falsifiability, and inversely related to its probability. Scientific hypotheses can be arranged on a continuum of falsifiability ranging from zero to one, bounded at one end by tautologies, which have a falsifiability equal to zero (they make no predictions about the empirical world and hence cannot be falsified), and at the other end by contradictions, which have a falsifiability of one (they say everything about the world and hence are certain to be falsified). (As an example of a contradiction consider the hypothesis 'It will rain and it will not rain tomorrow'. If it does rain tomorrow the second part of the statement will be falsified; if it does not rain the first part will be.) The more chances there are of a hypothesis being falsified the more information it contains. This may sound paradoxical but some intuitive insight can be gained by thinking of it in terms of surprise value. It is not very informative to discover that something very likely to happen has occurred; by contrast, it is informative to discover that something unlikely to happen has occurred.

Popper's recommendation then is that scientific hypotheses should be sought which are maximally falsifiable (bold, risky conjectures) and that persistent efforts should be made to seek falsification of existing hypotheses. In short, science should proceed by way of conjecture and refutation.

Popper was partly led to this conclusion as a result of examining Marxist theory and the psychoanalytic theories of Freud and Adler. What struck him about these was their imperviousness to falsifiability: no matter what happened, these theories seemed able to explain the results.

> I could not think of any human behaviour that could not be interpreted in terms of either theory. It was precisely this fact – that they always fitted, that they were always confirmed – which in the eyes of their admirers constituted the strongest argument in favour of these theories. It began to dawn on me that this apparent strength was in fact their weakness (Popper 1963).

Although the emphasis on testability and falsifiability in science is sound (intellectual honesty consists in specifying precisely the conditions under which one is willing to give up one's position), there are a number of modifications or qualifications that might be made to Popper's theory.

Some have argued that there is a place in science for untestable theories, either those that may become testable at a later stage, perhaps with the development of improved techniques, or those that, though not strictly testable, nevertheless aid understanding in some way, perhaps by unifying diverse material. Evolutionary theory is often cited in this context. Although not totally unfalsifiable, it does not rate high on falsifiability, and much of the relevant evidence is now inaccessible. Similarly, geological (and psychological) theories are often *post hoc* in form, seeking to explain, and testable primarily by reference to, events that have already occurred.

The absolute superiority of falsification over verification may also be questioned. 'Complete refutation is no more possible than complete proof' (Braithwaite 1953). Nagel (1967) has argued that refutation may be no more definitive than verification: it depends on the stability of the theories. There may be cases where refutation does not (and should not) lead to rejection of a theory. The novice experimenter failing to confirm a well established scientific law concludes that the experiment rather than the law was at fault. Popper in fact allows for this. His recommended methodology is what he terms critical falsification. Falsifications may be rejected in certain circumstances but systematic rejection of them is to be avoided. Lakatos (1970), in an important and extensive examination of falsification as a research methodology, concludes that falsification is neither a necessary nor a sufficient condition for the elimination of a theory, and in favour of what he calls sophisticated falsificationism (postitive outcomes can be informative as well as negative). All that is required of a new theory is that it should have verified excess content compared with the theory it is superseding. Moreover, all facts are theory-laden.

Popper's stress on logical factors in the development of science ignores non-logical factors, some of which are discussed in the last section of this chapter.

Perhaps even more serious than the logical criticisms of his theory are the psychological. Empirical work in psychology throws considerable doubt on the likelihood of Popper's recommendations actually being implemented by scientists. Experiments by Wason (e.g. Wason 1960), simulating scientific reasoning, have demonstrated a bias towards seeking confirming rather than infirming evidence. Very few intelligent young adults spontaneously tested their beliefs but rather adhered tenaciously to their own hypotheses when confirming evidence for them could be produced. Wason and Johnson-Laird (1972) conclude that the results were more consistent with Kuhn's view, that hypotheses are only abandoned when more adequate ones become available, to which we now turn.

Kuhn

Kuhn's ideas (1962) have been almost as influential as Popper's. His basic notion is that of a **paradigm**, which has been variously defined as a 'strong network of commitments, conceptual, theoretical, instrumental and methodological', 'the source of the methods, problem-field, and standards of solution accepted by any mature scientific community at any given time', and 'universally recognizable scientific achievements that for a time provide model problems and solutions to a community of practitioners'. It is essentially a sociological concept and refers to agreements amongst a group of scientific practitioners which range from metaphysical (basic assumptions on which the practice of science depends, such as the belief in determinism), through theoretical (agreements about theoretical frameworks and what questions can reasonably be asked, e.g. the belief that all behaviour is explicable in terms of conditioning), to methodological (closer to paradigm in the narrower more conventional sense of well tried procedures, what Kuhn describes as 'concrete exemplary solutions', e.g. paired–associate learning.)

Kuhn has attempted to describe the pattern of scientific progress. He suggests that initially there is a period of pre-paradigmatic science typified by multiple schools: there is no agreement as to what theoretical framework or approach should be adopted.

Once a paradigm is agreed upon, a stage of normal science can begin. Possession of a paradigm is a necessary condition for the conduct of normal science. This is typified by what Kuhn calls 'puzzle solving', i.e. the major issues as to what questions should be asked have already been resolved and relatively minor problems are tackled. An example is filling in the values of the atomic table. Possession of a paradigm has advantages and disadvantages. The advantage is that of precision: it enables the asking of precisely formulated questions; the disadvantage is one of limitation: only certain questions can be posed within a given framework.

Science proceeds in this way, Kuhn supposes, until a period of extraordinary science is entered. The point will come when anomalies within the existing system can no longer be tolerated and ultimately a paradigm shift occurs. An alternative conceptualisation is proposed. Examples are the Copernican, Newtonian and Einsteinian revolutions. Such revolutions involve a major re-orientation of the conceptual framework and, according to the original formulation (Kuhn 1962), paradigms are non-comparable. There will be some questions which can be asked under one paradigm but not under another. This non-comparability of para-digms led Kuhn to query the supposed cumulative progression in science and to propose instead that it was characterised by non-cumulative Gestalt switches. Indeed, his writing is of additional interest to a psychologist on account of its use of psychological illustrations. Paradigm revolutions are likened to Gestalt switches such as occur in the perception of reversible figures in that the same material is seen from an entirely different perspective. The way in which observations are never theory-free is illustrated by reference to Bruner and Postman's (1949) experiment which demonstrates the influence of expectation on set in perception.

Both Popper and Kuhn agree on the contribution of theoretical preconceptions to observations and on the role of criticism in science. Popper sees the latter as ever present; Kuhn sees it as the exception rather than the rule.

Kuhn's theory has not escaped criticism. First, it has been pointed out that the concept of a paradigm is extremely vague. Masterman (1970) claimed that Kuhn used it in 21 different senses, which could be classified into metaphysical, social and artefactual. Kuhn (1970a) himself later acknowledged two basic senses: (a) sociological – 'the entire constellation of beliefs, values, techniques, and so on shared by a given community', and (b) exemplary past achievements – 'the concrete puzzle-solutions which, employed as models or examples, can replace explicit rules as a basis for the solution of the remaining puzzles of normal science'.

Secondly, the relativity implied has not proved popular. Most scientists find it unpalatable to accept that their efforts are not progressive in any real sense.

Thirdly, the revolutionary character of science is exaggerated and the lines between normal and extraordinary science drawn too sharply. Revolutions are atypical, shifts are more gradual and the various stages less distinct than they are depicted.

Fourthly, as Shapere (1971) points out, in his efforts to meet his critics, Kuhn (1970b) has involved himself in contradiction and sacrificed what were the most important and novel aspects of his theory.

The application of the notion of paradigms to psychology

There has been much debate about whether Kuhn's proposals, based largely on a consideration of the history of the physical sciences, are applicable to psychology, and whether or not psychology has acquired a paradigm. Warren (1971) has argued that psychology is in a pre-paradigmatic state typified by multiple schools and uncertainty as to the best method of proceeding. Palermo (1971) on the other hand has argued that psychology has gone through several paradigms. The first paradigm to be adopted was structuralism, where the subject matter of psychology was immediate conscious experience, the subjects normal human adults and the approved method introspection. This was succeeded by behaviourism in which the agreed subject matter was behaviour, the subjects were extended to include children and animals and the approved method was objective observation. He goes on to suggest that anomalies have arisen within the behaviourist paradigm which is in turn being supplanted by alternative paradigms whose origins lie in linguistics and computer science. Warren (1971) has criticised this on the grounds that belief in behaviourism as the only dominant framework is parochial!

My own view is that behaviourism comes as close to the notion of a paradigm as anything could. It seems particularly easy to specify its assumptions with respect to: (a) fundamentals – determinism, the analysis of behaviour in terms of stimuli and responses, behaviour as a function of conditioning history in terms of reinforcement contingencies, (b) subject matter – behaviour rather than experience, emphasis on learning rather than more cognitive (i.e. perception and thinking) or physiological components, (c) method – objective observation, introspection only as verbal report, progress from simple to complex forms of behaviour, (d) explanation – functional analysis with the emphasis on prediction and control, general laws, conditioning as a pre-theoretic model (see e.g. Kendler & Spence 1971). It is also my view that cognitive psychology has not been specified sufficiently precisely to constitute an alternative paradigm (and that most of its changes are such as could be accommodated by a neo-behaviourism) and that currently the only candidate for one is likely to be found in the camp of humanistic psychology and its progenitors, which in some of its forms, notably phenomenology, contains fundamental challenges to aspects of behaviourism (see Ch. 13).

Non-rational factors

So far we have predominantly been considering views that emphasise logical factors in the development of science. What of non-logical factors? Although the role of imagination and intuitive processes in science has always been acknowledged, recently a number of writers have given explicit recognition to non-rational elements. Insofar as advances in science are novel, they involve creative problem solving and are inherently non-predictable. (This may be one reason why the scientific study of creativity has been limited in its progress.) Polanyi in a number of works (e.g. Polanyi 1966) has developed the theme of tacit knowing. He is convinced of the impossibility of the existence of strict rules for establishing knowledge, and the indeterminacy of science with respect to content, coherence and data. Using a perceptual analogy, he suggests that an integration of what he calls 'unconscious subsidiaries' (background knowledge or preconceptions) and focal awareness is always involved.

In similar vein Feyerabend (1975) has espoused what he refers to as an 'anarchist epistemology' in which 'anything goes'. In his view there are no absolute judgments, and no fixed method or theory of rationality. His argument is based on a consideration of the history of science which shows it to be complex and unpredictable, and the necessity of anarchy for the growth of knowledge. There is a need for revolutions in which the rules are broken. The importance of play in scientific creativity is stressed. He makes three recommendations:

(a)   A counter-inductive procedure: evidence that is relevant for the test of a theory can often be unearthed only with the help of an incompatible theory.

(b)   The principle of proliferation: the invention and elaboration of theories which are inconsistent with the accepted point of view is an essential part of critical empiricism.

(c)   A pluralistic methodology: a variety of approaches should be tried rather than the exclusive adoption of one. Fixed rules are unrealistic and vicious.

Feyerabend's views can be seen as an extension of Popper's taken to their logical conclusion, and in opposition to Kuhn's. It is tempting to think that in a subject as varied as psychology Feyerabend's approach is the more appropriate (but not everyone would agree). For a statement and critique of irrationalism, and a warning against the dangers of taking *this* approach to its extreme, see Frankel (1973).

Summary

We began this chapter by discussing evidence for the influence on the development of science of cultural and personal factors and of conceptual and technical advances. This was followed by a consideration of the relative contributions of factual discovery and theoretical interpretation. We saw how inductive answers had given precedence to deductive answers to both the logical and the psychological questions concerning the relation between facts and theories, although it seems clear that both processes take place. This led on to a consideration of the views of Popper and Kuhn on the nature of scientific theories. Popper's notion of the conjectural nature of knowledge and the importance of falsifiability, and Kuhn's concept of a paradigm and its applicability to psychology were discussed. The chapter concluded with a consideration of the role played by non-rational factors.

8

Theories and explanations

The next five chapters will be devoted to an evaluation of different types of theoretical explanation in psychology. In this chapter we shall first define certain theoretical terms and then consider what functions theories serve. This will be followed by a discussion of the dimensions on which theories may differ and criteria for choosing between rival theories. Finally we shall discuss the nature of explanation and review different types used in psychology.

What are theories?

It is first necessary to distinguish systems, theories and models.

A **system** is a general theory plus metatheoretical recommendations. McGeoch (1933) defines a system as 'a coherent and inclusive, yet flexible, organization and interpretation of the facts and special theories of the subject' and mentions six features by which they may be evaluated (definition of the field, explicit postulates, nature of data, mind–body position, organisation of data, principles of selection). Examples are the early schools of psychology, for example behaviourism, which not only attempted to provide a general theory of behaviour (as is indicated by some of the titles of the period, e.g. Hull's (1943) *Principles of behavior* or Skinners' (1938) *The behavior of organisms*) but also made metatheoretical recommendations about the subject matter, methods and theoretical explanations to be employed.

A **theory** has a narrower scope than a system. Bergmann (1957) defines a theory in the traditional way as 'a group of laws deductively connected' and Marx (1976) as 'a provisional explanatory proposition, or set of propositions, concerning some natural phenomena and consisting of symbolic representations of (1) the observed relationships among (measured) events, (2) the mechanisms or structures presumed to underlie such relationships, or (3) inferred relationships and underlying mechanisms'. A theory is essentially an abstraction and distinct from the data.

The term **'model'** has been variously used. In some cases it appears to be synonymous with 'theory', although generally a model is narrower in scope (thus: a theory of perception but a model of pattern recognition). Chapanis (1961) defines models as 'representations or likenesses of certain aspects of complex events, structures or systems, made by using symbols or objects which in some way resemble the thing being modelled'. Essentially models are analogies and typically involve the application of a better developed, better understood system to a less developed, less well understood one. Thus, although it is true that all theories are models in the sense that they are representations, their mutual identification hardly seems a usage to be recommended. Simon and Newell (1956) suggest that models may be distinguished from theories in the following ways: (a) They are useful rather than true. Models are intended as heuristic aids rather than as complete descriptions. (b) They are less data sensitive; disconfirming evidence is damaging to a theory but not necessarily so to a model. (c) They are more susceptible to type II errors, i.e. they are more liable to make false claims.

In psychology models have come to be used to refer to a particular subgroup of theories, those which employ structural explanations (see p. 102). These aim at describing the mechanisms involved, though usually only in an abstract form (see Ch. 10 for a fuller discussion of models).

A **law** refers to a relatively well established statement of regular predictable relations among empirical variables. They are noteworthy for their scarcity in psychology.

A **hypothesis** is a tentative law.

A **postulate** is an assumption of a theory not intended to be subjected to empirical test, e.g. that all behaviour is determined.

A **protocol statement** is a description of an observation, sometimes referred to as 'data language'.

A **primitive term** is a basic term not defined within a theory but external to it, if at all, e.g. stimulus, response, reinforcement.

A **construct** is a concept referring to relations between events or properties, e.g. anxiety (see Ch. 9 for fuller discussion).

The function of theories

Are theories necessary at all?

The case against
In a classic paper, Skinner (1950) put forward the view that theories, whether of a conceptual, neural or mental type, were not necessary in psychology. His arguments were that: (a) they create new problems of explanation which get covered up (it is true that

having a theory may lead to a false sense of security and tend to preclude further investigations, an example of the latter being the hypothesis that behaviour is innate); (b) they may generate wasteful research (an examination of the research on learning in the 1940s and 1950s tends to confirm this view); (c) more direct approaches exist (Skinner's own approach favours the pursuit of functional laws based directly on empirical research, whose merits and demerits are considered in Ch. 9).

However, many psychologists are not so pure-minded. For most of them theories are a psychological if not a logical necessity. If not unnecessary, are they desirable? What functions do they serve?

The case for

First, a good case can be made for the view that there are no such things as pure facts. In Chapter 7 we considered evidence which suggests that data are not theory-free and that all observation involves selection and interpretation. Facts do not speak for themselves. This is particularly true in psychology where much of the subject matter is not directly observable and involves inference to a greater rather than a lesser extent.

Broadbent (1961) has argued that even Skinner's approach, which seeks only to predict and not to explain behaviour, cannot be theory-free, on the grounds that, because no two events are identical, theoretical assumptions must be invoked to enable selection of the relevant dimensions on which generalisation is to be based. So it appears that even for the limited goal of prediction a theory is necessary.

Theories normally have both backward-looking (retrospective) and forward-looking (prospective) functions. They serve to summarise and organise data that have already been collected, which would otherwise be unmanageable and unassimilable. They bring order and coherence to material. For most people 'facts are useless unless one takes the intellectual risk of thinking about them'. Most theories are attempts at explanation. 'Theories are nets cast to catch what we call "the world": to rationalize, to explain and to master it' (Popper 1959).

Theories also serve a heuristic function of guiding research. 'Theory is the stage upon which experiments are conducted' (Allport 1955). They provide a means of selecting from the infinitude of possible experiments. It may be concluded that theories are both a logical and a psychological necessity.

Dimensions of theorising

In this section we shall consider broad dimensions on which theories may vary.

First, not all theories have the same *aim*. The primary aim of a theory is explanation, the main function of which is to increase understanding. The conventionally accepted form of this for scientific theories is deductive prediction. However, there may be other possible avenues to understanding. Some psychological (and other scientific) theories are essentially post-dictive; for example, psychoanalysis. Rycroft (1966) has gone so far as to claim that psychoanalysis is not intended as a scientific theory, whose purpose is to elucidate causes, but rather as a semantic theory, whose purpose is to provide a way of making sense of symptoms. Other theories seem to aim more at a type of understanding dependent on empathy. These occur primarily in literature (it is frequently claimed that more is learned about people from reading novels than by studying academic psychology) but also in some phenomeno-logically and socially based approaches (see pp. 103–4), a particular case in point being hermeneutics.

Secondly, theories may vary in their *mode of formulation*. Simon and Newell (1956) distinguish verbal, mathematical and analogical formulations. They give an example of the same information expressed in three different ways: (a) verbal – 'consumption increases linearly with income, but less than proportionately'; (b) mathematical – $C = a + bY; a > 0; 0 < b < 1$; (c) analogical – the flow of goods and money might be likened to that of a liquid. Psychological examples of verbal theories are Guthrie's theory of learning and Homan's theory of group behaviour, which have been given corresponding mathematical formulations by Estes (1950) and Simon (1952) respectively. Psychological examples of analogical theories are well reviewed in Miller, Galanter and Pribram (1960, Ch. 3) and range from Ashby's homeostat to Lorenz's hydraulics (see Ch. 10 for further discussion). It is important to distinguish the logical content of a theory, i.e. what it is possible to infer from it in principle, from the psychological content, i.e. what is actually inferred from it. Thus, theories may contain the same logical content but differ in psychological content. Simon and Newell (1956) claim that verbal formulations tend to have logical rather than psychological advantages, and mathematical formulations psychological rather than logical advantages. The logical advantages are a function of the theory, the psychological advantages more dependent on the theorist. The latter lies in the realm of differential psychology, which should be able to explain why different theorists prefer different modes of formulation.

In Chapter 7 we considered the roles of data and theory. It is clear that the *relation between data and theory* is a variable on which theories differ. Some are predominantly data determined, others predominantly conceptually determined. Various relations that may obtain between data and theory have been represented diagrammatically by Marx (1976) (see Fig. 8.1).

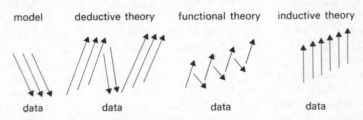

Figure 8.1 Relations between theory and data in four modes of theory construction (from Marx 1976).

He has considered (a) the direction of inference between theory and data (indicated by arrows), (b) whether the relation is static or dynamic (represented by vertical and slanted lines respectively), and (c) the scope, i.e. the extent of inference beyond the data (represented by the length of line). Time is represented on the horizontal dimension. Models and deductive theories tend to be theory oriented, functional and inductive theories to be data oriented. We shall consider the four types in turn. A *model* is a conceptual analogue, whose value is heuristic. Inferences exist in one direction only: from theory to data. It is not data-sensitive; no feedback is planned from data to theory, so there is no interaction. There are many examples of models in psychology (see Ch. 10), a simple one being Broadbent's filter theory of attention. A **deductive theory** involves two-way interaction: theoretical generalisations are induced from observations and predictions of future observations are deduced from theoretical hypotheses. An example in psychology is Hull's theory of learning. Such theories are prototypical in science but have been criticised as being premature in psychology. There is a danger of overformalisation, which may make the theory difficult to modify. An example of a theory which is predominantly conceptually rather than data-driven is Piaget's. Some work in mathematical psychology also gives the impression of the theorist having become obsessed with the mathematics and having lost touch with the data. In a **functional theory,** interaction is two-way but the scope is much narrower. The theory is merely a restatement of the data, theory and data being given equal weight. Examples in psychology are the Weber–

Fechner law and Ebbinghaus' empirical law of forgetting. Being closer to the data they are more data-sensitive and easily modifiable but because the theory does not go beyond the data they lack virility and seldom lead to new predictions. In an **inductive theory,** inference is only in one direction, namely, from data to theory. The facts are expected to speak for themselves, the theoretical statements being mere summaries of empirical findings. An example is Skinnerian theory. Such theories, like functional theories, are insufficiently complex and lacking in implications.

Another choice that faces a theorist is *level of analysis.* In psychology there is a wide range of choice from social to physiological. George (1953) has suggested that the psychologist is faced with speculating about the organism that intervenes between stimulus and response. The issue then becomes one of how detailed an analysis of the organism is undertaken. The molar theorist accounts for discrepancies between stimuli and responses by postulating constructs which represent organismic factors without analysing these in detail or observing the internal state of the organism. The molecular theorist attempts to reduce the vagueness and possible surplus meaning of these constructs by making them more explicit and suggesting possible mechanisms. They can then be tested not only as part of a molar theory but are also open to test by physiological evidence (these issues are more fully discussed in Chs 9 and 11).

Finally, Brunswik (1939) has raised the interesting notion of what he calls *conceptual focus.* If psychological theories are taken to be concerned with predicting responses as a function of stimuli, there is a choice as to what is selected as stimulus and response. This involves not only what might crudely be described as a spatial dimension (the size of unit of analysis just discussed) but also a temporal dimension, in terms of how far back in the history of the individual the cause is sought, and how far into the future effects are predicted. Brunswik confounds these two dimensions in suggesting the following range:

(a) the remote past of the organism; (b) manipulable physical bodies, distal stimuli; (c) proximal stimuli; (d) intra-organismic events and dispositions; (e) proximal reactions, molecular behaviour; (f) distal effects of reactions, molar behavioural achievements; (g) far reaching successes, products of life activities.

These he illustrates by reference to a comparison of classical schools in psychology.

Criteria for choosing between theories

Given the necessity of theories and the existence of several rival theories, what criteria may be used for choosing between them? This question has been considered by Goodson and Morgan (1976) and by Paxton (1976).

One relevant consideration is the *scope* of a theory, the range of data covered. Both breadth and completeness of coverage may be considered advantageous.

Parsimony is another requirement of a theory. Although nature may not be simple the goal of a theory should be to account for the maximum amount of data with the minimum number of theoretical hypotheses. The simplest account compatible with the data should always be preferred. The principle of parsimony was formulated in mediaeval times by William of Occam, after whom it came to be known as Occam's razor. In the early days of comparative psychology, Lloyd Morgan urged his canon in opposition to the anthropomorphism that had characterised 18th-century studies of animals. More recently, theories such as psychoanalysis have been criticised for their lack of parsimony.

The *clarity* with which a theory is formulated contains a number of aspects. The ease with which predictions can be derived has both logical and psychological implications, as we saw earlier in discussing modes of formulation, and will be inversely related to both complexity and ambiguity. Logical *consistency* is a necessity and maximum *precision* a desirability.

Both the scope and the clarity of a theory will have implications for its *testability*. The greater the empirical content and the more clearly specified the theory, the greater will be its potential for falsification. Sensitivity to data is partly a function of theories but also partly a function of theorists, as was indicated in Chapter 7.

The extent of *empirical support* for a theory is obviously another criterion by which theories may be evaluated. Popper has stressed the importance of variety as well as quantity of corroboration.

As was pointed out in the previous section, a theory has both retrospective and prospective functions. As important as accounting for past observations may be the ability to lead to novel predictions. A theory may be in error but nevertheless of heuristic value in leading to new discoveries. In the long term then, the *fruitfulness* of a theory may be an important criterion.

What are explanations?

'It is convenient to regard an explanation as any answer to a why question that is accepted by the questioner as making the event in question somehow more intelligible' (Boden 1972). She goes on to define a scientific explanation as 'an explanation that is justified by reference to publicly observable facts, and which is rationally linked to other, similar explanations in a reasonably systematic manner'. Some scientific explanations might better be regarded as answers to 'how?' questions. Given that explanations are answers to questions of some sort it seems reasonable to suggest that there may be as many different types of answers as there are types of question, and that the type of explanation adopted will depend on the following three factors:

(a) Who asked the question. An answer will be related to the present state of knowledge of the questioner. For example, an explanation of the motion of the planets given to a child will be different from that given to an atomic physicist. (b) What the question was aimed at. For what purpose is the knowledge required? Are there practical implications? For example, one suspects that Skinner's option for explanations of behaviour in terms of environmental rather than genetic factors may be motivated by possibilities of modification. Similarly, which explanation of pathological behaviour is preferred may depend on available treatments. (c) Who gave the answer. What are the personal biases of the theorist? The existence of psychological factors in theorising is beyond doubt (cf. Coan 1968, Caine, Wijesinghe & Winter 1981).

Explanations must supply new information. Ultimately what is accepted is a matter of subjective satisfaction as William James pointed out clearly in *Pragmatism*: 'Our commerce with the systems reverts to the informal, to the instinctive human reaction of satisfaction or dislike . . . We philosophers have to reckon with such feelings on your part. In the last resort, I repeat, it will be by them that all our philosophies shall ultimately be judged. The finally victorious way of looking at things will be the most completely impressive to the normal run of minds' (James 1907). In theory there is a wide choice; in practice, there is less. In science, as we have seen, certain kinds are preferred to others. The prototype has been a causal explanation embedded in a hypothetico-deductive theory. Whether different types of explanation are possible or whether, for example, only causal ones are acceptable is a much debated issue. Foss (1974) has put the case for multiple types in psychology. One thing to be avoided is evaluating one type of explanation from the viewpoint of another. Thus, it is inappropriate to reject evolutionary functional explanations on the grounds that they are not causal: they are not intended to be.

Deutsch (1960) has claimed that psychologists are confused about explanation: '. . . There is no concord among psychologists about what the facts they have accumulated are evidence for. This does not mean that they are merely in disagreement about the edifice they wish to erect; they have not even decided what constitutes a building. That is, not only do they disagree about the explanation of their findings, but they are not clear what it would be to explain them.'

Below we shall distinguish and discuss the relative merits of six different types of explanation.

Types of explanation

GENERALISATORY

Preliminary to explanation is description and classification. Phenomena to be explained must be identified and labelled. Whether classification as such can ever count as explanatory is a controversial issue. In certain cases it is not. The nominalist fallacy exposes the false belief that in naming something it has been explained, instanced in the statement 'pigs are so called because they are such dirty animals' or the peasants mentioned by Vygotsky who, it is claimed, could understand the discovery of the stars but expressed puzzled amazement at the discovery of their names. An example from literature is in Molière's *Le malade imaginaire,* where he mocks the doctors who suggested that what makes opium have its soporific effect is its *virtus dormitiva,* i.e. its soporific power. In psychology a similar case is the use of the concept of instinct criticised, for example, by Field (1921). Nor is it clear that its successor, drive, has escaped the same fate. In these cases the description may be tautologous. A classification becomes explanatory if it conveys additional independent information. Consider the example: 'Jones goes to parties because he is an extrovert'. This is not explanatory if party-going behaviour is the only way of identifying an extrovert, if going to parties is what it means to be an extrovert. If, however, extroversion has additional implications, either behavioural, such as taking relatively more involuntary rest pauses in tapping tasks, or physiological, such as greater cortical inhibition, then the circularity is avoided and it is explanatory.

Examples of generalisatory explanations in psychology, where events are explained by reference to a class of events of which they are members, include neo-behaviourist accounts in terms of drive reduction (which have been criticised by Deutsch 1960) and rule following models favoured by some social psychologists (cf. Goffman 1959, Harré & Secord 1972).

These draw attention to important aspects of behaviour, and classification is probably a necessary prerequisite but they need to be supplemented by other types of explanation. For example, with respect to rules: How did they come into being? How do they work in detail? What causal factors are involved?

FUNCTIONAL

The next step might be to establish associations between events, some form of correlation; for example, between smoking and cancer, or weight and mental age in the first few years of life.

The motivations for asserting a relation of contingency rather than cause may be various. In philosophy Hume argued that there was no logical necessity involved in cause, which could be reduced to contiguity:

> We have no other notion of cause and effect but that of certain objects, which have been always conjoined together, and which in all past instances have been found inseparable. We cannot penetrate into the reason of the conjunction. We only observe the thing itself, and always find that from the constant conjunction, the objects require a union in the imagination.

An even more critical analysis of the notion of cause has been provided by Russell (1913). In physics, Heisenberg's uncertainty principle has suggested limits to determinacy. In neurophysiology, Burns (1968) has claimed there are stochastic processes at the cellular level. In psychology, probability statements are the order of the day. Probability implies determinism but one that is imperfectly known. Whether the limits to knowledge are a function of the knower or of the known is an interesting question for speculation.

One of the main proponents of a functional approach in psychology is Skinner, who deems functional relations between stimuli and responses to be sufficient for prediction and control. 'I do not know why (food is reinforcing to a hungry animal) . . . and I do not care' (Skinner 1964). Other examples of functional relations are the Weber–Fechner law and Luce's preference law.

As we saw in the previous section, these have the advantages of being closely related to the data but more powerful explanations are required for most purposes.

CAUSAL

Causal explanations explain a given event by reference to a past event. They are equivalent to Aristotle's efficient causes. For example, 'the billiard ball moved because it was hit by the cue'. They are considered by many to be the preferred type of explanation in science, but as we shall see philosophers have not found it easy to give them precise specification. Essential ingredients appear to be conditionality and relevance. Thus, the occurrence of an event B is explained as being the result of an antecedent event A having occurred, A being a condition for B. A may be a sufficient condition for B if there are events other than A which are possible causes of B, or A may be a necessary and sufficient condition for B if there are no possible causes of B other than A. A necessary but not sufficient condition would not itself be a cause, if, for example, A only produces B when in conjunction with C. It is to be noted that this dependence is logical; there is no compulsion or mysterious force involved.

It may be debated whether events are uniquely caused, or whether the same effect can have different causes on different occasions; and whether an event can have multiple causes, more than one event contributing to its occurrence. Strictly, in a deterministic system the same cause must always lead to the same effect. But this appears contrary to common sense, which might suppose, for example, that subnormality could be caused by anoxia at birth or later insult to the brain. Presumably we must suppose either that the effects are in fact different or that they are mediated by the same mechanism, say the same kind of brain damage. But this latter conclusion merely reduplicates the problem (of same effect, different causes). A case in the literature that might be interpreted as a mistaken conclusion of unique causation is that of Watson (1907), who successively eliminated sight, hearing and touch in rats. On finding that learning was unimpaired for trained and untrained rats, he concluded that it must be mediated kinaesthetically. However, in 1929, Lashley managed to eliminate kinaesthesis surgically and, although their gait was awkward, his rats still managed to learn mazes. The conclusion must be that rats will use any sense the experimenter is generous enough to leave them with and/or that the critical factor lies elsewhere, as Tolman and his followers would have argued.

Turning to the question of multiple causation, a frequent situation is one of predisposing factors and precipitating events. This has been documented for psychiatric disorders, e.g. with respect to inherited and congenital factors in the aetiology of schizophrenia (Mednick 1970) and social factors in the development of depression

(Brown & Harris 1978). Freud certainly considered the possibility of overdetermination: the co-occurrence of two events each of which alone would have been sufficient to cause the effect, for example, an instruction given in hypnosis to open a window after returning to the normal waking state plus a stuffy atmosphere.

Russell (1913) argued that whether a many-to-one or one-to-many relation pertains depends on the precision and width of specification. The supposed asymmetry between cause and effect is illusory, and results from conceiving causes precisely and widely and effects vaguely and narrowly, in which case plurality of causes can be allowed. For example, it may be said that many antecedents, specified precisely and widely, 'caused' a man's death, specified vaguely and narrowly. But the opposite course could be adopted, e.g. it might be said that the drinking of a dose of arsenic, specified vaguely and narrowly, caused the whole state of the world five minutes later, in which case there would be plurality of effects.

It is clear that causal explanation potentially involves an infinite regress. As with the persistent child, the question 'why?' can always be repeated. It has been suggested that a cause which is the first event in a long chain is particularly satisfying. Comfort has distinguished what he calls hard- and soft-headed causal explanations in terms of the quantity of unknown factors tolerated between cause and effect. This may be part of the reason why psychological explanations are often considered softer than physiological.

Many of these difficulties may stem from the looseness inherent in causal accounts. Russell (1913) has examined the difficulty of giving a precise formulation of the notion of cause. The difficulty stems from the requirement of temporal contiguity between cause and effect. Absurdities result both from the assumption of dynamically changing causes, in which case the critical ultimate part, a change in which would alter the effect, can be diminished to zero; and from the assumption of static causes which, if they exist at all, would have to 'explode' into the effect at some arbitrary time. If cause and effect are not temporally contiguous there is always the possibility that something will intervene to prevent the effect occurring. When the antecedents have been given sufficiently fully to enable the consequent to be calculated with some exactitude, the antecedents will have become so complicated that they are unlikely to recur.

Russell concludes that causal explanations are only useful in the infancy of a science. In mature sciences they are superseded by statements of functional relations. Thus we may conclude, contrary to what might at first be supposed, that statements of association are crude and possibly inaccurate formulations which later give way to more powerful causal statements, that rather the opposite is the case: causal statements are essentially loose formulations of sequential regularities which precede more precise mathematical statements of functional dependence.

STRUCTURAL

An alternative and currently popular approach is explanation in terms of the mechanisms involved. This is equivalent to Aristotle's material cause, explaining something in terms of its composition. There are two levels at which this can be done, which may be referred to as software and hardware. The software approach is that favoured by Deutsch (1960), who contrasts it with the generalisatory approach discussed previously:

> An event is explained by being deduced as the property of a structure, system or mechanism and not as an instance of events in its own class . . . The precise properties of the parts do not matter; it is only their general relationships to each other which give the machine as a whole its behavioural properties. . . . This highly abstract system . . . can be embodied in a theoretically infinite variety of physical counterparts . . . Given the system or abstract structure alone of the machine, we can deduce its properties and predict its behaviour.

These approaches have gained much from cybernetics, information theory and computer science. They may be described as being concerned with the program that governs behaviour, a popular mode of representation being the flow chart. Examples are Deutsch's model of need and Newell and Simon's theory of problem solving. Deutsch recommends this structural approach as a middle road between what he calls 'positivism run wild' and 'neurophysiologising'. Its power is that it is sufficient for the prediction of behaviour and its advantage that it provides a link to physiology, which ultimately may provide an additional testing ground. Certain concepts from cybernetics such as feedback are crucial to the understanding of behaviour and the advent of computer simulation has led to a de-mystification and making precise of many previously mentalistic concepts, such as 'mind', for example. However, again it is only one approach among many and in particular lacks the historical dimension that a causal account might provide. Models and computer simulation are discussed in more detail in Chapter 10.

TELEOLOGICAL

In contrast to causal explanations, teleological or purposive explanations explain a given event by reference to a future event. It is equivalent to Aristotle's final cause. As Nagel (1961) describes it the focus is on the effect rather than the cause. Behaviour is explained as occurring in order that some future event (a goal) may be achieved. For example, 'the chicken crossed the road in order to get to the other side'; 'the man crossed the road in order to buy tobacco'. It is often advanced that evolutionary accounts are of this nature, e.g. 'hair stands on end because it frightens the enemy'. This is misleading if it is thought to preclude a causal account. The piece of behaviour evolved because members of the species who possessed it survived to procreate. The analogous case in ontogeny is the law of effect, which was criticised on the grounds of retro-action: how, it was asked, could a satisfying state of affairs strengthen a connection that had already occurred? But of course reinforcement affects the probability of the connection reoccurring in the future. Many psychologists in the past have stressed the purposive aspect of behaviour (notably McDougall, Tolman, Lashley and, in more recent times, Miller, Galanter & Pribram (1960), who suggest a feedback loop as the basic unit of behaviour). It is particularly appropriate where a variety of means may lead to a particular end, the behaviour thus being classifiable by reference to the end rather than the means. The flexibility of behaviour is one of its most distinctive characteristics, some would say its defining feature. Peters (1958), for example, has argued that purposive explanations are normally appropriate for behaviour, causal explanations only being resorted to when behaviour is abnormal in some way, e.g. under the influence of drugs or an obsessional compulsion. Similarly, Taylor (1964) has argued that causal explanations provide necessary but not sufficient conditions for behaviour, on the grounds that a goal may be achieved in a variety of ways. It is clear, however, that purposive explanations are not incompatible with causal explanations. These issues are discussed in detail in Chapter 12.

HERMENEUTIC

The methods of hermeneutics and *Verstehen* seek an interpretative understanding, which some have thought appropriate for the social sciences, distinct from causal explanation. Relying on empathic intuition and conceptual analysis, they aim to make the meaning of actions intelligible by reference to the part they play in larger structures, for example the social situation, and to explain the link between events whose correlation would otherwise be puzzling. An example is Weber's classic analysis of the link between the Protestant ethic and economic enterprise. Harré and Secord's (1972) approach in terms of rules and roles owes much to this, as does Gauld and Shotter's (1977) based on shared meanings. These approaches seek an empathic, intuitive understanding rather than one that enables deductive prediction. Abel (1948) has argued that the approach, although useful at the stage of formulating hypotheses, cannot substitute for subsequent testing. These points are taken up in Chapter 14.

Summary

We have distinguished explanations which explain events by relating them to increasingly higher order generalisations of classes of events of which they are members, and those that seek explanations by reference to the system, mechanisms and possibly materials involved. Other explanations seek to establish associative relations between events and may explain a given event either by referring it to an antecedent (causal) or subsequent (teleological) event, or by attempting to specify relations of functional dependence in mathematically precise terms. Yet other approaches seek an understanding which is not aimed at prediction but is based on empathic intuition and shared meaning. These types of explanation and their associated issues will be considered in more detail in the subsequent chapters.

9

The problem of the organism

The problem

The aim of psychology might be thought to be the prediction of responses as a function of stimuli. The problem with which we shall be concerned in this chapter is how to conceptualise the relations between stimuli and responses. If a hierarchy of sciences is accepted, then each level may be conceived of as making assumptions about the subject matter of the science at the next level down. Thus sociology makes assumptions about psychology and psychology makes assumptions about physiology. In Osgood's (1956) words, 'Behaviour theory is made up of hunches about how the nervous system operates to generate the lawful relations we observe among stimuli and responses.'

A strictly functionalist approach, which deals only with observable stimuli and responses, has a very limited range of application. Sooner rather than later, the unpalatable fact becomes apparent that behaviour cannot be predicted on the basis of the stimulus alone. Discrepancies arise between stimuli and responses, such that the same stimulus does not give rise to the same response, either between individuals or on different occasions within the same individual. It becomes necessary to postulate some processes intervening between stimulus and response.

The problem is compounded by the fact that these organismic processes are not directly observable and hence must be inferred. The issue becomes conceptual. **Conceptual behaviourism** is behaviourism with respect to concepts, i.e. the view that any constructs postulated should be tied to observations. According to the strict version these are completely reducible, and identical in meaning, to observations; according to a weaker version they must be related to observations but these do not necessarily exhaust their meaning. For example, hunger drive might be defined purely in terms of hours of food deprivation, or might be taken to refer to some internal processes not directly observed. Wertheimer (1972) labels these positions prescriptive and descriptive operationism respectively. In a classic paper, MacCorquodale and Meehl (1948) distinguished two types of constructs which they termed **inter-**

vening variables and **hypothetical constructs.** As examples of intervening variables they gave: Hull's concept of habit strength, Tolman's concept of demand, and Skinner's concepts of drive and reflex reserve (the number of responses to extinction); and as examples of hypothetical constructs: Hull's r_g and s_g, Mowrer's movement-produced stimuli, anxiety and ego. They stated that intervening variables do not go beyond what is observed whereas hypothetical constructs postulate events, entities or processes which are not observed. Thus an intervening variable does not have, but a hypothetical construct does have, surplus theoretical meaning over and above empirical content. From this it follows that the truth of an empirical statement (i.e. getting the facts right) is a necessary and sufficient condition for the truth of a statement involving an intervening variable, but a necessary but not sufficient condition for the truth of a statement involving a hypothetical construct. An intervening variable is a summary function strictly derivable from stimulus–response laws, whereas a quantifiable form of a hypothetical construct cannot be so derived. (Deutsch (1960) objects to the distinction on the grounds that it confounds unobservability in practice with unobservability in principle, and prefers a distinction between constructs which form part of general-isatory theories and those which form part of structural theories.)

The problem of the organism, i.e. how to deal with the organism conceptually, has been well described by Joynson (1970) (see also Kelvin 1956). Joynson points out that psychologists in the past have tended to evade the issue by concentrating on the stimulus. The formula R = f(S) was superseded by the formula R = f(S, O), but only lip service was paid to the organism. He discusses what he describes as two 'direct' and three 'indirect' methods for investigating the organism. The two methods, perhaps somewhat misleadingly called 'direct', following Woodworth and Schlosberg (1954), are introspection and physiology. *Introspection* was the subject of Chapter 5, where we saw there were two main problems: (a) most psychological data are not accessible to conscious introspection, and (b) introspection is by no means an infallible method, being no less and in some cases more susceptible to error than other methods. *Physiology* is at worst a form of intellectual displacement activity (Bannister 1968) and at best does not generally increase the explanatory power of a psychological theory (Deutsch 1960) (cf. Ch. 11).

The three 'indirect' methods are the use of *antecedent variables,* individual differences and cybernetic models. The first of these has been favoured by behaviourists who have attempted to index hunger drive, for example, by reference to antecedent conditions of hours of food deprivation. The essential difficulty with this is that it cannot be done (see below). Koch (1959) doubts the possibility of 'unambiguous linkage' to observable variables. If explanatory power sufficient for the prediction of behaviour is to be achieved, what is postulated must go beyond a specification of externally observable antecedent conditions. The internal representation of the stimulus does not correspond to the external stimulus. The way in which a stimulus is represented by an organism depends on its internal state, which in the case of higher animals depends increasingly on its past history (and the past history of two organisms is never identical). Organisms interact with and adapt to constantly changing environments. Antecedent conditions interact with each other and with organismic conditions. Attempts to pursue this approach have shown the necessity for multiple indexing of internal processes but these indices have usually been found not to agree. The non-unitary nature of the concept of hunger drive was demonstrated by Miller (1956) who showed that, as hours of food deprivation increased, tolerance of quinine in food and rate of bar pressing continued to increase while stomach contractions and water consumption did not. Another classic case of inconsistency between indices is that of arousal.

This suggests that Joynson's second indirect method, approaching the problem through *individual differences,* may hold more promise. Eysenck (1966), for example, has attempted to reduce the error variance in conventionally designed experiments by taking into account such factors as extroversion and neuroticism. (Indeed, he has pointed out that should these interact with the main variables under investigation, ignoring personality variables may lead to the total obscuration of the effect of experimental variables, see Ch. 14.) However, these approaches, although an improvement, have not been without their weaknesses too. Agreement about the main variables to be considered is not universal, though there is a measure of consistency between, for example, Eysenck's and Cattell's conceptualisations. It is to be doubted, in view of what was said above, whether the number of variables to be considered is finite and hence whether the programme could in fact be carried out adequately. This is an empirical matter; however, the proportion of variance accounted for in most psychological experiments (see Ch. 6) does not inspire optimism. Joynson objects that this method involves inference. But so do all the other methods and not least those labelled 'direct'. In my view this is inescapable and in the nature of the problem. All that can be sought is strong rather than weak inference.

Joynson's third indirect method is through the use of *cybernetic models.* Here psychological processes are accounted for by reference to an abstract system from whose properties the behaviour is deduced (e.g. Deutsch 1960, Newell & Simon 1972). This too is inferential but has the advantages of power and precision without involvement in the physiological hardware (this approach is fully discussed in Ch. 10). The problem is central to cognitive psychology where this approach has been most frequently adopted. Newell (1973) in a trenchant critique of the current state of the art bemoaned the immature, non-cumulative nature of the discipline in which issues are never settled. This he attributed both to narrowness of scope (variously described as 'phenomena driven' (Newell 1973), 'parochialism' (Allport 1975), and 'paradigm specificity' (Eysenck 1977)), the adoption of a piecemeal 'divide and conquer' strategy, but also to looseness of theoretical structure. Central to this is the fact that, 'Uncertainty over what method the subject is using drives a substantial amount of discussion of experimental results.' 'The same human subject can adopt many (radically different) methods for the same basic task.' This leads to selective and *ad hoc* treatment of results and enables endless debate over their interpretation. 'Much of the ability of the field continually and forever to dispute and question interpretations arises from the possibility of the subject's having done the task by a not-till-then-thought-of-method or by the set of subjects having adopted a mixture of methods so the regularities produced are not what they seemed.'

Averaging over methods conceals rather than reveals, providing garbage or spurious regularity. In Newell's view, behaviour is a function of the task structure, the subject's goal and what he calls the 'control structure' – the invariant structure of the processing mechanisms, which determines the possible sequences of operations and hence constrains the methods that can be employed, and without a knowledge of which the method actually used cannot be inferred. To what extent behaviour is a function of a general, invariant structure rather than situation-specific optional strategies is a matter of controversy (cf. Allport 1975). Specification of the control structure is necessary in order to provide a theoretical framework with which to limit the number of alternative explanations and hence tighten the inferential web that links experimental studies.

Osgood (1956) has suggested that the evolution of behaviour theory can be seen in terms of what is assumed to happen between stimulus and response. Following his suggestion, we shall adopt a historical perspective for the remainder of this chapter, to discuss the main solutions to the problem of the organism that have been offered in the development of psychology.

Faculty psychology

In the 19th century, a state existed in psychology which Osgood nicknames *'junk-shop psychology'*. He describes the situation that pertained as one in which phenomena were attributed to faculties, motives to instincts. There were as many explanatory devices as things to explain:

> Whenever something needed explaining, a new explanatory device was stuck inside the black box, and it rapidly became chock-full of ill-assorted, ill-digested demons . . . And, at least for communicating with his patients, Freud had big, flat-footed super-egos stomping around on red-slippery ids, while cleverly anxious little egos tried to arbitrate.

This approach had as an advantage the freedom to exercise intuition and it is worth bearing in mind that each approach probably had a contribution to make at the stage in the history of psychology when it was actively pursued. The disadvantage was a lack of parsimony with consequent loss of explanatory power. The aim of a scientific theory should be to seek the lowest possible ratio of explanatory statements to observations. Many of the concepts were circular, lacking independent operational definitions. A more recent example, for which Skinner takes Blanshard to task (Blanshard & Skinner 1967), is the statement that Hitler exterminated the Jews because he hated them. Explaining Hitler's behaviour in terms of his hatred is otiose if we have no independent evidence of his hatred of the Jews other than his instigation of their extermination.

Functionalist psychology

As might be predicted, the reaction this provoked was a swing to the opposite extreme in the form of radical behaviourism, what Osgood dubs *'empty organism psychology'*. This single-stage S–R theory permitted only functional relations between stimuli and responses. What was inside the black box it was not the business of the psychologist to investigate. This view, prominent in the 1920s and espoused by Weiss, Kantour and Watson, is currently held by Skinner. At the time it was proposed that it was a healthy antidote to the prevalent loose mentalism that had preceded it. It encouraged accurate measurement of stimuli and responses, promoted attempts to establish functional laws and was fruitful in such areas as psychophysics, reaction time and conditioning.

However, it became increasingly clear that there were severe limitations. A number of objections can be made on purely theoretical grounds. Insofar as no two events are identical, some theoretical abstraction is required in order to enable generalisation. Broadbent (1961) has argued that the Skinnerian approach is inadequate even for prediction, let alone explanation:

> So long as this implies that psychologists will confine themselves purely to stating what they observe, it is a genuine improvement on Hull's approach. But unfortunately one cannot confine oneself in this way for ever: all of us want to give a scientific account of behaviour in complex situations where more is involved than the frequency of some simple action. It is possible to make predictions in such situations on the basis of experiments carried out under simpler conditions: but we then often have a choice between various features of the complex situation, each of which might correspond to some feature of the simple one. We must therefore make theoretical assumptions in applying the results of the simple case, and as the followers of Skinner have no rules for doing this with greater caution than the Hullians, there is a danger that they may make just as rash pronouncements.

Insofar as it eschews any attempt to provide reasons for the occurrence of particular stimulus response contingencies, it fails to provide an explanation for them. Skinner has said that he does not know why food is reinforcing to a hungry animal and he does not care.

Humphrey (1951) has documented the way in which parallel objections were raised against both philosophical and psychological associationism. These may be roughly classified into those primarily concerned with the adequate treatment of stimulus, response and organismic variables respectively. It is clear on empirical grounds that there are a number of classes of phenomena which a functionalist approach is inadequate to handle.

STIMULI

Stimuli are actively processed such that the internal representation of a stimulus does not correspond to its external representation. Underwood (1963) distinguished the functional from the nominal stimulus. A basic phenomenon which testifies to this fact is that of selective attention.

Any account of stimuli in discrete or absolute terms is doomed to failure. The Gestalt psychologists' claim, that the critical properties of stimuli are configurational and cannot be predicted on the basis of a consideration of their component parts, has a venerable history of at least eight centuries and a philosophical counterpart in John Stuart Mill's illustration of the spectrum in which seven different colours generate white light. Animals typically respond to relative rather than absolute values of stimuli, as was emphasised by Köhler (1918) and Lashley (1942) and demonstrated by the phenomenon of transposition. Sutherland and Mackintosh (1971) have invoked the concept of 'analyser' to explain similar phenomena including the overlearning reversal effect. Moreover, it is now clear that responding in terms of such dimensions is not the prerogative of animals possessing language.

A similar point is of course made by consideration of the phenomenon of generalisation, which demonstrates that animals' responding is not restricted to absolute values of stimuli.

Osgood (1956) has argued that a functionalist approach is inadequate for handling phenomena which are best conceived in terms of stimulus–stimulus relations or sensory integration of some kind, such as closure. Bindra (1976) has argued that all learning is of this nature.

RESPONSES

Responses can no more be treated in an absolute and discrete fashion than can stimuli. One of the arguments to which Humphrey drew attention is that reproduction of responses does not occur. Conditioned responses are not exact replicas of unconditioned responses; for example, a conditioned avoidance reaction will be more restricted than the original unconditioned response to the shock. This is an example of the more general problem we have met that no two events are identical, with its implication that some theoretical content over and above mere association is required if statements are to be generalised and future events predicted.

In a notorious paper, Chomsky (1959) challenged Skinner's attempt to extend a functional analysis to verbal behaviour on several grounds. He pointed out that there were difficulties in deciding on the functional equivalence of responses, which certainly could not be predicted on the basis of a consideration of their physical properties. Secondly, he argued that indices of response strength such as frequency and recency could not be appropriately applied to all responses, in particular verbal responses. (This point seems arguable.) Thirdly, he drew attention to the fact that it is often difficult if not impossible to specify the stimulus for an utterance.

Behaviour is more commonly emitted than elicited. Apter (1973) described it as being synthesised or created. Thus recall is recon-structive (Bartlett 1932, Bransford *et al.* 1971 *et seq.*); speech is generated. Many psychologists have stressed the planned, pur-posive, rule-following characteristics of behaviour (e.g. Miller *et al.* 1960, Peters 1958, Harré & Secord 1972).

In Osgood's (1956) view a functionalist approach is inadequate for handling behaviour that involves response–response relations or motor integration. Lashley (1951) claimed that this applied to skills such as speaking and typing, where responses were emitted in such quick succession that there would not be time for stimulus control to intervene. Bindra (1976) has argued, however, that these must be under the control of central processes as several lines of evidence militate against the notion of response chaining. Flexibility and substitutability of linkage is necessary in response to environmental demands. The same act can be carried out by different movements and the same movements may occur in different acts. A simple associative theory cannot explain how the same response may be preceded or succeeded by different responses on different occasions, as in double alternation. Moreover, a number of workers have failed to obtain practice effects for sequences of movements repeatedly stimulated (Pinneo 1966, Delgado 1965). Pinneo elec-trically stimulated sites in the brain stem and cerebellar nuclei responsible for the production of specific movements. Sequences of movements could only be activated by successive stimulation and could not be triggered by activation of the first movement.

THE ORGANISM

Woodworth (1918) put back the organism into the stimulus–response formula and Hebb (1949) postulated a central autono-mous process. It is now generally accepted that stimuli modulate continuous activity in the nervous system. Thus the appropriate formula is $R = f(S \times O)$.

The mediating internal structure is inherited insofar as all learning is superimposed on an existing inherited structure and modifies an existing organisation (Lorenz 1966), and to the extent that there are built-in behavioural processes: reflexes, instinctive behaviour patterns, imprinting, maturation and species-specific predispositions, e.g. for language (Lenneberg 1967), or differential preparedness to learn contingencies (Thorndike 1935, Seligman 1970).

To a greater extent the internal structure is the result of learning. Organisms are continually adapting to changing environments. How an organism responds to a stimulus depends on its past experience. This has two important implications. First, it means that the relationship between stimuli and responses is dynamic rather than static, changing over time. Secondly, on account of the fact that no two organisms have the same past experience, these relations will differ between individuals. These two facts pose the most fundamental challenges to psychology.

Shorter-term changes are usually described as motivational. Humphrey (1951) pointed out that some account must be taken of 'direction' in addition to associative strength. This became apparent to the Würzburg psychologists who proposed that thinking was a function of determining tendences as well as association. For example, whether 'six' or 'eight' is given in response to the stimulus 'two and four' depends on whether an instruction was given to add or to multiply. The fact that a rat's hunger as well as its knowledge of the maze is relevant to predicting its performance in it was acknowledged by Hull in his neo-behaviouristic theory of learning which included drive and habit strength as intervening variables. De Bono (1967) remarks that the salesman may modify the probabilities of responses not by altering habit hierarchies but by manipulating motivation.

The most obvious class of phenomena that a functionalist approach is unable to handle is symbolic processes. The problem of describing unobservables is one of the greatest weaknesses of behaviour theory. Broadbent, who considers himself a behaviourist, writes (1961): 'It is almost universally admitted now that even the behaviour of rats requires us to think of mechanisms operating purely inside their brains, and revealing themselves only indirectly in action.'

Neo-behaviourists admitted that even a phenomenon as simple as avoidance conditioning required the postulation of mediating processes. In a typical experiment, the first stage involves the conditioning of an escape response to shock. In the second stage, a neutral stimulus such as a buzzer is associated with the shock but no escape is possible. In the third stage, presentation of the buzzer alone is tested and an escape response occurs. The problem for the functionalist is to explain how the response is produced in stage 3 when it has not previously been elicited by that stimulus. Neo-behaviourists solved the problem by postulating mediating responses and stimuli which they supposed were elicited by the shock in stage 1, became conditioned to the buzzer in stage 2 and served to elicit the escape response in stage 3.

Neo-behaviourist mediation theory

It seems to be clear then that something must be put back into the black box. The question is what? Parsimony dictates that as little as possible be put back; adequacy demands sufficient explanatory power.

The minimum replacement would be intervening variables as employed by Hull and Tolman. But as these are merely summary statements of observed relations between stimuli and responses and completely reducible to these they represent in fact no advance.

Hypothetical constructs have additional meaning over and above observed relations but they are vague and it is not clear whether they are observable in practice or not, nor what observations one could make to improve on them. There are also difficulties in anchoring these reliably (Miller 1956) and validly (Joynson 1970), as was discussed above.

Most neo-behaviourists opted for postulating internal stimuli and responses (represented by lower case 's's and 'r's) which were unobservable but subject to the same laws as external observable stimuli and responses (indicated by upper case 'S's and 'R's). Theorists who favoured such an approach were Mowrer (1954) and Osgood (1953). They claimed that external stimuli elicited internal symbolic responses which gave rise to internal stimuli which served to mediate external responses. The application of this scheme to the explanation of conditioning is shown in Figure 9.1. Osgood

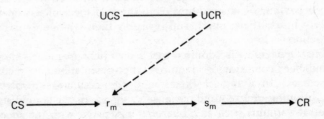

Figure 9.1 Formation of a representational mediation process (after Osgood 1956).

(1953) explains that the representational mediation process, r_m, is representational in that it is a fractional component of the unconditioned response, UCR, that would be elicited by the unconditioned stimulus, UCS; it is mediational because it produces self-stimulation, s_m, which is capable of eliciting a variety of instrumental acts, CR.

Such theoretical apparatus could be invoked to explain avoidance conditioning (e.g. May 1948), the combination of paths learned separately when occasion demands (e.g. Hull 1935), reversal shifts (e.g. Lawrence 1950) and vocabulary learning (e.g. Mowrer 1954, Osgood 1953, 1963).

However, Broadbent (1961) has drawn attention to a number of difficulties with this approach. First, covert responses do not in fact obey the same laws as overt responses. Overt responses can be reinforced by many rewards, but covert responses only by the specific reward to which they correspond. For example, an r_g corresponding to drinking can only be reinforced by water and not by food: a thirsty rat does not go to where it was last fed but to where it found water. Lawrence's work (1950) shows that reversal shifts are easier to learn than new discriminanda and hence suggests that it is easier to learn to attach a new overt response to an already learned internal response than to a new internal reponse. Thus covert responses may be more difficult to learn than overt responses. Secondly, there is a danger of identifying covert responses with too peripheral reactions (e.g. Wyckoff's (1952) observing responses or Watson's (1914) laryngeal movements). Thirdly, statements about unobservables can only be made by inference and hence demand caution. As we have seen, this is an inescapable problem. Finally, there is the difficulty of avoiding ambiguity in the description of internal processes. This is the reason why Skinner objects to introspection, i.e. there is inadequate knowledge of, and control over, the conditioning history of the use of terms referring to private states.

Fodor (1965) discusses the application of mediation theories to language. He argues that meaning could not be a mediating response on the grounds that two-stage S–R models are subject to the same objections as single-stage models. There is a dilemma in that either a one-to-one correlation between external stimulus and mediating response is assumed, in which case the two-stage model is no more powerful than a single-stage model; or this assumption is dropped, in which case sufficient conditions for linguistic reference and for predicting behaviour are lacking.

Cybernetic, information processing approaches

The main developments since mediation theory have been cognitive approaches based on an information processing analogy. These have borrowed ideas from information theory, cybernetics and computer science. A problem with early formulations of cognitive concepts such as Piaget's and Bartlett's schemata or Bruner's and Gregory's hypotheses was their ill defined nature. As Bindra (1976) has shown, cognitive theories are very inadequate when it comes to prediction. Their transformational, mediation processes are not specified; hence they remain descriptive rather than explanatory, *ad hoc* and untestable. They tend to be plausible but imprecise, whereas S–R theories tend to be precise but implausible. A contribution towards greater precision in cognitive theories has been made by the employment of terms and concepts from the disciplines mentioned above. A seminal approach in this direction was the book by Miller, Galanter and Pribram (1960), *Plans and the structure of behaviour,* in which the reflex model of behaviour was rejected, a single level analysis was considered inadequate and the feedback loop (which they called the TOTE, an acronym for test–operate–test–exit – see Fig. 9.2) was suggested as the basic unit of behaviour.

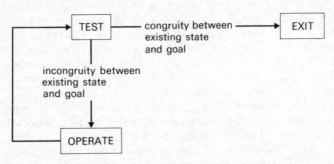

Figure 9.2 The TOTE unit (after Miller, Galanter & Pribram 1960).

A number of papers have attempted *reconciliations between cognitive and S–R theories.* Spence (1950) suggested the difference was merely one of emphasis. Thus S–R theorists, in contrast to cognitive theorists, concentrated on learning rather than perception and thinking, sought antecedent conditions in the past rather than the present, examined the effect of external rather than internal variables, viewed the organism as passive rather than active, attributed behaviour to nurture rather than to nature, stressed analysis rather than organisation and preferred explanations in terms of S–S rather than S–R relations.

Millenson (1967) has gone so far as to claim that the languages of S–R theory and information theory flow charts are in fact isomorphic and intertranslatable. To the extent that any flow chart represents a linear sequence of events this is a reasonable suggestion and Suppes (1969) has in fact demonstrated it formally. However, there will be some relations in the flow chart that will be obscured in the S–R description, and the flow chart is superficial and needs to become increasingly detailed. Like Spence, Millenson suggests that the differences are more apparent than real and principally reflect differences in emphasis and interest. S–R language is preferable when dealing with simple seqences, response contingencies or the acquisition of units; information theory descriptions are preferable for more complex contingencies.

In the next chapter we turn to a more detailed consideration of the information theory approach.

10

Models and computer simulation

Models

WHAT ARE MODELS?

In Chapter 8 it was pointed out that the term 'model' has been used in a number of different ways and three meanings were distinguished: (a) as synonymous with 'theory'; (b) as inferior to a theory on account of reduced scope and associated confidence; (c) as a particular type of theory, namely, structural, which seeks to explain phenomena by reference to an abstract system or mechanism. One of the foremost proponents of such an approach in psychology has been Deutsch (1960) who sees its advantages as compared with those of the descriptive approach as being qualitative rather than quantitative, possessing rigour rather than precision and logical cogency rather than mathematical formulation.

The essential feature of a model is the application of one (better understood and developed) system to another (less well understood and developed) system. Chapanis' (1961) definition of models, it will be recalled, was 'representations, or likenesses, of certain aspects of complex events, structures or systems, made by using symbols or objects which in some way resemble the thing being modelled'. In some cases a model may be an exemplar of a theory (Apter 1973), or a representation or embodiment of a theory (Frijda 1967). A model and a theory are not necessarily identical as is shown by the fact that the former may contain some aspects which are irrelevant to the latter. (For a more technical treatment of the relation between model and theory see Braithwaite 1953.)

The popularity of physical and mechanical models in science is due to the progress in the understanding of phenomena to which their employment has led. According to Radford and Burton (1974) the first scientific model was Anaximander's map. Other well known examples include Harvey's hydraulic metaphor for the circulation of the blood, Rutherford's planetary metaphor for the atom and Sherrington's telephone exchange metaphor for the central nervous system.

Psychology has been no exception, borrowing models from most other disciplines. Freud and the Gestalt psychologists borrowed from physics, the ethologists from biology, Estes from mathematics and Piaget from logic; cognitive psychologists have borrowed successively from cybernetics, communication theory, computer science and linguistics, and social psychologists from drama.

The borrowings have varied in nature from metatheories providing basic frameworks to piecemeal usage of specific concepts. In general terms, different psychological approaches can be characterised by reference to their model of man. Wiggins *et al.* (1971), for example, classify personality theories according to their model of man as an animal (in particular a rat, e.g. Skinner); an information processor (in particular a scientist, e.g. Kelly); a machine (in particular a computer, e.g. cognitive psychology); or an actor (e.g. Goffman). A dominant contrast has been between man as an active man (humanistic psychology) or as a passive machine (behaviourism) (see Fransella 1975, Joynson 1980, and Ch. 13). Examples of borrowings of more specific concepts are hydraulics (Lorenz 1950), vectors (Lewin 1951), filters (Broadbent 1957) and feedback loops (Miller, Galanter & Pribram 1960). A particularly popular form of modelling in recent years has been computer simulation. Accordingly, we shall devote the first part of this chapter to a consideration of models in general and the second part to a consideration of computer simulation in particular.

TYPES OF MODELS

Models can be distinguished both in terms of what is modelled, and of how it is modelled. In illustrating the first of these, Lachman (1960) distinguishes models of directly observed events from models of theoretical ideas. An example of the former is the treatment of perception as if it were a conditioned response (Howes and Solomon 1951), an example of the latter the treatment of r_g (Hull's fractional anticipatory goal response) as if it were a conditioned response (e.g. Spence 1951). It is also pointed out that more checks are provided by the data in the former than the latter case.

The form of a model can also be various. At the most concrete level there are models which are mechanical, what Chapanis (1961) describes as 'replicas'. Examples in psychology are Grey Walter's (1953) 'tortoises' or Ashby's (1948) homeostat. Mechanical analogies can also be employed at a more abstract level as in the case of flow charts. Some models are predominantly pictorial, such as Broadbent's (1957) filter theory, and possibly Lewin's (1951) topological vector theory of personality, of which it was said that it was a calculus that did not calculate (Braithwaite 1953). Symbolic models, which allow more powerful inferences to be made, may be verbal in form, as in the neo-behaviourist use of conditioning as a pre-theoretic model (see Kendler & Spence 1971), or mathematical as in Estes' (1959) mathematical learning theory, which treats the stimulus as a population of elements to which statistical sampling theory can be applied, and learning as a stochastic process to which probability theory can be applied. These different types suggest that models may serve a range of functions, to which we now turn.

Evaluation of models

ADVANTAGES

At the simplest level a model, by representing the phenomenon to be explained in a new way, may *aid understanding*. This may be the result of the model being better understood and/or more familiar (Young 1951). A model may reduce complexity by eliminating certain aspects from consideration. The didactic function of models is exemplified in Broadbent's filter theory, which provides a convenient mnemonic for the integration of a body of data and a crutch pending the formulation of a more rigorous theory.

Insofar as a model provides a new way of looking at things, it may serve a heuristic function of *generating new hypotheses to test*. For example, viewing man as a communication channel suggests the testing of capacity limitations. A more specific example from a concrete realisation of a model, comes from Grey Walter's (1953) 'tortoises', which produced behaviour that had not been predicted. In this way models may provide a framework for experimentation and here serve a function common to that of theories proper. They have the advantage that they enable consideration of the possible as well as the actual.

How explicitly this can be done depends on the nature of the model. Braithwaite (1953) claimed that the essence, and hence power, of a model lies in its inference rules rather than its symbolism. As Newell (1973) observed, many flow charts in cognitive psychology are insufficient for the performance of tasks. He suggests that a knowledge of the control structure (the invariant structure of the processing mechanism) yields explicit programming problems for the achievement of particular tasks, enabling inferences to be made about the methods used. Other cases where the model is sufficiently formulated to be used to interpret a theory or make specific predictions are mathematical learning theory and the behaviourists' application of the laws of conditioning to the explanation of other behavioural phenomena.

Thus, models may aid in the *evaluation of theories*. They may serve both to examine the logical consistency and completeness of a theory and its practical feasibility (e.g. Bush and Mosteller's 'stat rats' (1955)). This is particularly so in the case of computer programs, where implications can be worked out quickly and accurately.

If represented in concrete form, models may assist at a practical level in the *learning of skills* (e.g. simulated cockpits) and in engineering design.

Finally, models provide *amusement*. 'Scientists often entertain models because their models entertain them', as Chapanis (1961) observes, citing Hull as an example.

Thus models have a number of points of recommendation, whether logical or psychological. Braithwaite (1962), after discussing the issue, concludes that the advantages are all of the latter kind.

DISADVANTAGES

In that a model is necessarily a partial and imperfect represen-tation, the *danger of invalid inference* is ever-present. 'The price of a model is eternal vigilance.' There will always be areas of non-correspondence. There is a temptation to overgeneralise inappro-priately from aspects of the model which do not apply to the phenomenon modelled. The point is brought home by recognition of the fact that there are many possible models of a given phenomenon: the same end may be achieved by a variety of means. A possible explanation is not necessarily either *the*, or the best, explanation. Perhaps because the ultimate tests of models is useful-ness rather than truth they are insufficiently subjected to test.

There are specific respects in which a model may be *inaccurate*, namely, the *constants*, and the *relations between variables*. The latter may be the result of alterations in scale. There is also the problem of the validity of concepts. Examples in psychology are Estes' parameter theta, estimated from the data, and factors extracted in multivariate analysis. The validity of these may be merely mathematical and not psychological.

Finally, if theorising is *wasteful of energy* as Skinnerians suppose, how much more so must this be true of modelling. The answer to this hinges on whether the psychological advantages of modelling justify their use.

CRITERIA FOR EVALUATION

To some extent, the criteria for evaluating models are similar to those for evaluating theories. However, one criterion peculiar to models is that of *deployability*: the extent to which the terms or properties of a model can be applied to the phenomenon modelled. (Thus porridge is not a very good model of the brain. How much better is a computer?)

Secondly, the *scope* or range of data covered will also be a relevant consideration in the evaluation of a model. An increase in deployability will tend to lead to an increase in scope but the reverse is not the case.

Thirdly, *precision* is a dimension on which models differ greatly. Current psychology notwithstanding, those which enable unequivocal derivation of consequences and hence maximise testability are to be preferred. It is lamentable that, in psychology, 'model' has tended to be used in the sense of approximation or semi-formalised theory rather than in the sense of an interpretation of the theory's calculus. It would be better to call the former 'a *theoruncula* or (affectionately) a *theorita*' as Braithwaite (1962) suggests.

It was pointed out in Chapter 8 that the ultimate criterion of a model is usefulness, in contradistinction to that of a theory which is truth. So in the final analysis the question is whether the model serves its heuristic function and is fruitful in leading to new formulations, new predictions and new discoveries. It is not difficult to see the blind alleys that resulted from many of psychology's less appropriate borrowings, e.g. from physics (field theory turned out not to apply to the brain), information theory ('information' is used in very different senses in communications engineering and the psychology of communication), and linguistics (there are good reasons for holding that the linguist's constraints differ from those of the language user). One that looks as though it holds rather more promise is computer science, to which we now turn.

Computer simulation

Computer simulation has become increasingly popular as a model in psychology over the past 20 years, particularly in cognitive psychology but also in other areas, for example, personality, psychopathology and social psychology. Again the borrowings have been on various levels. On the one hand, the computer analogy is part of the metaview which treats man as an information processing system. On the other, a multitude of specific concepts have been employed. These include: hierarchical organisation and heter-archical control, linear and parallel processing, plan, compiler and

interpreter programs, subroutine, recursion, mini-maxing, iter-
ation, top-down and bottom-up processing, depth-first and
breadth-first search, procedural versus declarative representation of
knowledge, content-addressable memory, ring and list structures,
push-down stack.

Certain fears are associated with the employment of mechanistic
analogies in the explanation of human behaviour. What is involved
in the claim that the mind is a machine? In Chapter 3 two senses of
mind were distinguished: (a) conscious experience, and (b) the
system that governs behaviour. It is this latter sense that is
intended here. To say that the mind is a machine is merely to say
that there is a system according to which it works, whose rules can
be stated in principle. It may also imply that the principles which
govern physical phenomena can be extended to mental phenomena
(cf. Gregory 1961, Sutherland 1970). Scriven (1960) claims that
'machine' is a term, like 'science' or 'truth', which can be applied
correctly in typical cases but not explicitly defined. If the term
'machine' is applied to living systems, it may lose its main classifi-
catory function (Gregory 1961). There is a danger that explicit
definitions will presuppose answers to questions to be asked or be
either too imprecise or too restrictive. For example, making predictability of behaviour a defining property of a machine would
rule out roulette wheels and radium-driven randomisers (Scriven
1960). Boden has ably defended the computational metaphor in
psychology against the charge of dehumanisation, arguing that the
humanist's rejection of mechanism is partly the result of an
impoverished image of machine (Boden 1978), and that

> a psychology that looks to machines for some of its central
> concepts need not be crudely mechanistic in character, nor
> inhumanly reductionist in type. On the contrary, the comput-
> ational approach in psychology stresses (and helps to explain)
> important features of the mind, such as purpose and subjectivity,
> which many psychological theories have ignored – or even denied
> (Boden 1979).

In what sense, then, is the brain a computer? It is important to
stress the level at which the analogy is intended, and the distinction
between software and hardware. The software is the abstract level,
in this case the programme governing the system; the hardware is
the concrete level, what the system is made of in material terms, in
this case either organic tissue or electronic circuitry. The level at
which the analogy holds is that of the software. The hardware does
indeed have aspects in common, but it is not this that is meant but
rather that the workings of the mind can be likened to a program.

The ultimate aim is to construct programs whose fit is so good that they can be considered theories of behaviour. It may well be that the superiority of this model is due to the level of abstraction at which the analogy is employed.

SIMILARITIES BETWEEN BRAINS AND COMPUTERS

What kind of computer is the brain? What kind of brain is the computer? (Radford & Burton 1974.)

First, both consist of networks of connections which operate in *binary* fashion: thermionic valves or electromagnetic relays are on or off and neurons fire or do not fire according to an all-or-none principle. But Wooldridge (1963) has pointed out that this applies only to the axon: the body of the neuron works according to a summative principle and the threshold for firing may be affected by chemical and electrical changes. So it depends what level is considered: at lower and higher levels than the axon, functioning could be described as summative rather than all-or-none.

It might be argued that both computers and brains are pre-dominantly *digital* in nature. Representation in digital machines (e.g. most computers) is symbolic and discrete, whereas in analogue machines (an example of which is a slide rule) it is direct and continuously variable. However, computers can be made to function in analogue fashion by making the steps sufficiently small. Likewise, the nervous system is analogue in some aspects, e.g. endocrine secretion. Wooldridge (1963) suggests that it is unlikely, on the basis of logical considerations and empirical measures (e.g. EEG), that there are any purely digital circuits in the brain. Gregory (1961, 1970) has argued that in certain respects the brain (particularly the perceptual system) is analogue, on the grounds of speed of operation and type of errors. Analogue machines have faster transmission rates but limited precision (being subject to random error and dependent on the precision of their construc-tion); digital machines have no limits to their precision in principle but can be wildly wrong. Adaptive behaviour requires fast approximation: it is important to know (and quickly) that an object is, for example, a lion so that effective action can be taken, but its exact proportions are of less importance.

Both are *electrical* in nature though the brain is also chemical. However, these hardware similarities are without significance in the present context. Moreover, the differences between neurons and thermionic valves are more obvious (cf. von Neumann 1958).

More importantly, both are *information processors,* in particular symbol manipulators. Both have input and output mechanisms, storage systems and hierarchies of programs. Both perform complex operations by breaking them down into a series of small steps.

A second broad similarity is *similarity of output* or product. Computers and brains can achieve the same ends (e.g. the solution of problems). However, this is more pertinent to the domain of artificial intelligence, whose aim is to produce the same results as could be achieved by the human but usually much more quickly and efficiently, not necessarily and probably not by the same means.

The goal of computer simulation, in contradistinction, is to mimic the process as well as the product. Not only the end but also the means must be the same. The aim is to represent the operations in a program in such a way that it can be considered a theory of behaviour. It is these software similarities that are of importance. What of the differences?

DIFFERENCES BETWEEN BRAINS AND COMPUTERS

How far can the analogy be stretched? In what ways is it misleading?

We have already noted the marked differences in *hardware* between neurons and thermionic valves. These differences in themselves are relatively unimportant but they may be indicative of more significant implications.

Computers are predominantly *digital* in type of processing whereas, as Gregory (1970) and others have argued, brains are *analogue* in important respects. Dreyfus (1972) has attempted to base the claim that strong simulation of brain processes is impossible on such a distinction. Against this, Sutherland (1974) has pointed out that it is not proven, and indeed is in fact false, that analogue processes cannot be represented on digital computers. Furthermore, at the level relevant for understanding the overall working of the brain, digital may be more important than analogue processes. In some cases the processing of analogical information may be rather poor with continuously variable input being coded discretely, e.g. short term memory (Miller 1956) and categorical perception of consonant phonemes (Liberman *et al.* 1957).

Computers have a high degree of precision and accuracy but are peculiarly (excessively to the novice programmer) sensitive to *error* (a small change in input may have a large effect on output), and analogue machines are subject to random error. By contrast, brains approximate, are relatively insensitive to error at least at a fine level and are never subject to random error.

Computers generally *function sequentially* (though they can be programmed to function in parallel), whereas brains typically exhibit *parallel processing*. This suggests a reason why humour, insight, creativity and aesthetic appreciation (activities which depend essentially on parallel processing) seem distinctive of the human brain.

The last two differences considered have important implications for psychological simulation. Mathematical computation is easy to program on a computer but difficult for a human whereas the reverse is true of pattern perception. This suggests that the processes employed may be essentially different.

Memory is another function where there are obvious apparent differences. In the human, memory is necessarily selective and essentially constructive, whereas in the computer it is typically reproductive. Storing and processing tend to be separated whereas in the brain they are inextricably mixed. Human memory is messier and less reliable but more flexible (Wilding 1978). The data bases of current computers are severely limited, while even the solution of simple everyday problems requires much knowledge. One problem arises from the fact that there is no definable set of primitive facts from which all knowledge can be deduced, others from the need to organise and retrieve information. Severe problems of programming are raised by internal knowledge, strategies and the whole question of past experience. Forgetting is different too. In the computer, memories can be erased, whereas this is rarely so in the brain; rather they are tagged as false. Neisser (1963) suggests that computers are more docile in that there is greater control over what is learned and what is forgotten. Humans are not so easily able to select or avoid change.

Although an adequate simulation of *learning* poses one of the most serious programming challenges, the objection that computers cannot learn or modify their own programming as a result of past experience can no longer be defended. Several programs for pattern recognition (Selfridge & Neisser 1960, Taylor 1959, Uhr & Vossler 1961) succeed by discovering critical discriminative features of the stimuli. Samuel's (1959) program for draught playing improves its performance by storing and using information from past games. Zobrist and Carlson's (1973) chess program improves its heuristics by co-operating with a skilled player. Sussman's (1975) program HACKER which writes programs for solving problems learns to do better by possessing a general knowledge of the kind of mistakes that can occur and how to deal with them. It remembers what went wrong in the past and avoids it in future. Computers can learn by optimising probability weights and other internal parameters but important learning in humans involves changes in the structure of processing itself. It is difficult to simulate Piagetian accommodation adequately, and the cumulative and ordered sequence of cognitive development in which natural learning occurs is lacking in the computer which is not dependent on maturational sequence (Neisser 1963).

It is often said that computers can only do what they are programmed to do. It is true that computers follow instructions and that all their behaviour is *predictable* in principle but from this it does not follow that all their behaviour either could be or was predicted in fact. Programs often surprise their programmers, as in man–machine dialogues (e.g. Colby *et al.* 1971). Newell *et al.*'s Logic Theorist found an original proof for one of the theorems from Russell and Whitehead's *Principia mathematica*. There is no reason why computers cannot produce unpredicted and *novel* results. These are more likely to arise from quantity rather than quality of processing as current computers tend to be poor at complex analogical reasoning. It is more difficult to achieve controlled imprecision than precision in a computer. The reverse might be said to be true of humans.

The limitations in *complexity* of current computers can hardly be held against the analogy as what is at issue is whether computers can in principle be programmed to carry out tasks in the same way as humans. Already there is an impressive list of achievements that were thought *a priori* impossible. These include: holistic perception; the creative use of language; musical composition; translation from one language to another by way of language-neutral semantic representation; planning action in broad and sketchy fashion, the details being decided only in execution; and distinguishing between different species of emotional reaction according to the psychological context of the subject. In general, the limits of artificial intelligence and simulation cannot be specified in advance.

Purposiveness is fairly easy to accommodate in machines, from the simple examples of thermostats and guided missiles to programs where goals are pursued by a variety of means, e.g. GPS (General Problem Solver, Newell & Simon 1961). Hence purposiveness cannot be a basis for distinguishing brains from computers (see also Ch. 12). Neisser (1963) indeed observes that machines are in general more persistent than humans.

Brains are part of biological organisms, composed of living tissue. They are open systems constantly fighting the second law of thermodynamics. They are motivated by self-preservation and show a certain amount of plasticity in response to damage (as in restitution of function) though ultimately they wear out. Computers might be considered rational and brains selfish. For the latter, the pleasure principle precedes the reality principle (Neisser 1963). Stimulus information is assimilated largely with reference to needs; human thinking is intimately associated with emotions.

Singlemindedness has been thought a distinctive characteristic of machines, whereas almost all human behaviour simultaneously serves a multiplicity of motives (Neisser 1963). For example, a chess player's desire to win may be motivated by hope of success or fear of failure (either private or public), intellectual or aesthetic pleasure, aggression or affiliation, or any combination of these. His motivation could never be the chess program's: merely to win. Most artificial intelligence programs have a single overall end but a few have been developed with the aim of simulating the multi-dimensional nature of human motivation. For example, ARGUS (Reitman 1965) embodies various goals which compete for computational resources available, priority being given to the one which, in the current situation, is most strongly activated. In this case there are conflicting motives but only one functioning system.

It is often advanced that a distinctive feature of the brain which the computer necessarily lacks is *consciousness*. However, as became clear in Chapter 4, the resolution of this depends on an adequate account of the nature of consciousness not yet in existence. Boden (1979) suggests that the charge is misplaced, that no sense can be made of computers seeing, wanting, feeling or knowing (even if true): computer simulations are theories whose aim is to understand rather than to mimic experience and behaviour. It is no more to be expected of a psychological theory that it see or feel than 'of a chemical theory that it fizz if put into a test tube'.

Boden (1978) claims that one respect in which computers are lacking is in the possession of intrinsic interests (implied by a strong sense of moral dignity). Intrinsic interests pertain to the individual and cannot be explained further in purposive terms though they could be in evolutionary or physiological terms. The purposes of machines are not intrinsic to them but derive from those of the programmer. But this is due to their artificial rather than their mechanistic nature. Computers are dependent on brains in a way in which the reverse is not true. Computers are made and operated on by men. Who made and operates on men?

Thus certain differences between brains and computers stem from the distinction between natural and artificial machines. In other cases the differences may be more a matter of degree rather than kind. Despite the gaps, the similarities are sufficiently significant for the analogy to be mutually fruitful for artificial intelligence and psychological theory. It is the deficiencies of computers (lack of cognitive development, an emotional base and subtlety of decision-making) rather than their superiorities that are the true cause of humans' fear of them (Neisser 1963).

EXAMPLES OF SIMULATIONS

Apter (1973) suggests that simulations may arise from three sources:

(a) *Theories*, examples of which are the simulation by Colby (1963) of Freudian theory, by Rochester *et al.* (1956) of Hebb's (1949), by Abelson (1963) of Heider's (1958) balance theory, and by Gullahorn and Gullahorn (1963) of Homan's (1961) model of social interaction.
(b) *Behavioural data*, either introspections or performance responses, examples of which are Laughery and Gregg (1962), the simulation of problem-solving in symbolic logic and cryptarithmetic by Newell and Simon (1972), and of decision-making by Feldman (1962) and Smith (1968).
(c) *Artificial intelligence,* examples of which are programs to play chess (e.g. Newell & Simon 1972), draughts (Samuel 1959), and prove geometry theorems (Gelernter 1959).

Evaluation of simulation

ADVANTAGES

The advantages of computer simulation are related to those of structural theories, of which they form a special case. Perhaps the most important of these is the provision of descriptions, and hence understanding and explanation of *processes,* the fundamental aim of psychology. Moreover, it demands precision, thus enabling processes to be made explicit and theories to be formulated unambiguously. In this respect it has the advantage over verbal theories. Colby's (1963) formulation of Freudian theory might be given as an example.

It assists in the *testing of theories* both by examining *logical consistency* and *empirical adequacy.* On the one hand, it checks the specification of the model: it uncovers implications and derives predictions, revealing whether or not they are as intended. Consequences may be unforeseen (e.g. Feigenbaum 1959). On the other hand, running the program shows whether or not it works and whether it is sufficient to generate the predicted behaviour. If it is, it is a candidate for a theory. By varying the conditions under which it is run, empirical investigation can be extended and the effect of variables examined (e.g. Gelernter *et al.* 1960).

This may result in new insights being gained into the process under study and the *generation of new hypotheses.* For example,

Rochester *et al.*'s computer simulation of Hebb's theory revealed inadequacies which led to Milner's (1957) reformulation incorporating inhibitory (in addition to excitatory) connections.

In addition, computer simulation has made many *conceptual contributions*. On a general level it has suggested how psychological characteristics can be compatible with mechanisms. It has suggested resolutions of old philosophical problems, in particular the mind–body problem, and hence thrown light on issues such as substance, causation and volition. The proposal is that an intelligible way of formulating the relation between mind (at least in the sense of the program governing behaviour) and body is as that between program and hardware. It provides descriptions at an appropriate level for psychology (i.e. in terms of software rather than hardware) without the need to specify detail at more molecular levels. It has encouraged a more unified view of cognition (Wilding 1978), thinking being seen as a series of operations on symbols.

It has also contributed a large number of specific concepts, many of which were listed earlier in the chapter. Boden (1979) has provided some interesting illustrations of the way in which computer language can be used to aid conceptualisation in specific areas, e.g. dissociated states of consciousness such as cases of so-called 'split-personality' (e.g. Thigpen & Cleckley 1957). The two personalities can be viewed as two subroutines or modules of the same overall computational system, alternately using the same motor facilities and sensory apparatus but having different degrees of access to each other's information and data store.

DISADVANTAGES

On the one hand, it is difficult to build into the computer program human inferiorities (for example, being influenced by a multitude of motivational factors), although some beginnings have been made (e.g. Reitman 1965); on the other hand, it is difficult to build in human superiorities (for example, not being led into error by small changes, and the ability to make richly subtle comparisons). Most current computers are severely limited and serious problems are posed by the organisation, retrieval and inferential use of information.

Computer simulation is an aid to understanding rather than a means in itself (Sutherland 1974). It does not guarantee understanding, which requires inference beyond the observed to the unobserved.

EVALUATING THE ADEQUACY OF A SIMULATION

When does a simulation amount to a theory? In the final analysis the problem is the same as that for evaluating a theory. The conclusion rests on whether adequate tests have been made. Some of the criteria used for evaluating a simulation will be the same as those for theories in general, such as scope (e.g. the value of GPS depends on the range of problem areas in which it can be applied); fruitfulness in giving rise to new findings (e.g. Quillian's (1968) Teachable Language Comprehender gave rise to much empirical work on semantic memory); and success in prediction. A central problem is evaluating the fit with behaviour. Frijda (1967) remarks: 'As much ingenuity as has been invested in the making of programs, as little has been spent on the assessment of their value.'

A well known test was suggested by Turing (1950), viz. whether a judge could discriminate between a machine and a human, both hidden from view, on the basis of their output consisting of answers to any questions of the judge's devising put to them. Turing's criterion was that if the judge could not discriminate between them then the program in the computer was an adequate theory of the performance of the human. Fodor (1968) (as have others) claims that this criterion is either insufficient (what needs to be established is that they both do it in the same way), or question begging (what aspects are theoretically relevant?).

Total correspondence is not required (in the limit it would amount to identity) but rather abstraction of relevant features. This raises the important problem of *selection*. There is no algorithm for deciding which are the critical features of the system and the model that are intended to match. As Frijda (1967) points out, there is nothing in the program to indicate which features are relevant and which irrelevant.

Fodor (1968) distinguishes two levels of adequacy:

(a) *weak equivalence,* i.e. similarity of products, and
(b) *strong equivalence,* i.e. isomorphism or functional equivalence of the underlying processes. The former can be examined by comparing performance (in computers and humans). However, what is required is that any potential products be the same (i.e. similarity with respect to competence). Ultimately this amounts to strong equivalence.

Possible quantitative methods for comparing simulations with behavioural data have been discussed by Reitman (1965) and Frijda (1967). Frijda describes three levels of correspondence: with respect to (a) *problem solution*, as in question answering programs (e.g. Green 1963); (b) *quantitative performance measures,* such as time, errors, or order of difficulty, as in recognition (Uhr *et al.* 1962), immediate memory (Bower 1963), or serial reproduction (Feigenbaum & Simon 1962); and (c) *qualitative details of process,* as in introspections or intermediate results, e.g. in binary choice (Feldman 1962) or general problem-solving (Newell & Simon 1959).

He goes on to point out that significance testing is in general inappropriate on account of the large number of degrees of freedom in a program. It may be necessary instead to rely on the construction of alternative models (e.g. Clarkson 1961), or on a common-sense impression of similarity, which is often so striking as to render coincidence unlikely (e.g. Newell & Simon 1961, Simon & Kotovsky 1963).

In this chapter we have been concerned with attempts to explain behaviour by reference to abstract properties of the system governing it, i.e. with descriptions at the level of the software. In the next chapter we turn to a consideration of approaches which have focussed attention on the hardware and sought the explanation of behaviour in terms of the physical embodiment of the system.

11

The relation of physiology
to psychology

Introduction

As we saw in Chapter 1, one of the assumptions of science is that
different disciplines are related in a hierarchical way varying from
high level sciences at one end, such as sociology, which deal with
large units of analysis, to low level sciences at the other, such as
physics, which deal with small units of analysis. Thus, a possible
ordering might be: sociology, psychology, physiology, chemistry,
physics. What is relatively molecular for the high level scientist is
relatively molar for the low level scientist. At each level the
scientist makes assumptions about that which is the business of the
scientist at the next level down. For example, the sociologist when
theorising about the economic behaviour of a society or the
language of a culture makes assumptions about the individual man's
motivations and acquisition of language; the psychologist when he
theorises as opposed to merely observing makes assumptions about
what goes on inside the organism. As Osgood (1956) puts it:
'Behaviour theory is made up of hunches about how the nervous
system operates to generate the lawful relations that the psychologist observes between stimuli and responses.' There are also
different levels of description within each discipline: explanations
may be relatively molar or molecular. In psychology, a response
may be related to the role it plays in a larger unit of behaviour or to
the muscular movements of which it is composed.

As we saw in Chapter 9, looking inside is a possible solution to
the problem of how to deal with the organism. It is one common
type of explanation, Aristotle's 'material' cause, mechanistic
explanation where reference is made to the physical embodiment of
the system governing the behaviour.

Views on the relation of physiology to psychology

The relation of physiology to psychology is an area of much

controversy. We shall consider various views in order of increasing closeness of the posited relation.

No relation

The most extreme position at one end is that there can be no relation. Bannister (1968), who has argued that physiological psychology is impossible, gives the impression of holding such a view. 'In terms of a logic of sciences, there are reasons for believing that no form of physiological psychology can be a science or part of a science,' he writes. 'Psychological and physiological concepts stem from such different semantic networks that they cannot be meaningfully related into a subsystem', where a subsystem is a group of constructs which has a great many internal lines of implication and relatively few relations with other systems.

He presents four arguments in support of his case:

(a)   The constructs of physiology and psychology have partially non-overlapping fields of convenience, they deal with different phenomena, or in Kellyan jargon: 'they link down to different subordinate constructions'. Physiology traffics in subskin phenomena while psychology traffics in molar movement phenomena. They have different subject matters. This is undeniable but does not rule out the possibility of their being related.

(b)   Physiology need not be, but psychology needs to be reflexive, i.e. self-referring. Doing psychology is part of the subject matter of psychology in a way that doing physiology is not part of the subject matter of physiology. Again, this is true, and suggests that psychology may have some peculiarities, but does not seem sufficient to establish his case.

(c)   Physiological processes of individuals are largely independent of and unrelated to each other whereas psychological processes are interactive between individuals. In this case the distinction is probably invalid. Though it is true that 'no man is an island', it is not the case that 'all psychology is social psychology'. There are large areas of psychology where social factors are relatively unimportant, e.g. physiological psychology and some aspects of cognitive psychology. Conversely, in some cases physiological processes are affected by social factors, e.g. pheromones (see e.g. McClintock 1971).

(d)   Physiology uses a mechanistic, deterministic model, whereas this has failed in psychology, Bannister argues, because of the existence of concepts such as consciousness and choice and the paradox that an experimenter's prediction about a subject's behaviour may be invalidated by his having made it (for example the publication of Gallup poll results may influence the electorate's behaviour in such a way as to invalidate them). On this last point, as indicated previously, I think we are faced with complexity rather than indeterminism. Most psychologists would reject the charge that the deterministic model had failed in their discipline. Consciousness and choice can be given interpretations which are consistent with a deterministic framework (see Chs 2 and 4 for discussions of these concepts).

In summary, although Bannister's article draws attention to some of the differences between physiology and psychology, it is not sufficient to establish his case that physiological psychology is impossible.

He believes that the 'myth' of physiological psychology depends on verbal trickery. The illusion that physiology and psychology can be meaningfully related rests on the false assumption that concepts such as 'arousal', 'stimulus', 'response', 'inhibition' and 'threshold' have the same meaning in the two disciplines whereas in fact they have quite different meanings. Indeed, as Kelvin (1956) points out, certain phenomena such as selective attention and subliminal perception depend on discrepancies of this kind.

Double aspect
This may lead to the adoption of a double aspect view of the relation between physiology and psychology. Thus, Kelvin (1956) suggests that psychology and physiology provide descriptions of the same events from different points of view, and gives the example of a movement of the hand, which may be described in terms of a series of muscle contractions, some kind of response or as an expression of sadness. An 'event' is in this sense like a cube seen from different angles, or a playing card whose significance changes with the rules of different games.

Similarly, Bannister (1968) writes:

In line with Kelly (1955) it is assumed that it is not useful to talk of physiological events or psychological events but only of physiological and psychological modes of construing events

and gives the following illustration:

Thus if we contemplate a young lady crossing a bridge (a lay construction) then we may equally well construe her as 'a series of movements of force about a point' (engineer's construing), as 'a poor credit risk' (banker's construing), as 'a mass of whirling electrons about nuclei' (physicist's construing), as 'a soul in peril of mortal sin' (theological construing) or as 'a likely dish' (young man's construing). We do not have to assume that she is really any of these. We can accept that they are all constructions which have some explanatory value and predictive utility, depending on the networks of constructs from which they stem.

On this view, experiments in physiological psychology are cues to translation (Kelvin 1956). They tell one where to look in the other discipline's language for the alternative description of the event; for example, mass action experiments tell one that the physiologist's account of learning will be concerned with the total cortex, not just one part of it. They are akin to the pointing and exchanging of words that might occur between an Earthman and a Martian, to use Kelvin's analogy.

Irrelevance

Another possible view might be to allow that physiology could be related to psychology but to claim that it is irrelevant. An exponent of this position is Skinner (1950) who argued that in the case of theories of learning there was no need for those of a mental, conceptual or neural kind, on the grounds that all that is required for the prediction and control of behaviour are functional laws between stimuli and responses. Theories of any kind, he argued, create new problems of explanation which get covered up, generate wasteful research and can be replaced by more direct methods. This approach avoids the pitfalls of extreme physiological theories which may be wrong and generally do not lead to an increase in explanatory power. However, there are cases where physiological findings may have implications for psychology (see pp. 137–8). The inadequacies of functionalism as a general approach were discussed in Chapters 8 and 9.

Hypothetical construct

A third view recognises the existence of the organism but goes no way towards exploring the nature of the processes involved. In this case physiology takes the form of a hypothetical construct in psychology. Hull (1943) was a famous representative of such a position, but there has been a long line of concepts postulated as intervening between stimuli and responses: schemata, implicit stimuli and responses, representational mediation processes, insight, images, set, expectations, cognitive maps, etc. Frequently, however, these have served little more than a labelling function. Cognitive concepts have generally had few predictive implications and neobehaviourist concepts mainly empirically falsified predictions. In favour of the approach is the recognition that the postulation of internal mediating processes is required but it does not go far enough. It is misleading if it suggests that physiological events intervene between psychological events in a causal sequence.

Causal interaction

Some phenomena make it appear as if there were causal interaction between physiological and psychological processes. Examples of apparent behavioural causes having physiological effects are activity and increased heart rate, eating and obesity, stress and ulcers, life style and cardiac disease. Examples of apparent physiological causes of behavioural effects are mongolism, phenylketonuria, epilepsy and the Pülfrich phenomenon. In these latter cases, explanations in physiological or physical terms seem to be largely satisfactory. Possibly Valins' (1966) demonstration that perceived changes in sounds alleged to be recordings of heart beats resulted in subjects rating slides of semi-nudes as more attractive, or simply putting on more clothes when cold, are other examples. However, cause is a relatively crude concept and there are conceptual difficulties with statements of causal relations between different realms of discourse. These statements result from selective attention to the physiological aspect and neglect of the psychological or vice versa.

The claim that physiological events cause psychological ones is particularly common and perhaps due to the belief (probably correct) that physiological statements are better incorporated in a body of knowledge. However, in general it is misleading to speak of physiological events causing psychological events. In principle, a causal account could be given at either level. Physiological events do not universally precede psychological ones, which would be required if it were to be said that the former cause the latter (Kelvin 1956). Further evidence against the view that physiological events cause psychological ones is the fact that we see neither wavelengths nor nerve impulses but colours; we hear not frequencies but tones.

PSYCHOLOGICAL AND PHYSIOLOGICAL CONSTRAINTS

Psychological and physiological descriptions must be compatible and hence impose mutual constraints: neither discipline can put forward a theory which has implications which conflict with what is known or possible in the other discipline. Pavlov's theory of generalisation as irradiation of excitation in the cortex, the Gestalt electrical field theory of perception and Hebb's original formulation were all physiologically flawed (cf. Bass & Hull 1934, Lashley, Chow & Semmes 1951, Milner 1957, respectively) and could only be salvaged by a reformulation compatible with known physiology.

McFie (1972) has described cases where physiological findings may make contributions to psychological theory. For example, it may aid in the analysis of abilities with respect to their:

(a) *Nature*: the discovery that impairment of the ability to calculate is associated with right-sided hemispheric lesions might lead to the conclusion that calculation involves spatial ability; conversely, the discovery of an association between an impairment in reading and left hemispheric lesions would lead to the conclusion that there was little spatial involvement in such performance.

(b) *Differentiation*: neuropsychological studies of brain-damaged patients showing specific impairments of long and short term memory processes led Shallice and Warrington (1970) to argue for double dissociation of function within the memory system.

(c) *The discovery of new ones,* e.g. an aspect of performance on picture arrangement tasks sensitive to right fronto-temporal lesions.

Similarly, physiological theories must postulate mechanisms capable of accounting for psychological phenomena; for example, a three-colour receptor theory is faced with the problem of accounting for the perception of yellow (in the periphery beyond the areas for the perception of red and green). Likewise, physiological theories of learning and memory must be capable of accounting for the known psychological facts in these areas.

In addition to providing evidence which may have implications for theories of the other discipline, each may be able to supply methods to the other. Thus the psychologist may use drugs to study personality differences (e.g. individual differences reflected in reaction to alcohol) or clinical disorders; conversely, the pharmacologist may use behavioural measures in the analysis of drugs.

THE COMPUTER ANALOGY

An increasingly popular way of conceiving of the relation between physiology and psychology is to use a computer analogy and to suggest that psychology's concern is with the *software* that governs behaviour whereas physiology is concerned with the *hardware*. Essentially this is what Deutsch (1960) called a structural approach and (ironically) what Thomas (1978) and Fodor (1981) refer to as functionalism. Central to this is the view that behavioural processes should be described in terms of relations between states of a system. This can be done at an abstract level (e.g. in the form of a flow chart, program or Turing machine operations) without specification of the physical embodiment. Indeed, it is assumed that the same system can be physically represented in a variety of different ways (which leaves open the possibility of assigning mental states to machines). Deutsch sees the approach as a middle road between 'the sterility of positivism run wild' and 'the absurdities of the pseudo-physiologist'. Its advantages are that it is adequate for the prediction of behaviour, it enables use to be made of discoveries in cybernetic theory and computer science, and ultimately is mappable onto physiology which can provide another empirical check.

CORRELATION

Many experiments in physiological psychology seem to have as their aim the discovery of correlations between behaviour and physiology. Examples range from early attempts at cortical localisation of function and Funkenstein's (1955) work relating aggression and fear to the secretion of noradrenalin and adrenalin respectively, to more recent attempts to trace concomitant physiological and behavioural changes in the orienting response and Lassen *et al.*'s (1978) work relating sensory and motor functions to increased blood flow in cortical areas.

NEUROPHYSIOLOGISING

'The problem of understanding behaviour is the problem of understanding the total action of the nervous system and vice versa,' wrote Hebb (1949) who saw his book as a 'sedulous attempt to find some community of neurological and psychological conceptions'. In favour of this view may be stated the assumption that psychological processes are related to physiological ones and ultimately some physiological basis must be found for them, and that mutual interrelation between them is likely to increase as discoveries continue to be made. However, it depends on there being a one-to-one correlation between psychological and physiological states which has not been established. Against it, it may be argued that psychology exists in its own right, that specifying the physical embodiment does not generally lead to an increase in explanatory power and that neurologising is merely a form of intellectual displacement activity.

Reduction

Reduction refers to a relation between propositions. A weak form (empirical reduction) should be distinguished from a strong form (strict reduction). In the case of **empirical reduction**, terms in the two disciplines are taken as having different meanings, in the sense that different kinds of evidence are relevant to their truth. For example, the evidence for the existence of a piece of behaviour is different from the evidence for the existence of a certain brain state. A psychological statement is empirically reducible to a physiological statement if the truth of the latter is a sufficient (or necessary and sufficient) condition for the truth of the former. An important requirement for empirical reduction is the establishment of bridging laws stating the empirical correlations between terms or statements in one discipline with those in the other. Such a state of empirical reduction has in fact been achieved in the case of thermodynamics and statistical mechanics. In order for this to be achieved for psychology and physiology, complete accounts of each plus bridging laws would be required. These are nowhere near to being achieved but it is possible to speculate about the likelihood of their being so. I think it is doubtful if they ever will be.

Although all psychological events are mediated by physiological processes, there is no *a priori* reason why the two descriptions should map onto one another. This is because to some extent there are arbitrary and pragmatic factors involved in descriptions and what is useful in one discipline may not correspond with what is useful in another (a similar situation pertains between linguistics and the psychology of language). Empirical evidence of mismatch is provided by neural plasticity, equipotentiality and restitution of function. The same psychological function may be carried out by different physiological systems and the same physiological event may have differing psychological significance.

Even if it were possible to give, for example, a biochemical account of wine tasting it might not always be very useful. This is partly because it may not refer to relevant aspects or accessible variables, and partly because it may be too detailed or clumsy. Similarly, even if it did turn out to be possible to provide a biochemical account of memory, this might not be useful in helping to decide to which school to send a child. Another example comes from psychotherapy: which explanation is useful may depend on the practical possibilities of treatment (e.g. drugs versus group psychotherapy).

Strict reduction involves equivalence of meaning or logical derivability. For a psychological statement to be reducible to a physiological, two conditions must hold: (a) logical equivalence in the form of mutual entailment between the two statements, and (b) the physiological propositions must be on a lower epistemological plane and involve fewer concepts (Burt 1962). The psychological statement could be considered a shorthand for the physiological statement, which provides a more detailed account and might be said to 'explain' the psychological (for more formal definitions see Nagel 1961). Jessor (1958) suggests that reduction involves four essential ingredients: (a) the possibility of a hierarchical ordering of the sciences, (b) translation without loss of meaning from statements of one discipline into those of another, (c) unidirectionality of derivability, namely, propositions in higher level sciences are reduced to or deducible from those of lower level sciences, and (d) preferential evaluation of statements in lower level sciences as being more basic. According to this view psychology is merely part of physiology: once physiology is complete, psychology will become redundant. The motivations for such a view may be desire for membership of the science club, physiology being considered more respectable (Bannister 1968), or the result of an obsession with methodology (Kelvin 1956).

The main arguments in favour of strict reduction are parsimony and the unity of science. It would be aesthetically pleasing (at least to some) if it turned out to be the case that statements in different disciplines could be related to each other such that statements in one could be derived from statements in another. It would remove the puzzling element from bridging laws which otherwise appear irreducible and not further explicable.

However, there are at least two main arguments against strict reduction. First, psychological and physiological statements are different in meaning. The same action may be achieved by a variety of different movements and the same movement may be described in a number of different ways. Responses are normally defined in terms of consequences rather than constituent movements (Bindra 1976). Secondly, lower level sciences lack some of the concepts of higher level sciences. For example, physiology lacks concepts dealing with the functional environment and the context of behaviour that are required by psychology (Jessor 1958).

Summary

In summary, a variety of descriptions at different levels is possible within psychology and within physiology. Strict reduction of one to the other must be rejected on the grounds of a difference in meaning. Empirical reduction may sometimes be possible where perfect correlations can be established. The view variously known as structural or functional, based on an analogy from computer science, allows the possibility that a system can be physically embodied in a variety of different ways. Double aspect theory is most in line with views expressed elsewhere in this book: insofar as descriptions are relative no one-to-one correspondence can be guaranteed.

12

Teleological explanation

Introduction

In this chapter we shall be concerned with the nature and function of teleological explanations and in particular with the problem of whether the laws of the physical sciences that govern inorganic matter are adequate to account for the behaviour of living organisms, the subject matter of the biological sciences, or whether laws of a fundamentally different kind are required. It has frequently been argued that human behaviour has certain essential characteristics such as that it is purposive, goal-directed or self-determined, which render a mechanistic account inappropriate. This has sometimes been the motivation for the postulation of teleological explanations of behaviour, explanations which make reference to an end or goal (from Greek *telos* meaning 'end') but there has been a good deal of controversy about the status of teleological explanations and about their relation to mechanistic ones. In addition, some of these apologias have not been very clearly expressed.

Perhaps one of the most obvious characteristics of the behaviour of living organisms and one which increases as the phylogenetic scale is ascended is *plasticity*. Key biological concepts involve the notion of change over time, e.g. adaptation, modifiability, growth, maturation, development and learning. Indeed, such phenomena are the basis of survival. Most of the behaviour of living organisms is *sensitive to consequences*. Phylogenetic adaptation in evolution by means of natural selection is paralleled in ontogenetic development by reinforcement in learning, which may be interpreted in terms of the law of effect (Thorndike 1911) or, in the case of human learning, as extrinsic feedback in the form of knowledge of results (Annett 1969). More particularly, much of behaviour is goal-directed. Ends may be valued independently of the means whereby they are achieved. Such phenomena range from homeostasis where a fixed state is continuously maintained within certain limits, possibly by comparatively simple and rigid operations, to the active seeking of goals which can be realised in a variety of different ways. 'So long as people are behaving, *some* Plan or other must be executed' (Miller, Galanter & Pribram 1960).

The concept of purpose

Purposive behaviour may be defined as behaviour *directed towards a goal,* whose attainment results in the termination of the behaviour in question. That subsequent quiescence is not a distinguishing feature, however, can be seen by considering cases such as volcanic eruptions which are followed by periods of quiescence but would not be said to be purposive (Braithwaite 1947).

> Coming to a definite end or terminus is not *per se* distinctive of directive activity, for inorganic processes also move towards a natural terminus . . . What *is* distinctive is the active persistence of directive activity towards its goal, the use of alternative means towards the same end, the achievement of results in the face of difficulties (Russell 1945).

Nagel (1953) defines the characteristic feature of systems which have a goal-directed organisation as that, 'they continue to manifest a certain state or property G, or to develop "in the direction" of attaining G, in the face of a relatively extensive class of changes in their external environments or in some of their internal parts'. The essential ingredient is thus the attainment of a goal despite variations in initial conditions which are likely to necessitate the employment of different means. Behaviour is modified as a result of its consequences with reference to the goal.

The attribution to behaviour of purposive characteristics requires a *molar* analysis. As early as 1896 Dewey, in a famous paper which antedated much later Gestalt criticisms of behaviourism, recognised the need for a more holistic description of behaviour in which stimulus and reponse are seen as integrated into one act: 'The fact is that stimulus and response are not distinctions of existence, but teleological distinctions, that is, distinctions of function, or part played, with reference to reaching or maintaining an end.'

Some of the difficulties which a purposive analysis poses for behaviourism were pointed out by Perry (1918): 'In the case of hunting for a pin, the organism is not, strictly speaking, responding to an object or fact of its environment. The organism is not hunting for any particular pin; and is quite capable of carrying on the hunt, even though there be as a matter of fact no pin in its environment.' The fact that the goal does not exist objectively, and indeed may never materialise, indicates that an *intensional* analysis is required (cf. Boden 1972). A crucial feature of purposive behaviour is an internal representation of the goal which guides behaviour. Whether or not such an intention need be conscious is a matter of controversy. Nagel (1953) and Miller *et al.* (1960) argue that it need not be and I would agree with them; Boden (1972) and common sense, on the other hand, argue that intentions are necessarily conscious. The attribution of consciousness may be objectionable on several grounds: (a) if it is implausible (did the chicken have a conscious intention to cross the road?); (b) if there is no means of identifying it independently of the ensuing behaviour, in which case it is circular: cf. Skinner's objection to Blanshard's statement that Hitler ordered the extermination of the Jews because he hated them, if we have no evidence of his hatred other than his having given the order (Blanshard & Skinner 1967); or (c) if metaphysical properties are implied, as in the case of McDougall's (1932) *hormē*.

History

In Greek science, the categories of explanation for inorganic phenomena were derived from those for organic phenomena, the difference between the two realms being one of degree rather than kind. Functional explanations have been popular in accounts influenced by evolutionary theory, where attention has been focussed on the survival value of behaviour patterns, e.g. the ethologists' concepts of appetitive behaviour and consummatory acts. Some of these behaviours, however, may be insufficiently flexible to merit the predicate 'purposive'. Biologically oriented theorists have generally recognised the need to take account of the modifiability of behaviour, e.g. Piaget based his theory of cognitive development on the adaptive mechanisms of accommodation and assimilation.

McDougall, for whom the concept of purpose was a cornerstone in his theory, claimed that, 'the manifestation of purpose or the striving to achieve an end is, then, the mark of behaviour' (1912). He listed seven objective marks of purpose: spontaneity; persistence; variation of means; cessation of movements when, and not until, they result in the attainment of the goal; anticipation; improvement in efficiency; molarity: 'that is to say, it is an activity in which the whole organism takes part so far as necessary' (1925).

Lashley (1930) concluded that, 'the facts of both psychology and neurology show a degree of plasticity, or organisation and of adaptation in behaviour which is far beyond any present possibilities of explanation'. His physiological work and analysis of skilled movements such as language convinced him that the units of cerebral function were 'modes of organisation' rather than conditioned reflexes.

Tolman's 'purposive behaviourism' attempted to take account of the purposive aspect of behaviour while yet subscribing to the behaviourist program. 'Wherever the purely objective description of either a simple or complex behavior discovers a "persistence until" character there we have what behaviorism defines as purpose. And upon further analysis, we discover that such a description appears whenever in order merely to *identify* the given behavior a reference to some "end object" or "situation" is found necessary' (1925). Later, the status of purposive concepts took on an explanatory role in the form of intervening variables which, together with independent variables, determined behaviour. These former consisted of demands such as food and sex, and cognitions such as intentions and expectations, and were operationally defined in terms of behavioural dispositions. Tolman admitted that they were drawn from everyday common-sense terms and they have been much criticised for their failure to lead to precise, quantitative predictions.

Perhaps the most important development in the history of the purposive analysis of behaviour has been cybernetics, which restored respectability to teleology. It demonstrated that machines can possess teleological characteristics and that it is possible to give a mechanistic account of goal-directed systems, which may show considerable flexibility of behaviour before the target is reached, e.g. guided missiles. The notion of a servo-mechanism was foreshadowed in Dewey's (1896) analysis of James' (1890) example of the child learning to avoid fire. The concept of the feedback mechanism was introduced by Ashby (1940). Rosenblueth *et al.* (1943) argued for a uniform functional analysis applicable to machines and living organisms. They defined teleological behaviour as behaviour controlled by negative feedback.

All purposeful behavior may be considered to require negative feedback. If a goal is to be attained, some signals from the goal are necessary at some time to direct the behavior . . . The behavior of an object is controlled by the margin of error at which the object stands at a given time with reference to a relatively specific goal.

Wiener (1948) developed the analogy, demonstrating the relevance of cybernetics to biology, and to neurophysiology and psychology in particular. One of the most influential theoretical applications of the concept of the feedback loop to psychology was that of Miller, Galanter and Pribram (1960), who defended what they called the 'cybernetic hypothesis', that the fundamental building block of the nervous system is the feedback loop, or

TOTE (an acronym for test–operate–test–exit) as they call it, which is an incongruity sensitive mechanism.

The TOTE represents the basic pattern in which our Plans are cast, the test phase of the TOTE involves the specification of whatever knowledge is necessary for the comparison that is to be made, and the operational phase represents what the organism does about it.

Their suggestion was that behaviour as a whole is capable of description in terms of hierarchies of feedback loops.

The application of the concept of the feedback loop to behaviour ranges from relatively simple cases such as homeostatic mechanisms (e.g. temperature regulation) and sensorimotor coordinations (cf. von Holst's (1954) theory, according to which any discrepancy between reafference and the 'efference copy' produces a perceptual or motor effect on the system), to more complex cognitive skills. Rosenblueth *et al.* (1943) describe predictive behaviour which requires the discrimination of at least two coordinates, a temporal and at least one spatial axis, e.g. the pursuit of a moving object; and higher order cases, such as throwing a stone at a moving target. Goals may be fixed or flexible, and set externally or internally to the system. Mackay (1981) distinguishes a simple level of evaluation where the standard is externally specified and fixed (involving an open loop at the normative level but a closed loop at the executive level) from more complex cases where goals are set internally by the system (involving closed loops at both the normative and the executive levels), the analogue for flexible self-determination. One part of a system may transfer information to another part (transfer of control). More powerfully, one process within a system may modify the operation of another process (adaptive control). Broadbent (1977) presents evidence on decision making in complex environments which requires the postulation of the operation of a closed loop on an open chain.

The nature of teleological explanations

Mechanistic explanations imply a deterministic, i.e. rule-governed system and focus on past events (see Nagel 1961 for an extended discussion). They state the sufficient (or necessary and sufficient) conditions for the occurrence of an event. Given the antecedent condition, it should be possible in principle to predict the consequent. In addition, there is an assumption that the laws will be of the kind that have so far worked in the physical sciences.

An example of a mechanistic explanation is 'the chicken crossed the road because someone pushed it'. **Teleological explanations**, on the other hand, focus on future events; they explain events by reference to future events, ends or goals. An example of a teleological explanation is 'the chicken crossed the road in order to get to the other side'. They represent Aristotle's 'final' cause, the end for the sake of which an event occurs, e.g. walking for the sake of health. There is a sense in which teleological explanations are ultimate, particularly if they refer to natural goals, whereas mechanistic explanations can be pursued indefinitely.

The notion that a future event is somehow involved in current behaviour has appeared problematical to some, because it seems to imply that time goes backwards. (Similar difficulties arose over the supposed retroflex action of the law of effect, see Postman 1947.) However, this would only be so if it is held that the future event has a causal effect on current behaviour, in the generally accepted sense of cause (i.e. Aristotle's 'efficient' cause). 'Final' causation, if it involved the influence of later events on earlier events, would be an absurd notion. Rather, it is some representation of a future event or the result of past contingencies that is effective. Whether or not conscious intentions can be said to play a causal role is a controversial issue. As we have noted before, there are a number of difficulties with such a view (see Chs 3 & 4). Some current philosophers have preferred to consider the relation between intention and action as conceptual rather than contingent (see p. 151).

Braithwaite (1947) maintains that teleological explanations are distinguishable from mechanistic ones on epistemological as well as logical grounds. They tend to be discovered inductively by inference from past experience of similar behaviour patterns, rather than being deduced from causal laws. Skinner (1953) points out that we cannot attribute the purpose of posting a letter to a man walking down the street unless either we have seen him post it or we have observed similar behaviour and consequences before.

The relation between teleological and mechanistic explanations

Opinion has varied both on the relation of teleological to mechanistic accounts and on which is or are to be preferred in explaining behaviour. Those who consider the two to be incompatible are faced with the choice of which to adopt. Those who consider them to be compatible are faced with the problem of what the relation between them is. Three views may be distinguished: (a) those who prefer only mechanistic explanations, (b) those who prefer only teleological explanations, and (c) those who consider that both are required.

MECHANISTIC EXPLANATIONS AS SUFFICIENT

Most psychologists, particularly behaviourists, would probably take the view that *mechanistic explanations of behaviour are sufficient and* that *teleological ones are unscientific*. For example, Skinner (1953) writes:

> There is, therefore, no violation of the fundamental principle of science which rules out 'final causes'. But this principle is violated when it is asserted that behavior is under the control of an 'incentive' or 'goal' which the organism has not yet fulfilled. Statements which use such words as 'incentive' or 'purpose' are usually reducible to statements about operant conditioning, and only a slight change is required to bring them within the framework of a natural science. Instead of saying that a man behaves because of the consequences which *are* to follow his behavior, we simply say that he behaves because of the consequences which *have* followed similar behavior in the past. Purpose is not a property of behavior itself; it is a way of referring to controlling variables.

On this view, purposive accounts of behaviour are lay shorthands to be replaced by mechanistic accounts in a scientific description.

TELEOLOGICAL EXPLANATIONS AS SUFFICIENT

The opposite extreme view, espoused more by philosophers than psychologists, is that *mechanistic and teleological explanations are incompatible and* that *the latter are to be preferred in the explanation of behaviour*. This is the common-sense view. If people are asked what they are doing they will nearly always answer in terms of goals or purposes, which itself requires explanation. Amongst early psychologists, Tolman and McDougall defended the primacy of purposive over mechanistic descriptions.

> Behavior as behavior, that is, as molar, *is* purposive and *is* cognitive. These purposes and cognitions are of its immediate warp and woof. It, no doubt, is strictly dependent upon an underlying manifold of physics and chemistry, but as a matter of first identification behavior as behavior reeks of purpose and cognition (Tolman 1932).

Active striving towards a goal is a fundamental category of psychology, and is a process or a type that cannot be mechanistically explained or resolved into mechanistic sequences (McDougall 1936).

More recently, Peters (1958) has expressed the view that the appropriate type of explanation for most human behaviour is the 'rule-following, purposive model'. He describes the paradigm case of human action as when something is done in order to bring about an end. For example, the answer to the question: 'Why did Jones cross the road?' might be: 'To buy tobacco'. Such a model is normative, e.g. in this case it assumes that crossing the road is a reasonable way of achieving this aim, and logically distinct from causal explanations. In the case of actions which can be described in terms of the rule-following model, causal explanations (which imply the statement of sufficient conditions), are said to be not only otiose but also inappropriate. The point is that an exhaustive account of the necessary and sufficient conditions for an action cannot be given, e.g. all sorts of movements are possible in signing a contract, but we can say that Jones signed a contract in order to gain possession of a house.

On this view causal explanations are not irrelevant but their contribution is strictly limited. They may be able to state the necessary conditions for the occurrence of human actions, to show that some individual differences in performance are dependent on slight differences in these necessary conditions, or to give sufficient conditions for breakdowns in behaviour. The causal model, Peters argues, is only appropriate when behaviour has deviated from the normative, purposive model and can be viewed as having broken down in some way, as in an obsessional state, where we would be more likely to characterise the person as suffering or as something having happened to him. Thus the possibility of an all embracing theory of human behaviour, particularly of the mechanical kind espoused by Hobbes and Hull, is rejected.

This position has been developed by Taylor (1964) who argues that mechanistic accounts state sufficient conditions for abnormal behaviour but that in the case of normal behaviour they state necessary but not sufficient conditions, on the grounds that there is an infinite set of sufficient causal conditions. (There may not be an infinite set but it may be impossible to specify them.) A teleological account, he claims, can provide sufficient conditions for normal behaviour by referring the response to a goal state (the one that is required by the goal state given the current situation). However, as Sutherland (1970) points out, there is something odd about this account of teleological explanation: there is no known system of which it is true to say that an event's being required for a goal is a sufficient condition of its occurrence.

A related point of view has been put forward by Harré and Secord (1972), who reject the claim that the mechanistic model is the only scientific one and argue that rule-following can be scientific. They deny that the most scientific conception of cause is one which focusses on external stimulation and urge a shift from explanations in terms of substances and qualities to those in terms of powers and potentialities. Most social behaviour, they claim, requires explanation by reference to rules, roles and meanings. They recommend a dramaturgical model as employed by Goffman (1959).

Other defenders of this general line of argument are Gauld and Shotter (1977), who support a hermeneutical approach to the study of human behaviour (see Ch. 14), which involves the interpretation of actions in terms of goals, purpose and intentions.

MECHANISTIC AND TELEOLOGICAL EXPLANATIONS AS COMPLEMENTARY

A compromise position between these two extremes is the claim that *teleological and mechanistic explanations are different but compatible*. Perhaps one of the clearest, most thorough exponents of such a view is Boden (1972). Her thesis is that teleological and mechanistic accounts are compatible but complementary. Their compatibility implies that empirical reduction is true: teleological phenomena are dependent on causal mechanisms. Causal mechanisms provide necessary, but are unlikely to provide sufficient, conditions for teleological phenomena. The complementarity between teleological and mechanistic accounts implies that strict reduction is false. Different languages are involved: the two accounts are not intertranslatable. Different logics are involved: teleological accounts are subject to intensional logic (see Chisholm 1967, for a technical exposition), mechanistic accounts to extensional logic. The relation between intention and action is held to be conceptual, i.e. the meaning of one is part of the meaning of the other, whereas that between cause and effect is contingent. However, Davidson (1963) has pointed out that the question of whether two events are logically related depends on how they are described. Conklin (1943) suggests that

> . . . the relation of mechanism to finalism is not unlike that of structure to function – they are two aspects of organisation. The mechanistic conception of life is in the main a structural aspect, the teleological view looks chiefly to ultimate function. These two aspects of life are not antagonistic, but complementary.

Nagel (1953) has gone so far as to argue that '. . . teleological (or functional) explanations are equivalent to non-teleological ones' and that the difference is merely

> one of emphasis and perspective in formulation. Teleological explanations focus attention on the culminations and products of specific processes . . . They view the operations of things from the perspective of certain selected wholes to which the things belong . . . Non-teleological explanations, on the other hand, place chief emphasis on certain conditions under which specified processes are initiated and persist, and on the factors upon which the continued operation of such systems are contingent. They represent the inclusive behaviour of a thing as the operation of certain selected constituents into which a thing is analysable.

The uses of teleological explanation

In what situations are teleological explanations likely to be useful? According to Braithwaite (1947) they are only valuable when discovered independently of knowledge of causal laws. Foss (1974), arguing the necessity of different types of explanation for a full understanding of human behaviour, points out that in the case of ends functionally important for survival there is likely to be a variety of means serving them, e.g. body temperature is regulated by a number of built-in devices such as sweating and shivering, as well as learned processes such as adjusting the amount of clothing worn. In such cases it may make sense to focus on the common function and search for different means by which it is achieved.

Sutherland (1959) suggests that the behaviour of systems, for which we prefer an explanation in terms of ends, changes systematically in such a way as to achieve different ends at different times (we would not use a teleological explanation for water finding its own level because its final state does not vary from one piece of water to another nor from one time to another), and the same end under a very wide variety of initial circumstances. Hence, an explanation of the behaviour of a system in terms of ends is useful to the extent to which these two conditions are fulfilled. Teleological explanations are likely to be favoured where we are more interested in the result rather than in the details of the behaviour (which might be too complex or less useful for prediction). Braithwaite (1947) observes that an advantage of teleological explanations is that the exact time taken to attain a goal is not specified.

Conclusion

In this chapter we have discussed some of the controversial issues concerning teleological explanations and their relation to mechanistic accounts of behaviour. We have seen that they are best considered as complementary approaches. Teleological accounts are not reducible to mechanistic ones but neither are they mutually incompatible as developments in cybernetics have clearly shown. They cannot be used as a criterion for distinguishing organic from inorganic phenomena. Insofar as each account provides intellectual satisfaction (in the form of the appreciation of connections and the formulation of generalisations) and enables predictions, they are valid and useful explanations of behaviour.

13

Humanistic psychology

> When we take a man as he is, we make him worse;
> but when we take a man as if he were already what
> he should be, we promote him to what he can be
> (Goethe).

In this chapter we shall consider a diffuse movement, which merits
singling out for attention because it presents a serious challenge to
conventionally accepted behaviouristic psychology. This is the
movement known as humanistic psychology, an umbrella term for a
congeries of various loosely defined groups, which nevertheless
have recurring themes. Its main historical antecedents are phenomenology and existentialism, a prior consideration of which is
necessary for an adequate understanding of humanistic psychology.

Phenomenology

The term **phenomenology** was coined in the mid-19th century
(from the Greek *phenomenon* meaning appearance, that which
shows itself) to refer to the study of the essential nature of
consciousness. It is to be distinguished from 'phenomenalism', the
metaphysical theory that only phenomena or appearances need to
be postulated as existing, as distinct from some underlying reality,
noumena or things-in-themselves. According to phenomenology,
reality is relative to consciousness but transcends it. It is also to be
contrasted with introspection, which studies facts within consciousness. The goal of phenomenology is the systematic description of
the invariant structures of consciousness which constitute the
necessary preconditions for experience and knowledge. In this
sense it is prior to other studies. Its aim is to discover 'what the
mind has to be in order for the world of objects to exist for it'
(Bolton 1979), or in their terminology, how the objective is subjectively constituted. Consciousness is both presupposed by, and
reveals, reality.

In order to reach *zu den Sachen Selbst* (to the things themselves), it is necessary to pursue the phenomenological method of

reduction, a graded series of alterations in perspective. The *naturalistic standpoint* is exemplified by the natural sciences which investigate objective reality. In *descriptive phenomenology* consciousness itself becomes the object of study. Spiegelberg (1971) distinguishes three phases:

(a) intuiting – intense concentration on, and attentive internal gaze at, phenomena; (b) analysing – finding various constituents of phenomena and their relationship; (c) describing – providing an account of intuited and analysed phenomena such that they can be understood by others.

Transcendental phenomenology involves the intuiting of essences by means of eidetic reduction, in which an idea of something can be attained by studying instances of it; the method can be extended by examining imagined variations in order to determine the limits and hence the essential nature of the object.

The phenomenological method requires the elimination of presuppositions as far as possible. Central to this is the operation of **bracketing** (i.e. putting in brackets) or setting aside assumptions characteristic of the naturalistic attitude, e.g. belief in the existence of objective reality, space, time and the self. If this suspension of judgment (or *epochē,* after the Greek word meaning abstention) is perfectly achieved, then only the stream of pure consciousness is revealed. Experience is retained but its mode of apprehension is transformed. (It is interesting to compare this with certain forms of meditation.)

A central tenet of phenomenology is the interdependence of knower and known. Science constitutes rather than discovers the world. No view has ontological priority. Essentially a dialectical model is involved. Both a dualism between subjective and objective and the reduction of one to the other is rejected, thus avoiding the extremes of rationalism which overemphasises the contribution of the mind, and empiricism which overemphasises the contribution of the world. For a contrast of phenomenology with Piagetian interactionism see Bolton (1978). As applied to psychology, it has led to the focussing of attention on the subject's perspective and the meaning of the situation to him, which is considered crucial for understanding his behaviour; and to the study of intersubjectivity or shared meanings. Emphasis has been placed on understanding rather than explanation, and an anti-reductionist stance taken.

The origins of phenomenological thought can be traced to Augustine and Aquinas, and to *Kant* who was concerned with the preconditions of knowledge. He concluded that there were twelve *a priori* categories of understanding such as substance and cause, and two fundamental 'forms of intuition' namely space and time. These were presupposed by both analytic and synthetic knowledge.

The other precursor was Franz *Brentano* (1838–1917) who introduced the notion of *intentionality,* according to which mental acts (such as seeing, thinking or desiring) necessarily intend or imply objects (something seen, thought or desired), though these need not necessarily exist in the external world.

The founder of phenomenology was Edmund *Husserl* (1858–1938), who provided a formal statement of the system in *Logical investigations* (1901) and *Ideas* (1913). A central concept was the *Lebenswelt,* literally 'life-world', i.e. the world of everyday experience. The idea of the *Lebenswelt* as the world of lived experience and the dynamic relation between consciousness and reality was developed by Merleau-Ponty in *The structure of behaviour* (1942) and *Phenomenology of perception* (1945).

A number of psychologists became interested in phenomenology, particularly with a view to its methodological implications. Goethe and Purkinje had applied what might be described as phenomenological methods to the study of colour perception; and similarly Stumpf with respect to tone perception. David Katz, whose work together with that of E. R. Jaensch and Edgar Rubin anticipated Gestalt psychology, was directly associated with Husserl, as was Karl Buhler, a member of the Würzburg school of psychologists. Both they and the Gestalt psychologists favoured a procedure of 'naïve' observation. Wertheimer, Koffka and Köhler worked at Göttingen contemporaneously with Husserl but did not acknowledge him initially, and Köhler later dissociated himself from him philosophically. Others who have employed phenomenological methods include: Buytendijk, E. Strauss and Michotte on the continent; Goldstein, Snygg, and MacLeod in the USA; and in more recent times Rogers, Goffman and Shotter. A group who share some of their methodological ideals, though forming a distinct tradition, are the ethologists who take the view that the description of behaviour in its natural environment should take precedence over the explanation of behaviour in artificial laboratory conditions.

EVALUATION

Phenomenology studies the nature of consciousness. The issue of conscious experience as subject matter in psychology was discussed in Chapters 4 and 5 where it was concluded that it was legitimate subject matter and although raising methodological difficulties these were not insuperable nor radically different from those posed for other subject matters. Insofar as phenomenology is concerned with the essential characteristics of consciousness necessary to constitute the world of objects, it is more closely related to epistemology than to psychology, but fundamental to all science.

The concept of intentionality has, in my view, closer affinities with philosophical than psychological frameworks. It has, nevertheless, led to important developments in the notion of representation central to cognitive psychology (see, e.g. Fodor 1981). For a sympathetic treatment of its application to the explanation of behaviour see McGinn (1979).

The concept of the 'life-world', involving the rejection of both subject–object dualism and the reduction of one to the other, represents a radically different framework which has not been fully acknowledged in psychology, although moves towards consideration of the subject in interaction with his environment may be seen in Piagetian developmental psychology and some models of social psychology (e.g. Mischel 1973). The dialectical model implied by phenomenology (see Rychlak 1977) stands in radical opposition to the causal model pursued by psychology. Philosophical difficulties in giving a coherent account of the notion of causation, current work in social science and particularly developments in modern physics (see Capra 1975, for a popular treatment) suggests that the phenomenological perspective may be the more appropriate.

The need to focus on subjective meaning, anathema to the behaviourist and problematic for any scientist, has been increasingly realised in psychology, attempts to take cognisance of it having been made particularly in cognitive, social and dynamic psychology. for the view that ethology constitutes the application of this phenomenological perspective to animal psychology see Thinès (1977).

Phenomenology recommends a method of theoretically neutral observation and description, which it shares with functionalist psychology and the early stages of ethology. Although unattainable in the limit (presuppositions cannot be entirely eliminated nor can non-conceptualised experience be communicated), it is laudable as an aim. It is particularly desirable at an initial stage in a complex discipline and too often bypassed in psychology.

Existentialism

Existentialism was a movement in philosophy and literature, the seeds of which were sown in the mid-19th century, although the label (which takes its meaning from the Latin *ex-sistere* meaning to stand out, emerge, become) did not appear until the 1920s, coming into general use by the 1940s. The original stimulus was a lecture given by Schelling in which he criticised Hegel. Existentialism constitutes a reaction against Hegelian philosophy in particular and western philosophy in general, with its emphasis on positivism, materialism, pragmatism and a distinction between subject and object.

It has been said that if one reads the existentialists without exasperation one is almost certainly misreading them and that their chief works are intellectually accessible only to those who are trained in abstract speculative discourse and are thoroughly schooled in the history of philosophy. They are certainly non-homogeneous and difficult. Ayer (1969) remarks that they some-times give the impression of trying to whistle what they cannot say.

As their label suggests the emphasis is on existence (i.e. conscious experience), in contra-distinction to classical philosophy's preoccupation with essence (i.e. the analysis of the nature of things). In their view all man's characteristics and properties are consequences of his existence. The central concern is with man rather than the world and in particular with the human condition and the meaning of life. Barrett (1964) defines existentialism as a philosophy 'that confronts the human situation in its totality to ask what the basic conditions of human existence are and how man can establish his own meaning out of these conditions'. This represents a shift in question from Plato's and Aristotle's 'What is man?' to Augustine's 'Who am I?' Interest is centred on the individual and subjective experience, which is accepted as valid and con-sidered a sufficient criterion for truth. Non-rational processes are acknowledged and the supremacy of reason denied. The negative aspects of the human condition are mortality and the subjugation of the individual by society. The positive aspect is freedom. It is an essential part of the existentialist credo that choice is real: people are self-determining agents who create their own destiny. In the words of Karl Jaspers: 'What man is, he ultimately becomes through the cause which he has made his own'. The emphasis is on potential, 'becoming', the possibilities of existence. The goal is to seek authenticity.

Those most often designated as existentialists are the following:

Søren Kierkegaard (1813–55), whose main books *Either/Or, The concept of dread* and *Sickness unto death* were dominated by the themes of man and his conflicts especially those arising from finitude.

Martin Heidegger (1899–1976), whose main work *Being and time* dealt with human existence (*Dasein*) tied inseparably to the

world ('being-in-the-world'). Man is distinguished by his awareness of existence and death which brings dread and anguish
which he tries to escape through convention.

Jean-Paul Sartre (1905–80), whose best known books are *Being
and nothingness* and *La Nausée*, which explored the existentialist themes of the meaning of man's existence and the reality of
freedom and choice; and his most psychological: *Imagination*
and *Emotions*.

Karl Jaspers (1883–1969), a psychiatrist turned philosopher,
whose *General psychopathology* (1913) stressed the importance of
the patient's subjective experience and the therapist's empathy,
themes taken up later by Carl Rogers. He wrote of the 'becoming
self', and supported *Verstehende* psychology (see Ch. 14).

Others who are often included among existentialists are: Marcel,
Nietzsche, Dostoyevsky, Scheler, Tillich, de Beauvoir, Tolstoy,
Rilke, Dilthey and Kafka.
Existentialism had a greater influence on psychiatry than psychology. Particular mention should be made of *Ludwig Binswanger*
(1881–1966), originally a Freudian, who developed *'Daseinanalyses'*
('being analysis') which promoted self-actualisation; and *Viktor
Frankl* (1905–   ) who developed 'Logotherapy' based on the 'will-
to-meaning', which he described in *Man's search for meaning*. In
this tradition might also be seen Erikson, Fromm and Laing.

EVALUATION

Existentionalism has been criticised as being metaphysical nonsense
(Carnap), unintelligible and excessively subjective. Its philosophy
is frequently considered confused and its psychology too general to
be of use. Piaget (1971) writes:

We have seen Sartre project his self into consciousness . . . to
discover there that its 'causality' is magic, and we see Merleau-
Ponty end by concluding that subjectivity is basically ambiguous.
This is, then, what is given to us as knowledge of Man and
which is opposed to the psychology of conduct, because the latter
is intellectualist and only 'scientific'.

Existentialism's main contribution has been to provide new foci
of attention. Its emphasis on the meaning of life and striving for
authenticity have made a significant impact, predominantly in
clinical psychology and psychotherapy. The study of positive

aspects of the human condition, particularly self-actualisation, has been developed by humanistic psychologists.

Its only methodological contribution to psychology has been insistence on the validity of subjective experience, a faith which is not always justified (see Ch. 5).

The existentialist claim that choice is real is in conflict with a deterministic psychology unless a coherent account of self-determinism can be given. This issue was discussed in Chapter 2, where it was concluded that although there is an interpretation of free will which can be reconciled with determinism it is not the sense usually intended. Moreover, the findings of scientific psychology suggest there are severe limitations to choice and freedom.

Humanistic psychology

The term 'humanistic psychology' was coined by Cantril in 1955 with its aim as the building of 'a science *of* man that is *for* man' (Brewster Smith 1969). Maslow introduced the term 'third force' in 1958, reflecting dissatisfaction with the other two forces, namely, psychoanalysis and behaviourism which was considered by many to be dehumanising (mechanistic and reductionist) and narrowly based ('ratomorphic' to use Koestler's term).

Its themes centre on man and in particular the study of characteristics deemed to be distinctively human, such as experience, uniqueness, meaning, choice and dignity. Human nature is positively evaluated and attention focussed on superior qualities and their development; hence the human potential movement and the stress on personal growth and self-actualisation. Concentration is directed towards the present (and the future) rather than the past. Humanistic psychology adopts a phenomenological attitude towards individual experience and emphasises uniqueness within an organismic and holistic theoretical framework. Meaningfulness of problems is valued over rigour and objectivity.

The immediate factor leading to the development of humanistic psychology was the emigration of continental Europeans to a receptive atmosphere in the United States where there was dissatisfaction with the first and second 'forces', and disenchantment exacerbated by the world wars. The movement gathered momentum with the translation of continental books especially into English. It was formally established in the United States in the 1950s, Maslow providing a general sketch in 1954 and a paper specifically on humanistic psychology in 1956. The *Journal of Humanistic Psychology* appeared in 1962 and the Association for

Humanistic Psychology was formed the following year.

Humanistic psychologists have much in common with neo-Freudians such as Jung, Adler, Rank, Horney and Fromm and with defenders of the tradition of *Verstehen* and idiographic psychology (discussed in Ch. 14).

Probably the most central humanistic psychologist has been A. H. *Maslow*, whose major work was *Motivation and personality* (1954), in which he postulated a hierarchy of needs: physiological, safety, belonging and love, esteem and self-actualisation, claiming that satisfaction of the lower ones was a necessary prerequisite for satisfaction of the higher. He made an exploratory study of self-actualisation, based on an examination of people selected by him as self-actualised, resulting in the description of fifteen characteristics of self-actualised people. He also described peak experiences, moments of the highest happiness and fulfilment.

One other person who perhaps should be singled out for special mention is *Carl Rogers*, the developer of client-centred therapy and an independent originator of encounter groups. His work includes an account of what he calls the 'fully functioning person'. Conditions necessary for successful therapy are considered to be positive regard for, empathy with, and unconditional acceptance of, the client by the therapist. One of his main contributions has been the conduct of empirical research in support of these claims, although inadequacies still remain (see Shapiro 1976). Nevertheless his approach calls for optimism with regard to the possibility of combining humanistic ideas with rigorous research.

EVALUATION

On the credit side, it may be said that humanistic psychology has focussed attention on positive characteristics of man and been prepared to study aspects ignored by other approaches, thus somewhat redressing the imbalance created by a pessimistic behaviourism. Humanistic psychologists have had the courage to face the challenge of relevance and to tackle significant and meaningful issues. Its applications have been far reaching through encounter groups, the Esalen Institute and other developments of the Human Potential Movement.

On the debit side, humanistic psychology may be criticised for its loose-knit and vague conceptualisation. It is to be doubted whether its optimism is justified and whether its methods are scientific. Ineffable experience cannot be communicated; rigour and controls are often lacking. Even Maslow (1969) writes of humanistic psychologists that they 'hover on the edge of antiscience and even irrational feelings in their enthusiasm for "experiencing"'. In general, there have been deficiencies in evaluative criteria and a lack of empirical support.

Can phenomenology be reconciled with behaviourism?

The answer to this question depends largely on what is meant by 'phenomenology' (continental or American) and 'behaviourism' (methodological or radical). If the original continental formulations of phenomenology and existentialism are taken then, as we have seen, there are serious areas of conflict at the conceptual level with respect to the relation between subject and object, choice and determinism, and dialectical and causal models. In my view these are irreconcilable.

However, much of the literature suggests that a reconciliation between them is possible. For example, of the six contributors to the Rice symposium on behaviourism and phenomenology (Wann 1964) four were in favour of a reconciliation in some form. Brody and Oppenheim (1966) in considering tensions between the two schools suggest two forms of rapprochement: terminological and complementary roles. The latter, they suggest, could consist of the use of either behaviourist methods to construct theoretical systems and phenomenological methods to test them, or vice versa: phenomenological methods to construct theoretical systems and behaviourist methods to test them. The second of these alternatives, namely the application of behaviourist methods to phenomenological problems, is proposed by Day (1969), who is of the opinion that 'there are numerous ways in which a flourishing phenomenology and radical behaviourism need each other'.

It is clear that many of these reconciliations involve a very much watered down version of phenomenology. Kvale and Grenness (1967), in an extremely interesting paper, point out that phenomenology in the Rice symposium is taken to mean merely the study of experience and the acceptance of verbal reports. They then go on to develop the thesis that Skinner's radical behaviourism shows some remarkable similarities to Sartre's and Merleau-Ponty's views on psychology. They present evidence to document the claims that both schools reject a dualism between private and public or the psychologist and his subject. 'The "boundary" for public–private is not the skin but the line between the verbal community's being able to reinforce behaviour differentially and its not being able to, or able to only with great difficulty' (Skinner 1964). Both reject what Kvale and Grenness refer to as the illusion of the double world, the view that the inner world is a copy of the external world (on this see also Still 1979); the prejudice of the objective world, the view that physics is more 'real' than perception; and the flight to the inner man, the explanation of behaviour based on the assumption that it is an index of and/or caused by an inner process. Both emphasise adequate description, stress behaviour in relation to the environment as the fundamental subject matter of psychology, and conceive of knowledge as action. The message is that Skinner is trying to be a phenomenologist but sometimes slips from the path!

In conclusion, a reconciliation between phenomenology and behaviourism in the form of the application of behaviourist methods, with their advantage of rigour, to phenomenological problems, with their advantages of relevance and significance, is possible and desirable; but at the level of conceptual framework there are fundamental differences between behaviourism and phenomenology. Nevertheless, contrary to expectation, there are some striking parallels between Skinner's radical behaviourism and phenomenology.

Central to all the movements considered in this chapter has been the importance of the individual. Many have based on this the claim that the approach appropriate to the social sciences is radically different from that of the natural sciences. Not only has it been argued that different methods are required but also that the nature of the enterprise is fundamentally different. These claims are the subject of the final chapter.

14

Idiographic approaches

The problem

The final movement to be considered which raises questions about the foundations of experimental psychology is the tradition of *Verstehen* and idiographic psychology. They raise a number of issues in personality and social psychology concerned with the appropriate treatment of the individual. The problem arises from the fact that science is concerned with generalities: means and probability statements. According to an old adage: *scientia non est individuorum*, i.e. science does not deal with individual cases. We shall consider whether a science of the individual is possible and what role can be played by the study of individual cases.

> In every concrete individual, there is a uniqueness that defies all formulation. We can feel the touch of it and recognize its taste, so to speak, relishing or disliking, as the case may be, but we can give no ultimate account of it, and have in the end simply to admire the Creator (James 1912).

The scientific study of the individual has been thought problematical on the grounds that the individual constitutes a unique pattern which is more than the sum of component parts and not fully represented by, for example, scores on dimensional tests.

> We spend scarcely one per cent of our research time discovering whether those common dimensions are in reality relevant to Bill's personality, and if so, how they are patterned together to compose the Billian quality of Bill . . . The organization of Bill's life is first, last, and all the time, the primary fact of his human nature (Allport 1962).

These problems have led to the relative neglect of the study of individual differences and failure to integrate experimental and differential psychology, the consequences of which have been discussed by Eysenck (1966). His own solution to the problem is through the compromise position of studying typologies.

Allport, who rejects the view that assigns the unique to art and the general to science, has called for an **idiographic** psychology of personality (from the Greek *idios* meaning own or private as distinct from public) whose function is to study the individual, in addition to *nomothetic* psychology (from the Greek *nomos* meaning law) which is concerned with dimensions, norms and general laws. We shall be considering the validity of this distinction. Allport's claim is that idiographic interpretations can be made testable, communicable and predictable but that special morphogenic methods (from the Greek *morphē* meaning form), suited to studying the pattern of individuals, are required in addition to dimensional ones.

The tradition of *Verstehen* is based on the premiss that different methods are required by the social sciences from those used in the natural sciences, the former demanding empathic, intuitive understanding in contrast to the latter's preoccupation with prediction and explanation based on general causal statements. Its supporters are likely to be sympathetic towards the view that more is to be learned about human nature by reading novels than by studying academic psychology.

James (1907) pointed out that much of the variance between thinkers can be accounted for by reference to a dimension he labelled tough–tendermindedness, for which experimental support, with respect to psychological theorists, has been provided by Coan (1968). Idiographic psychologists belong to the latter group or to use Boring's terms to the 'something more' rather than the 'nothing but' school. In general they are opposed to mechanistic quantification and reductionist analysis of holistic qualities.

Origins

The origins of these movements lie in 19th-century Germany, as part of a general swing away from classicism (represented by objectivity, positivism, materialism and mechanism) towards romanticism (represented by subjectivity, intuitionism and vitalism) (Holt 1962). A central theme was the claim that the social sciences were distinct from the natural sciences and demanded different methods, notably that of *Verstehen* (understanding). Eighteenth-century precursors can be found in *J. S. Mill,* who distinguished the science of character ('ethology') from the science of mind in general (psychology), the task of the former being to study the operation of psychological laws in specifically individual combinations, e.g. the pattern of a particular person or culture; and *Kant,* who suggested that the study of the mind required the method of intuition of the whole in addition to the analytic and generalising methods of the natural sciences devised for the study of matter.

In 1851, *Cournot* distinguished the exact sciences in which precise laws were possible from history which he believed to be dominated by chance so that it could only be probabilistic in nature. This distinction between *Naturwissenschaften* – the natural sciences – and *Geisteswissenschaften,* which covered the social sciences plus philosophy, history, jurisprudence and the humanities, was developed by several writers:

Windelband introduced the terms 'nomothetic' to refer to the kind of science that dealt with general laws and 'idiographic' to refer to the kind of science that dealt with structured patterns (terms which Holt (1962) dismisses as pretentious jargon, 'mouth-filling polysyllables to awe the uninitiated'). The former was said to give knowledge of being (*Sein*), the latter consciousness of relatedness to norms (*Sollen*). It was claimed that different methods were appropriate in the two cases: analysis, quantification and explanation in the former but understanding in the latter. 'We explain nature but we understand human beings' (Dilthey 1937).

Rickert distinguished the historical and cultural from the generalising, natural sciences on the grounds that the former was concerned with individuals and values.

Simmel stressed the subjective understanding of meanings by reference to typical cases and the need to acknowledge plurality of interpretations.

Dilthey (1833–1911) thought the difference between the social and the natural sciences lay in their content, the subject matter of the former being characterised by mental activity. In this context he introduced the concept of *Verstehen,* himself beginning with what might be described as psychological understanding but moving towards a more cultural endeavour. In his view *Verstehen* psychology strove for direct insight into the vital nature of things as articulated wholes ('*Strukturzusammenhang*'), involving the systematic description of the nature and development of consciousness and the inner unity of individual life. Experienced relations were stressed over analysis into elements. The most important unifying forces in man were seen as purpose and moral character and human character as intimately related to, and an outgrowth of, social institutions. An important follower of Dilthey was *Spranger,* whose *Types of men* was published in 1922. He distinguished descriptive from explanatory psychology favouring the former '*Struktur Psychologie*', whose concern was intelligible wholes grasped through the method of *Verstehen.* A person's values were of primary interest and Spranger is probably best known for his six ideal values: theoretical, economic, aesthetic, social, political and religious, on which Allport, Vernon and Lindzey (1960) based their test.

Weber employed the psychological understanding of motives, as well as the identification of actions through the understanding of meaning by recourse to complex conceptual structures such as 'the spirit of capitalism'. His distinction between direct and explanatory understanding is similar to Jaspers' between static understanding ('the presentation to oneself of psychic states, the objectifying to oneself of psychic qualities') and genetic understanding, of an empathic kind.

In the post-war years, the positivist line held sway but recently there has been a resurgence of doubts about the method appropriate for the social sciences (see in particular Harré & Secord 1972, Outhwaite 1975, Gauld & Shotter 1977).

Is a science of the individual possible?

There are a number of issues raised under this head. One concerns the question of whether the individual can be studied in science and if so, what role case studies play in such a discipline. An individual case can be and often is the subject of scientific investigation. No-one objects to astronomy studying the Moon or geology a particular rift valley. However, it alone is insufficient to establish general laws.

> No matter how intensively prolonged, objective and well-controlled the study of a single case, one can never be sure to what extent the lawful regularities found can be generalised to other persons, or in what way the findings will turn out to be contingent on some fortuitously present characteristic of the subject – until the investigation is repeated on an adequate sample of persons. As excellent a way as it is to make discoveries, the study of an individual cannot be used to establish laws (Holt 1962).

The individual is subject to laws but study of particular cases, like the method of *Verstehen*, is useful for hypothesis formation rather than testing.

The reasons for supposing that a scientific study of the individual is impossible or that some important aspects must necessarily be neglected are various. It may be argued that science deals with general statements whereas the individual is *unique*. However, as

Grünbaum (1952) and others have pointed out, all particulars are unique. Scientific laws relate only certain aspects of events which are classified together on the basis of some common feature(s). Total identity is not required. Individuality is a matter of degree. Kluckholn and Murray (1953) observe that every man is in certain respects (a) like all other men, (b) like some other men, and (c) like no other men. (a) and (b) are no less significant for predicting behaviour than (c). If there were no commonalities between individuals then an idiographic discipline must be dumb or incomprehensible (Holt 1962). Holt has argued that, paradoxically, the greater the degree of abstraction and generality of conceptualisation the better the fit to the individual case. Moves towards the concrete and particular sacrifice flexibility and hence explanatory power.

It may be objected that *qualitative properties* of individuals cannot be subjected to quantification. For a discussion of the view that psychologists have sacrificed quality for quantity, see Hudson (1972). Meanings and values can be measured and great progress has been made in their objective investigation as the more inspired work in personality and social psychology testifies. It must be left to the reader to assess its significance.

It is frequently argued that individuality lies in the unique combination of traits and that a whole person cannot be reduced to the sum of scores on a set of dimensions, which ignores their pattern or *structure*. It is ironical that those who called themselves 'structuralists' were some of the worst offenders. However, science can and does study structure and the problem of different levels of analysis is common to all its departments. Personology has focussed attention particularly on individual patterns. The problem becomes serious if there are interactive effects, if the expression of a trait is differentially affected by the combination of other traits with which it occurs, for which there is indeed plenty of evidence. The issue then becomes an empirical one.

Whether there can be a science of individual differences depends on whether these effects are systematic. It seems likely that they are but that their complexity and extent is such that practical investigation of them may be impossible. Eysenck (1966), for example, has suggested that, as a minimum, experiments should have 27 cells: three levels (high, medium and low) of intelligence × three levels of extraversion × three levels of neuroticism.

Only when we have relatively pure-bred strains of animals representing these three dimensions, and all possible combinations of them, will we be able to devise experiments which come up to the requirements of scientific investigation. Until then we cannot properly specify, identify or duplicate our experimental subjects, and will for ever be at the mercy of strain differences of an accidental kind yielding results which may not be duplicated when other strains are used (Eysenck 1966).

This is only considering the variables which he thinks are important. Others might want to add more.

No doubt our designs will be much more complex and difficult, experiments will be more time consuming and expensive, and background knowledge will have to be more extensive and less idiosyncratic; but all this is inevitable if we are serious in our scientific quest (Eysenck 1966).

To what extent has the individual been neglected in psychology?

In Chapter 9 we noted the examination of individual differences as a strategy for dealing with organismic variables. However, in general, experimental and differential psychology have maintained an apartheid and attempts to integrate them have been few (see, e.g. Cronbach 1957, Eysenck 1977). Individual differences are customarily excluded from experimental designs. Taken together with the fact that, as we saw in Chapter 6, only a small amount of the variance is accounted for by main experimental variables, Eysenck's (1966) warnings about *the consequences of neglecting individual differences* may be heeded:

(a) The failure of experimentalists systematically to investigate individual differences opens the door to non-scientific theory and practice in the field of personality. Although remedying the former may not prevent the latter it does at least provide a weapon against it.
(b) Main effects apply only to means and do not enable predictions about the individual case to be made.
(c) Theories and explanations based on one type of subject may not be replicated on another type. This is the problem of atypical sampling and non-replicability.
(d) Failure to consider individual differences may lead to main effects being swamped (e.g. Hovland 1939), or obscured (e.g. Eysenck & Slater 1958, where systematic functional differences accounted for only 1 per cent of the variance).

Obscuration of main effects may be caused by their interaction with personality variables. For example, it has been found that extroverts work to obtain light and noise whereas introverts work for darkness and quiet (Weisen 1965), and that the effect of performance under frustration is differentially affected by heart rate (Doerr & Hokanson 1965). Interactive effects with neurosis have been shown for rate of stimulus presentation (Jensen 1962), and for the effect of drugs such as meprobamate on mood and performance (Munkelt 1965, Janke 1964). Similarly the strain of animal has been shown to interact with the size and duration of the effect of a drug (McClearn 1962) and with prenatal stress.

According to Jones and Fennell (1965) such differences might have been responsible for the long controversy between Hullians and Tolmanians. They discovered that Spence used animals descended from C. S. Hall's 'non-emotional' strain whereas Tolman's were less selected and probably closer to the 'emotional' strain. In their own studies they found that the latter were much slower in latency and running time than the former. They comment: 'These differences between the two strains of rats are strikingly congruent with the theoretical accounts of the investigators who used them', and go on to suggest that such differences may even have been responsible for differential choices of experimental equipment and design, as in their own work they found that neither strain settled very well in the apparatus used by the opposite camp. They conclude: 'The possibility that there may exist genetic differences between them cannot be dismissed; nor can we be sure that hereditary differences may not have played some role in the great debate between S–R and S–S theorists.'

When linear correlations with single personality dimensions cannot be found, conceptualisations which take account of more than one personality variable may be required. These include zone analysis (Furneaux 1961), based on the hypothesis that different combinations of traits produce different types of behaviour, so that means on tests will differ according to zone, zones being produced by combining two or more traits; and its mathematical equivalent, moderator variables (Ghiselli 1963). Kogan and Wallach (1964), for example, used anxiety and defensiveness as personality variables to moderate correlations with risk taking measures. One of their findings was that low anxious, low defensive subjects showed post-decision satisfaction proportional to their winnings whereas high anxious, high defensive subjects showed the opposite: the less they won the more satisfied they were. They write:

It is clear that the consideration of personality dispositions of test anxiety and defensiveness as moderator variables has rendered clear a psychological picture that otherwise would have been totally ambiguous. Overall sample correlations that were nonsignificant or, although statistically significant, so low as to be of doubtful psychological value have been found to be substantiated in one moderator subgroup, negligible in another. In some cases, these overall correlations have been found to be significant in a positive direction in one moderator subgroup, significant in a negative direction in another. Such findings require the conclusion that consideration of potential moderator variables is nothing less than essential in psychological research involving the study of correlations (Kogan & Wallach 1964).

Eysenck (1966) sees typology as a compromise between the false extremes of the experimentalist, who seeks to establish general functional relations, and the idiographic personologist, who 'embraces the concept of the individual so whole-heartedly that it leaves no room for scientific generalization, laws, or even predictability of conduct'. The experimentalist has the advantage of control and objectivity but runs the risk of sterility and irrelevance. He is liable to neglect individual differences on the grounds that they are negligible, unsystematic, or systematic but incapable of investigation. The personologist has the merits of significance and understanding but runs the risk of making statements that are untested, and so perhaps untrue, or untestable. Eysenck applauds Spence, Cattell and himself for having made efforts in the typological direction.

The questions as he points out, are (i) whether people can in fact be sorted into groups such that they perform differentially in an experiment of the $a = f(b)$ kind (an empirical issue), and (ii) whether the relationship between (a) and (b) can be predicted on the basis of a personality theory (a theoretical issue). He and others have produced a large body of evidence favouring an affirmative answer to the former. By constructing a theoretical superstructure for the dimensions of extroversion and neuroticism and frequently invoking the Yerkes–Dodson law, he has attempted to do the same for the latter. However, any result can be explained *post hoc* by the use of the Yerkes–Dodson law. It is crucial that the levels of the dimensions are established independently and the theoretical predictions made *a priori*.

Idiographic psychology

A prime champion of the idiographic approach has been *Gordon Allport*. Following Meehl (1957), he has pointed out some of the limitations of the dimensional approach in personality. First, it is restricted in its application to circumstances where the dimensions can be objectively defined, reliably measured, validly related to the prediction target and normed for the appropriate population. Secondly, there may be a mismatch between the dimensions measured and those relevant to the individual, in that some measured may not be particularly relevant, and conversely other important ones may be omitted. Finally, there is the problem of weighting the scores on the dimensions, which is an empirical matter. The crucial question is whether there is something left unaccounted for when the weighting has been achieved.

He goes on to suggest a number of so-called **morphogenic methods.** The basic idea underlying these is that they should serve to study the pattern or structure of an individual without reference to nomothetic norms, instead being subjectively validated. Their 'basic emphasis is upon the individual as a unique being-in-the-world whose system of meanings and value orientation are not precisely like anyone else's' (Allport 1962).

The morphogenic methods suggested by Allport are:

(a) *Matching* (Allport 1961) in which correlations between different records of personal expression e.g. voice and handwriting are examined.

(b) *Personal structure analysis* (Baldwin 1942), in which the letters of one subject were analysed for such things as associative complexes and feeling tone.

(c) *Questionnaires* designed after intensive interview specifically for use with one patient (Shapiro 1961). These can then be used longitudinally during the course of therapy to evaluate progress. Comparisons are made within rather than between subjects.

(d) *Structural foci,* i.e. major themes and intentions, usually essential motivational or stylistic characteristics. The number and range of these for a given life can be examined.

(e) *Direct questioning* about value systems or peak experiences.

(f) *Self-anchoring scales* (Kilpatrick & Cantril 1960), in which the subject rates his position on a scale anchored at both ends, e.g. 'worst possible' and 'best possible'. These can be used to increase objectivity.

A number of **semi-morphogenic methods,** which involve the adaptation of dimensional methods for the study of the individual, were also suggested. These include:

(a) *Rating scales.* Conrad (1932) showed that agreement between observers on traits rated of central importance to the individual was 0.95 compared with 0.45 for traits overall, suggesting the possible irrelevance of non-central traits, the inclusion of which may merely serve to increase error. The simple adjective checklist, in which only traits that seem appropriate to the primary trends of an individual's life are rated, takes advantage of this.

(b) *The repertory grid* (Kelly 1955), which is nomothetic in its requirement that significant others be specified, in mode of response and in measures obtained, but allows for some morphogenic discovery.

(c) *Ipsative scores,* introduced by Broverman (1960) for use in the measurement of cognitive style. Standard tests are given but within subject comparisons made in that the performance of a subject on a given test is related to his/her performance on other types of test.

(d) The Allport–Vernon–Lindzey *study of values,* which also makes within rather than between subject comparisons.

(e) *The Q-sort* (Stephenson 1953), which is dimensional in its use of standard propositions and the injunction usually given to produce a quasi-normal distribution among sorts but might be considered morphogenic in that it makes use of self-report and can be used for measuring changes in the self-concept (Nunnally 1955).

EVALUATION

Holt (1962) has argued that the idiographic–nomothetic issue is based on a false dichotomy, and that 'these mischievous and difficult terms . . . had best disappear from our scientific vocabularies'. Truly idiographic methods cannot exist in science. A scientific method must be communicable and in principle generalisable. Allport's so-called idiographic methods are merely more or less nomothetic methods applied to individual cases. With reference to one of the semi-morphogenic methods he says:

> The Q sort is quite unacceptable in the traditional meaning of the term idiographic, and the use of the term to signify the fact that it is applied to individuals is simply grandiloquent prose (Holt 1962).

Idiography is merely a label indicating that interest is focussed on the individual, but this is a question of subject matter. As different methods are not required and science is defined by its methods rather than by its subject matter, idiography, in Holt's view, does not constitute a distinct science.

Clinical versus statistical psychology

Similar to the idiographic–nomothetic issue in psychology is that labelled clinical versus statistical. Here it is argued that experimental conclusions apply to means which enable only actuarial predictions to be made and not exact outcomes with respect to the individual case. But as far as the individual is concerned the conclusion is either true or not true. Even though it may be impossible in practice to predict exactly the events of an individual life this does not mean they are not determined.

Clinical and statistical approaches may be contrasted with respect to methods and aims. The clinical can be distinguished from the statistical *method* at both the stages of data collection and decision procedure (Meehl 1954). The clinician favours a flexible, under-standardised procedure such as the interview or case study, whereas the statistician favours a rigorous procedure such as the administration of tests with standardised norms. The advantage of the former is that the procedure can be modified to suit the individual case; the advantage of the latter is that individual scores can be compared with generalised norms. At the stage of decision procedure the clinician interprets the data relying on his own judgment whereas the statistician employs a mechanical procedure, e.g. applying a formula to weighted scores. Meehl (1954) reviewed 20 empirical studies which compared the predictive success (with respect to recidivism, psychiatric prognosis or benefit from training programmes) of statistical and clinical methods of combining data. The results of his survey were that in about half the cases the statistical method gave superior results to the clinical, in the other half there was no significant difference between them and in only one was the clinical possibly superior to the statistical. However, Meehl comments that the third ear may pay off therapeutically while not leading to predictive success of the kind studied, namely, choice among a few predetermined, crudely socially defined outcomes rather than the creation and selection from among an unlimited set of concrete, specific predictions more typical of the therapeutic situation. In Holt's view, the spheres of activity of the statistician and the clinician overlap very little. Where the same task is performed it could be argued that the clinical method only differs from the statistical in that it is covert rather than overt. The clinician may not be able to formulate the basis on which he makes his judgments but insofar as they are valid there must be a basis and one that is nomothetic, i.e. in principle generalisable.

With respect to *aim* it might be argued that the clinician is concerned with empathic understanding and the statistician with explanation and prediction. However, this is to oversimplify.

Prediction, control and understanding are inextricably mixed. The experimentalist seeks understanding (though of a different kind) and the clinician may predict and/or control.

The method of Verstehen

The method of *Verstehen* or interpretative understanding is central to the debate about whether the social sciences are distinctively different from the natural sciences (some of the features claimed as distinguishing the former being subjectivity, value, meaning, purpose, mental activity, agency, actions and intention). *Hermeneutic understanding* (from the Greek *hermeneutikos* meaning interpreter) was first applied in theology to the interpretation and clarification of the meaning of biblical texts, where its aim was to grasp the intentions of the author. It became popular in philology and history, where it was hoped that it would reveal 'cultural objects'. Its application to social phenomena is based on the assumption that they are in some important way analogous to texts. Proponents of the method believe that as humans we have a special ability to understand human behaviour and that appropriate explanation of social phenomena should remain close to everyday concepts and common sense. Droysen (1858) voiced the opinion of many who followed when he claimed that the data of social science are already partially interpreted and hence the role of the scientist is to systematise, deepen and qualify. A similar view is expressed by Schutz (1932): objective science can have no other basis than 'the already constituted meanings of active participants of the social world'. A community of outlook is presupposed, language being seen as having a particularly important role to play, in that it embeds everyday concepts.

There are perhaps two aspects: empathic identification of motives, which may involve either participatory dialogue or solitary imagination, and interpretation of the social significance of actions. Typical is the emphasis on structure and explanation of the parts by reference to the whole.

> Explanation is nothing other than the incorporation of this structure, as a constituent element, in an immediately embracing structure . . . in order to render intelligible the genesis of the work (Goldmann 1959).

The aim is to identify the meaning of an action in terms of the role it plays in the social situation. For example, the writing down of a formula might be explained as being part of the task of balancing a ledger or solving a mathematical problem. People's marching in the street might be explained by the fact that there is a demonstration going on, in terms of the reasons people go on demonstrations or by reference to the private motives of individuals.

Abel (1948) describes the operation of *Verstehen* as involving two stages: (a) the internalisation of factors in a behavioural situation, analysed in such a way (usually in terms of 'feeling states') that they parallel some personal experience of the interpreter, and (b) the hypothetical interpolation of a behaviour maxim (a generalisation based on personal experience, e.g. that frustration tends to lead to aggression or aggression to guilt), which makes an otherwise puzzling connection between two observed events relevant or meaningful. He gives several examples. To explain the link between a drop in temperature and a man lighting a fire it might be assumed that the reduction in temperature decreases body temperature, the feeling state imputed being that of feeling cold, and that lighting a fire will produce heat. The behaviour maxim that is applied is that feeling cold leads to seeking warmth. The correlation between a changing and hostile world and belief in eternal truths might be explained by assuming that the former gives rise to feelings of inadequacy and by applying the behaviour maxim that these lead to seeking feelings of security which are provided by the belief in eternal truths. Similarly, a correlation between crop failure and a fall in the marriage rate may be made intelligible by assuming that the former results in a reduction of income which gives rise to a feeling of anxiety and that this leads to fear of new commitments which marriage would bring. Weber's famous application was the explanation of the link between the Protestant ethic and capitalist enterprise by reference to feelings of the sacredness of worldly calling, leading to such virtues as honesty being valued. However, as von Schelting (1934) pointed out, rather more is required in this case, including a consideration of the Calvinist conception of God.

EVALUATION

The method of *Verstehen* may satisfy curiosity and relieve apprehension in the case of unfamiliar or unexpected behaviour. In its favour it may be said that it recognises the problem of meaning, and the hermeneutic base of, and importance of language in, social behaviour. There is a sense in which interpretation of meaning is prior to any causal analysis. It has an important role to play in hypothesis formation and it is interesting to speculate whether it is indispensable in this respect.

However, there are a number of limitations. Many are agreed that it is inadequate alone. Sympathetic imagination is relevant to the origin but not the validity of explanatory hypotheses. Empathic identification may serve a heuristic function but it does not guarantee knowledge. Conjecture is not fact nor plausibility probability. The logical canons of the social sciences are no different from those of the natural sciences (Nagel 1961). Objective evidence is required through the application of experimental and statistical tests. Outhwaite (1975) distinguishes between the psychological understanding of motives 'from below' which he thinks can and should be incorporated within a natural science framework and the hermeneutic interpretation 'from above' which he is less confident about.

The criteria of *Verstehen* appear rather to be coherence and consistency. There is a problem of circularity, known as the hermeneutic circle.

We understand the whole from the part and the part from the whole. We derive the 'spirit of the epoch' from its individual documentary manifestations – and we interpret the individual documentary manifestations on the basis of what we know about the spirit of epoch (Mannheim 1952).

Dilthey (1937) describes it as the 'central difficulty of the art of interpretation':

The totality of a work must be understood through its individual propositions and their relations, and yet the full understanding of an individual component presupposes an understanding of the world.

There is difficulty in verification, both with respect to testing the validity of the subjective mental states and the objectivity of the behavioural maxims. Abel (1948) comments that there is no objective method for the internalising of either the stimulus or the response, which is largely a matter of imagination. The motives are inferred from their consequences and constrained by the total situation into which they must fit. Similarly, the behaviour maxims, the generalisations which link the feeling states and imply functional dependence between them, are constructed *ad hoc* on the basis of introspection and self-observation rather than being experimentally established. Interpretation is much dependent on the observer. To what extent it is dependent on his own experience and hence how far it is limited in its application to societies and experiences with which he is familiar is a controversial issue. Parallel problems arise in cultural anthropology and comparative psychology.

Nor does *Verstehen* add to our store of knowledge as it merely involves the application to observed behaviour of knowledge we already possess from personal experience. In my view its fruitfulness has yet to be demonstrated.

The problem of the relation of understanding by means of *Verstehen* to causal explanation has been the subject of much debate (see Ch. 12). The most extreme view (Peters 1958, Winch 1958) is that the method of *Verstehen* is necessary and sufficient for the study of behaviour, and distinct from causal explanation. Davidson (1963) and his followers have argued that rationalisation, i.e. the explanation of action by reference to an agent's reasons, intentions, beliefs and desires is a legitimate species of causal explanation. Most of the original exponents of *Verstehen*, e.g. Dilthey and Rickert, saw it as a complementary method distinct from but a necessary supplement to the method of causal explanation traditional to the natural sciences. For Weber *Verstehen*, involving intuition, a wordless act of identification with the object or some attempt to live in it without analysing its Gestalt, is merely the first of three stages in the scientific investigation of anything. The positivist view (Abel 1948, Nagel 1961, Holt 1962) is that it is a preliminary method helpful at the stage of formulating hypotheses but inadequate for testing them.

Empathic understanding

Artistic empathy is distinct from scientific explanation (Grünbaum 1952, Holt 1962, Kendler 1970). *Verstehen* in art involves subjective, empathic feeling, direct non-intellective knowing, non-explanatory understanding; scientific explanation on the other hand involves the grasp of structure and is concerned with how things work and their necessary and/or sufficient conditions. They have different aims and criteria.

An artist's quest for 'truth' differs from a scientist's in being a striving not for strict verisimilitude but for allusive illumination. The criterion of this kind of understanding is the effect on some audience; the ultimate criterion of scientific understanding may be verified prediction, or . . . an elegant and comprehensive account of facts already available, like the Darwinian theory of evolution (Holt 1962).

Intuition and empathy are desirable in deciding what to study and what strategies to use, in formulating hypotheses and making discoveries. But they are not sufficient.

The methodology of verification, the hypothesis testing phase of scientific work, involves well-developed rules and consensually established procedures, and . . . intuition and empathy have no place in it (Holt 1962).

In some ways, however, the dichotomy between science and art is less than the nomothetic–idiographic controversy would have us believe. Scientists need to be artistic in theory construction and communication and the best of them combine traits from both art and science. As Holt observes: 'The more secure scientists are in their methodological position, the more respect they usually have for intuition.' Art can inform and science be beautiful.

Bibliography

Abel, T. 1948. The operation called *Verstehen*. *Am. J. Sociol.* **54,** 211–8.

Abelson, R. P. 1963. Computer simulation of 'hot' cognition. In *Computer simulation of personality,* S. S. Tomkins and S. Messick (eds), 277–98. New York: Wiley.

Allport, D. A. 1975. Critical notice: the state of cognitive psychology. *Q. J. Exp. Psychol.* **27,** 141–52.

Allport, F. H. 1955. *Theories of perception and the concept of structure.* New York: Wiley.

Allport, G. W. 1961. *Pattern and growth in personality.* New York: Holt, Rinehart and Winston.

Allport, G. W. 1962. The general and the unique in psychological science. *J. Personality* **30,** 405–22.

Allport, G. W., P. E. Vernon and G. Lindzey 1960. *A study of values,* 3rd edn. Boston: Houghton Mifflin.

Anand, B. K., G. S. Chhina and B. Singh 1961. Some aspects of electro-encephalographic studies in yogis. *Electroenceph. Clin. Neurophysiol.* **13,** 452–56.

Annett, J. 1969. *Feedback and human behaviour.* London: Penguin.

Antrobus, J., J. S. Antrobus and C. Fisher 1965. Discrimination of dreaming and non-dreaming sleep. *Archs Gen. Psychiat.* **12,** 395–401.

Apter, M. J. 1973. The computer modelling of behaviour. In *The computer in psychology,* M. J. Apter and G. Westby (eds), 125–49. London: Wiley.

Argyris, C. 1968. Some unintended consequences of rigorous research. *Psychol Bull.* **70,** 185–97.

Armstrong, D. M. 1968. *A materialist theory of mind.* London: Routledge and Kegan Paul.

Aserinsky, E. and N. Kleitman 1953. Regularly occurring periods of eye motility and concomitant phenomena, during sleep. *Science* **118,** 273–4.

Ashby, W. R. 1940. Adaptiveness and equilibrium. *J. Ment. Sci.* **86,** 478–83.

Ashby, W. R. 1948. Design for a brain. *Electron. Engng* **20,** 379–83.

Ayer, A. J. 1946. Freedom and necessity. In *Philosophical essays,* 271–84. London: Macmillan.

Ayer, A. J. 1959. Privacy. *Proc. Br. Acad.* **45,** 43–65.

Ayer, A. J. 1969. Reflections on existentialism. In *Metaphysics and commonsense,* 203–18. London: Macmillan.

Ayer, A. J. 1973. Body and mind. In *The central questions of philosophy,* 112–36. London: Weidenfeld and Nicholson.

Bacon, F. 1620. *Novum organum,* T. Fowler (ed.). Darby, Pennsylvania: Arden Lib., 1979.

Baddeley, A. D. 1976. *The psychology of memory.* Harper International.

Baddeley, A. D., S. Grant, E. Wight and N. Thomson 1975. Imagery and visual working memory. In *Attention and performance,* P. M. A. Rabbitt and S. Dornic (eds), vol.V, 205–17. London: Academic Press.

Baldwin, A. L. 1942. Personal structure analysis: a statistical method for investigation of the single personality. *J. Abnorm. Soc. Psychol.* **37**, 163–83.

Bannister, D. 1968. The myth of physiological psychology. *Bull. Br. Psychol Soc.* **21**, 229–31.

Barber, T. X. and M. J. Silver 1968. Fact, fiction, and the experimenter bias effect. *Psychol Bull. Monogr. Suppl.* **70**, 1–29.

Barrett, W. 1964. *What is existentialism?* New York: Grove Press.

Bartholow, R. 1874. Experimental investigation into the functions of the human brain. *Am. J. Med. Sci.* **67**, 305–13.

Bartlett, F. C. 1932. *Remembering.* Cambridge: Cambridge University Press.

Bass, M. J. and C. L. Hull 1934. The irradiation of a tactile conditioned reflex in man. *J. Comp. Psychol.* **17**, 47–65.

Beach, F. A. 1955. The descent of instinct. *Psychol Rev.* **62**, 401–10.

Bem, D. J. and H. K. McConnell 1970. Testing the self-perception explanation of dissonance phenomena: on the salience of premanipulation attitudes. *J. Pers. Soc. Psychol.* **14**, 23–31.

Bentley, E. 1947. *The cult of the superman.* London: Hale.

Berger, R. J. and I. Oswald 1962. Eye movements during active and passive dreams. *Science* **137**, 601.

Bergmann, G. 1957. *Philosophy of science.* Madison: University of Wisconsin Press.

Berkeley, G. 1710. *A treatise concerning the principles of human knowledge.* LaSalle, Illinois: Open Court, 1963.

Bindra, D. 1976. *A theory of intelligent behavior.* New York: Wiley.

Binet, A. 1903. *L'étude experimentale de l'intelligence,* Paris: Schleicher Frères.

Binet, A. and J. Passy 1895. Etudes de psychologie sur les auteurs dramatiques. *Ann. Psychol.* **1**, 60–118.

Blanshard, B. and B. F. Skinner 1967. The problem of consciousness – a debate. *Philosophy Phenom. Res.* **27**, 317–37.

Boden, M. 1972. *Purposive explanation in psychology.* Cambridge, Mass.: Harvard University Press.

Boden, M. 1978. Human values in a mechanistic universe. In *Human values,* G. A. Vesey (ed.), 135–71. Hassocks, Sussex: Harvester Press.

Boden, M. 1979. The computational metaphor in psychology. In *Philosophical problems in psychology,* N. Bolton (ed.), 111–32. London: Methuen.

Bogen, J. E. 1969. The other side of the brain. *Bull. Los Ang. Neurol Soc.* **34**, 73–105, 135–62, 191–220.

Bolton, N. 1978. Reflecting on the pre-reflective: phenomenology. In *Thinking in perspective,* A. Burton and J. Radford (eds), 203–23. London: Methuen.

Bolton, N. 1979. Phenomenology and psychology: being objective about the mind. In *Philosophical problems in psychology,* N. Bolton (ed.) 158–75. London: Methuen.

Boring, E. G. 1927. The problem of originality in science. *Am. J. Psychol.* **39**, 70–90.

Boring, E. G. 1937. A psychological function is the relation of successive differentiations of events in the organism. *Psychol Rev.* **44**, 445–61.

Boring, E. G. 1942. Human nature *vs.* sensation: William James and the psychology of the present. *Am. J. Psychol.* **55**, 310–27.

Borst, C. V. 1970. *The mind–brain identity theory*. London: Macmillan.

Bower, G. 1963. *A model of immediate memory*. Working paper at Summer Institute in Heuristic Programming, Santa Monica. (Cited in Frijda 1967.)

Braithwaite, R. B. 1947. Teleological explanation. *Proc. Aristotelian Soc.* 1946–7, i–xx.

Braithwaite, R. B. 1953. *Scientific explanation*. Cambridge: Cambridge University Press.

Braithwaite, R. B. 1962. Models in the empirical sciences. In *Logic, methodology and philosophy of science,* E. Nagel, P. Suppes and A. Tarski (eds), 224–31, Stanford: Stanford University Press.

Bransford, J. D. and J. J. Franks 1971. The abstraction of linguistic ideas. *Cog. Psychol.* **2**, 331–50.

Brentano, F. 1874. *Psychologie vom empirischen Standpunkt*. Leipzig: Duncker and Humbolt.

Bricker, P. D. and A. Chapanis 1953. Do incorrectly perceived tachisto-scopic stimuli convey some information? *Psychol Rev.* **60**, 181–8.

Bridgman, P. W. 1928. *The logic of modern physics*. New York: Macmillan.

Broadbent, D. E. 1957. A mechanical model for human attention and immediate memory. *Psychol Rev.* **64**, 205–15.

Broadbent, D. E. 1961. *Behaviour*. London: Eyre and Spottiswoode.

Broadbent, D. E. 1977. Levels, hierarchies, and the locus of control. *Q. J. Exp. Psychol.* **29**, 181–201.

Brody, N. and P. Oppenheim 1966. Tensions in psychology between the methods of behaviorism and phenomenology. *Psychol Rev.* **73**, 295–305.

Broverman, D. M. 1960. Cognitive style and intra-individual variation in abilities. *J. Personality* **28**, 240–56.

Brown, G. and T. Harris 1978. *Social origins of depression*. London: Tavistock.

Bruner, J. S. 1957. Going beyond the information given. In *Contemporary approaches to cognition,* H. Gruber, K. R. Hammond and R. Jesser (eds). Cambridge, Mass.: Harvard University Press.

Bruner, J. S. and L. Postman 1949. On the perception of incongruity: a paradigm. *J. Personality* **18**, 206–23.

Brunswik, E. 1939. The conceptual focus of some psychological systems. *J. Unif. Sci.* **8**, 36–49.

Brunswik, E. 1947. *Systematic and unrepresentative design of psychological experiments with results in physical and social perception*. Berkeley: University of California Press.

Buchanan, J. 1812. *The philosophy of human nature*. Richmond, Kentucky: Grimes.

Burns, B. D. 1968. *The uncertain nervous system*. London: Edward Arnold.

Burt, C. 1962. The concept of consciousness. *Br. J. Psychol.* **53**, 229–42.

Bush, R. R. and F. Mosteller 1955. *Stochastic models for learning*. New York: Wiley.

Caine, T. M., O. B. A. Wijesinghe and D. A. Winter 1981. *Personal styles in neurosis: implications for small group psychotherapy and behaviour therapy.* London: Routledge and Kegan Paul.

Capra, F. 1975. *The tao of physics.* London: Wildwood House.

Carlson, V. R. 1960. Overestimation in size-constancy judgments. *Am. J. Psychol.* **73**, 199–213.

Carnap, R. 1934. *The unity of science* (transl. M. Black). London: Routledge and Kegan Paul.

Carr, E. H. 1961. *What is history?* London: Macmillan.

Castaneda, C. 1968. *The teachings of Don Juan: a yaqui way of knowing.* Berkeley: University of California Press.

Chapanis, A. 1961. Men, machines, and models. *Am. Psychol.* **16**, 113–31.

Chisholm, R. M. 1967. Intentionality. In *The encyclopaedia of philosophy,* P. Edwards (ed.), **IV**, 201–4. New York: Macmillan.

Chomsky, N. 1959. Review of *Verbal behavior* by B. F. Skinner. *Language* **35**, 26–58.

Clark, J. H. 1972. A map of inner space. In *Six approaches to the person,* R. Ruddock (ed.), 155–98. London: Routledge and Kegan Paul.

Clarkson, G. P. E. 1961. *A simulation of trust investment.* Englewood Cliffs, NJ: Prentice-Hall.

Coan, R. W. 1968. Dimensions of psychological theory. *Am. Psychol.* **23**, 715–22.

Cochrane, R. and J. Duffy 1974. Psychology and scientific method. *Bull. Br. Psychol Soc.* **27**, 117–21.

Colby, K. M. 1963. Computer simulation of a neurotic process. In *Computer simulation of personality,* S. S. Tomkins and S. Messick (eds), 165–79. New York: Wiley.

Colby, K. M., S. Weber and F. D. Halif 1971. Artificial paranoia. *Artif. Intell.* **2**, 1–26.

Comte, A. 1842. *Cours de philosophie positive.* Paris: Bachelier.

Conklin, E. G. 1943. *Man: real and ideal.* New York.

Conrad, H. S. 1932. The validity of personality ratings of pre-school children. *J. Educ. Psychol.* **23**, 671–80.

Coombs, C. H., R. M. Dawes and A. Tversky 1970. *Mathematical psychology: an elementary introduction.* Englewood Cliffs, NJ: Prentice-Hall.

Cronbach, L. J. 1957. The two disciplines of scientific psychology. *Am. Psychol.* **12**, 671–84.

Davidson, D. 1963. Actions, reasons and causes. *J. Phil.* **60**, 685–700.

Day, W. F. 1969. Radical behaviorism in reconciliation with phenomenology. *J. Exp. Analysis Behav.* **12**, 315–28.

Day, W. F. 1976. The case for behaviorism. In *Theories in contemporary psychology,* M. H. Marx and F. E. Goodson (eds), 534–45. New York: Macmillan.

De Bono, E. 1967. *The use of lateral thinking.* London: Cape.

De Groot, A. D. 1965. *Thought and choice in chess.* The Hague: Mouton (first published in Dutch in 1946).

Deikman, A. J. 1973. The meaning of everything. In *The nature of consciousness,* R. E. Ornstein (ed.), 317–26. San Francisco: W. H. Freeman.

Delgado, J. M. R. 1965. Sequential behavior induced repeatedly by stimulation of the red nucleus in free monkeys. *Science* **148**, 1361–3.

Dement, W. C. 1955. Dream recall and eye movements during sleep in schizophrenics and normals. *J. Nerv. Ment. Dis.* **122**, 263–9.

Dement, W. C. 1972. *Some must watch while some must sleep.* San Francisco: W. H. Freeman.

Dement, W. C. and N. Kleitman 1957. The relation of eye movements during sleep to dream activity: an objective method for the study of dreaming. *J. Exp. Psychol.* **53**, 339–46.

Descartes, R. 1641. *Discourse on method* (transl. J. Veitch). London: Dent, 1953.

Deutsch, J. A. 1960. *The structural basis of behaviour.* Cambridge: Cambridge University Press.

Dewey, J. 1896. The reflex arc concept in psychology. *Psychol Rev.* **3**, 357—70.

Dilthey, W. 1937. *Historik.* Munich: Oldenbourg.

Doerr, H. O. and J. E. Hokanson 1965. A relation between heart rate and performance in children. *J. Pers. Soc. Psychol.* **2**, 70–7.

Dreyfus, H. L. 1972. *What computers can't do.* New York: Harper and Row.

Droysen, J. G. 1858. *Grundriss der Historik.* Halle-Saale: Niemeyer, 1925. Translated as *Outlines of the principles of history.* Boston: Ginn, 1893.

Dulany, D. E. Jr 1962. The place of hypotheses and intention: an analysis of verbal control in verbal conditioning. In *Behavior and awareness,* C. W. Eriksen (ed.), 102–29. Durham, North Carolina: Duke University Press.

Duncker, K. 1945. On problem solving. *Psychol Monogr.* **58**, whole no. 270, 1–113.

Eccles, J. C. 1951. Hypotheses relating to the brain–mind problem. *Nature* **168**, 53–7.

Eddington, A. S. 1935. *New pathways in science.* Cambridge: Cambridge University Press.

Elashoff, J. D. and R. E. Snow 1971. *Pygmalion reconsidered.* Worthington, Ohio: Jones.

Erickson, M. H. 1965. A special inquiry with Aldous Huxley into the nature and character of various states of consciousness. *Am. J. Clin. Hypnosis* **8**, 17–33.

Estes, W. K. 1950. Toward a statistical theory of learning. *Psychol Rev.* **57**, 94–107.

Estes, W.K. 1959. The statistical approach to learning theory. In *Psychology: a study of a science,* S. Koch (ed.), Vol. 2, 380–491. New York: McGraw-Hill.

Evans, J. St B. T. 1980. Thinking: experiential and information processing. In *Cognitive psychology,* G. Claxton (ed.), 275–99. London: Routledge and Kegan Paul.

Evans, J. St B.T. and P. C. Wason 1976. Rationalization in a reasoning task. *Br. J. Psychol.* **67**, 479–86.

Eysenck, H. J. 1966. Personality and experimental psychology. *Bull. Br. Psychol Soc.* **19**, 1–28.

Eysenck, H. J. and P. Slater 1958. Effects of practice and rest on fluctuations in the Müller–Lyer illusion. *Br. J. Psychol.* **49**, 246–56.

Eysenck, M. W. 1977. *Human memory: theory, research and individual differences.* Oxford: Pergamon.

Feigenbaum, E. A. 1959. *EPAM: An elementary perceiver and memoriser.* RAND Report 1817.

Feigenbaum, E. A. and H. A. Simon 1962. A theory of the serial position effect. *Br. J. Psychol.* **53**, 307–20.

Feigl, H. 1958. The 'mental' and the 'physical'. In *Concepts, theories and the mind–body problem,* H. Feigl, G. Maxwell and M. Scriven (eds), 370–497. Minneapolis: University of Minnesota Press.

Feigl, H. 1960. Mind–body, *not* a pseudo-problem. In *Dimensions of mind,* S. Hook (ed.), 33–44. New York: New York University Press.

Feldman, J. 1962. Computer simulation of cognitive processes. In *Computer applications in the behavioral sciences,* H. Borko (ed.), 336–56. Englewood Cliffs, NJ: Prentice-Hall.

Feyerabend, P. K. 1975. *Against method: an outline of an anarchistic theory of knowledge.* London: NLB.

Field, G. C. 1921. Faculty psychology and instinct psychology. *Mind* **30**, 257–70.

Fishbein, M. 1967. Attitude and the prediction of behavior. In *Readings in attitude theory and measurement,* M. Fishbein (ed.), 477–92. New York: Wiley.

Flourens, P. 1842. *Recherches expérimentales sur les propriétés et les fonctions du système nerveux dans les animaux vertébrés,* 2nd edn. Paris: Baillière.

Fodor, J. A. 1965. Could meaning be an r_m? *J. Verb. Learn. Verb. Behav.* **4**, 73–81.

Fodor, J. A. 1968. *Psychological explanation: an introduction to the philosophy of psychology.* New York: Random House.

Fodor, J. A. 1981. The mind–body problem. *Scient. Am.* **244** (4), 124–32.

Foss, B. M. 1974. On taking sides. *Bull. Br. Psychol Soc.* **27**, 347–51.

Foulkes, W. D. 1962. Dream reports from different stages of sleep, *J. Abnorm. Soc. Psychol.* **65**, 14–25.

Foulkes, W. D. and G. Vogel 1965. Mental activity at sleep onset. *J. Abnorm. Psychol.* **70**, 231–43.

Frankel, C. 1973. The nature and sources of irrationalism. *Science* **180**, 927–31.

Fransella, F. 1975. *Need to change?* London: Methuen.

Franz, S. I. 1902. On the functions of the cerebrum: the frontal lobes in relation to the production and retention of simple sensory habits. *Am. J. Physiol.* **8**, 1–22.

Freud, S. 1895. *The origins of psychoanalysis: letters to Wilhelm Fliess, drafts and notes.* New York: Basic Books.

Frijda, N. H. 1967. Problems of computer simulation. *Behavl Sci.* **12**, 59–67.

Fritsch, G. and E. Hitzig 1870. Ueber die elektrische Erregbarkeit des Grosshirns. *Arch. Anat. Physiol.* 300–32.

Funkenstein, D. H. 1955. The physiology of fear and anger. *Scient. Am.* **192** (5), 74–80.

Furneaux, W. D. 1961. Neuroticism, extraversion, drive and suggestibility. *Int. J. Clin. Exp. Hypnosis* **9**, 195–214.

Galdston, I. 1956. Freud and romantic medicine. *Bull. Hist. Med.* **30**, 489–507.

Garner, W. R., H. W. Hake and C. W. Eriksen 1956. Operationism and the concept of perception. *Psychol Rev.* **63**, 149–59.

Gauld, A. and J. Shotter 1977. *Human action and its psychological investigation.* London: Routledge and Kegan Paul.

Gazzaniga, M. S. and J. E. LeDoux 1978. *The integrated mind.* New York: Plenum Press.

Gelernter, H. 1959. Realization of a geometry-theorem proving machine. In *Computers and thought,* E. A. Feigenbaum and J. Feldman (eds), 134–52. New York: McGraw-Hill, 1963.

Gelernter, H., J. R. Hansen and D. W. Loveland 1960. Empirical explorations of the geometry-theorem proving machine. In *Computers and thought,* E. A. Feigenbaum and J. Feldman (eds), 153–63. New York: McGraw-Hill, 1963.

George, F. H. 1953. Formalization of language systems for behavior theory. *Psychol Rev.* **60**, 232–40.

Ghiselli, E. E. 1963. Moderating effects and differential reliability and validity. *J. Appl. Psychol.* **47**, 81–6.

Globus, G. G. 1973. Unexpected symmetries in the 'world knot'. *Science* **180**, 1129–36.

Goethals, G. R. and R. F. Reckman 1973. The perception of consistency in attitudes. *J. Exp. Soc. Psychol.* **9**, 491–501.

Goffman, E. 1959. *The presentation of self in everyday life.* New York: Anchor Books.

Goldmann, L. 1959. *Recherches dialectiques.* Paris: Gallimard.

Goodson, F. E. and G. A. Morgan 1976. Evaluation of theory. In *Theories in contemporary psychology,* M. H. Marx and F. E. Goodson (eds), 286–99. New York: Macmillan.

Gordon, R. 1950. An experiment correlating the nature of imagery with performance on a test of reversal perspective. *Br. J. Psychol.* **41**, 63–7.

Grant, D. A. 1968. Adding communication to the signalling property of the CS in classical conditioning. *J. Gen. Psychol.* **79**, 147–75.

Gray, J. A. 1971. The mind–brain identity theory as a scientific hypothesis. *Phil Q.* **21**, 247–54.

Green, B. F. 1963. *Digital computers in research.* New York: McGraw-Hill.

Gregory, R. L. 1961. The brain as an engineering problem. In *Current problems in animal behaviour,* W. H. Thorpe and O. L. Zangwill (eds), 307–30. Cambridge: Cambridge University Press.

Gregory, R. L. 1970. On how little information controls so much behaviour. *Ergonomics* **13**, 25–35.

Grünbaum, A. 1952. Causality and the science of behavior. *Am. Scient.* **40**, 665–76, 689.

Gullahorn, J. T. and J. E. Gullahorn 1963. A computer model of elementary social behavior. In *Computers and thought*, E. A. Feigenbaum and J. Feldman (eds), 375–86. New York: McGraw-Hill.

Gunter, R. 1951. Binocular fusion of colours. *Br. J. Psychol.* **42**, 363–72.

Gustav, A. 1962. Students' attitudes towards compulsory participation in experiments. *J. Psychol.* **53**, 119–25.

Haber, R. N. 1965. Effect of prior knowledge of the stimulus on word-recognition processes. *J. Exp. Psychol.* **69**, 282–6.

Haber, R. N. and R. B. Haber 1964. Eidetic imagery: I Frequency. *Percept. Mot. Skills* **19**, 131–8.

Haldane, J. B. S. 1927. *Possible worlds*. London: Heinemann, 1940.

Haldane, J. B. S. 1954. I repent an error. *Literary Guide* 7 April, 29.

Haldane, J. B. S. 1963. Life and mind as physical realities. *Penguin Science Survey B*, 224–38.

Harré, R. and P. F. Secord 1972. *The explanation of social behaviour*. Oxford: Blackwell.

Hayes, J. R. 1973. On the function of visual imagery in elementary mathematics. In *Visual information processing*, W. G. Chase (ed.), 177–214. London: Academic Press.

Heather, N. 1976. *Radical perspectives in psychology*. London: Methuen.

Hebb, D. O. 1949. *The organization of behavior*. New York: Wiley.

Hebb, D. O. 1968. Concerning imagery. *Psychol Rev.* **75**, 466–77.

Heider, F. 1958. *The psychology of interpersonal relations*. New York: Wiley.

Heisenberg, W. 1927. Uber den anschlaulichen Inhalt der quantentheoretischen Kinetik und Mechanik. *Z. Phys.* **43**, 172–98.

Herbart, J. F. 1824. *Psychologie als Wissenschaft*. Leipzig.

Hobbes, T. 1651. *Leviathan*. London: Dent, 1914.

Holmes, D. S. 1967. Amount of experience in experiments as a determinant of performance in later experiments. *J. Pers. Soc. Psychol.* **7**, 403–7.

Holst, E. von 1954. Relations between the central nervous system and the peripheral organs. *Br. J. Anim. Behav.* **2**, 89–94.

Holt, R. R. 1962. Individuality and generalization in the psychology of personality. *J. Personality* **30**, 377–404.

Holt, R. R. 1964. Imagery: the return of the ostracized. *Am. Psychol.* **19**, 254–64.

Homans, G. C. 1961. *Social behavior: its elementary forms*. New York: Harcourt, Brace and World.

Hook, S. 1943. *The hero in history*. New York: Doubleday.

Horgan, T. 1976. Reduction and the mind–body problem. In *Theories in contemporary psychology*, M. H. Marx and F. E. Goodson (eds), 223–31. New York: Macmillan.

Hovland, C. I. 1939. Experimental studies in rote learning theory. V. Comparison of distribution of practice in serial and paired-associate learning. *J. Exp. Psychol.* **25**, 622–33.

Howes, D. H. and R. L. Solomon 1951. Visual duration threshold as a function of word-probability. *J. Exp. Psychol.* **41**, 401–10.

Hubel, D. H. and T. N. Wiesel 1962. Receptive fields, binocular interaction and functional architecture in the cat's visual cortex. *J. Physiol.* **160**, 106–54.

Hudson, L. 1972. *The cult of the fact.* London: Cape.

Hull, C. L. 1935. The mechanism of the assembly of behavior segments in novel situations suitable for problem solution. *Psychol Rev.* **42**, 219–45.

Hull, C. L. 1943. *Principles of behavior.* New York: Appleton–Century–Crofts.

Hume, D. 1740. *Treatise of human nature.* Oxford: Clarendon Press, 1888.

Humphrey, G. 1951. *Thinking.* London: Methuen.

Husserl, E. 1901. *Logische Untersuchungen,* 2 vols. Niemeyer: Halle. *Logical investigations* (English translation, J. N. Findlay). New York: Humanities Press, 1970.

Husserl, E. 1913. *Ideen zu einer Reinen Phaenomenologie und Phaenomenologische Philosophie* (transl. W. R. Boyce Gibson). London: George Allen and Unwin, 1931.

Huxley, A. 1954. *The doors of perception.* New York: Harper and Bros.

Huxley, T. H. 1874. On the hypothesis that animals are automata, and its history. *Fortnightly Rev.* **16**, 555–80.

Hyman, R. 1964. *The nature of psychological inquiry.* Englewood Cliffs, NJ: Prentice-Hall.

Idhe, A. J. 1948. The inevitability of scientific discovery. *Scient. Monogr.* **67**, 427–9.

Jackson, C. W. and J. C. Pollard 1966. Some nondeprivation variables which influence the 'effects' of experimental sensory deprivation. *J. Abnorm. Psychol.* **71**, 383–8.

Jackson, J. H. 1878. On affections of speech from disease of the brain. In *Selected writings of Hughlings Jackson,* Vol. II, 155–70. New York: Basic Books, 1958.

James, W. 1880. Great men, great thoughts and the environment. *Atlant. Mon.* **46**, 441–59.

James, W. 1890. *The principles of psychology.* New York: Holt.

James, W. 1907. *Pragmatism.* New York: Longman.

James, W. 1912. *Memories and studies.* New York: Longman, Green.

Janis, I. L. and B. T. King 1954. The influence of role-playing on opinion change. *J. Abnorm. Soc. Psychol.* **49**, 211–18.

Janke, W. 1964. *Experimentelle Untersuchungen zur Abhangigkeit der Wirkung psychotroper Substanzen von Persönlichkeitsmerkerkmalen.* Frankfurt: Akademische Verlagsgesellschaft.

Jaspers, K. 1913. Allgemeine psychopathologie. *General psychopathology.* Manchester: Manchester University Press, 1962.

Jeans, J. 1933. *The new background of science.* Cambridge: Cambridge University Press.

Jensen, A. R. 1962. Extraversion, neuroticism and serial learning. *Acta Psychol.* **20**, 69–77.

Jessor, R. 1958. The problem of reductionism in psychology. *Psychol Rev.* **65**, 170–8.

Johnson, L. C. 1977. Psychophysiological research: its aims and methods. In *Psychosomatic medicine*, Z. J. Lipowski, D. R. Lipsitt and P. C. Whybrow (eds), 253–61. New York: Oxford University Press.

Jones, E. 1955. *Sigmund Freud: life and work*. London: Hogarth.

Jones, M. B. and R. S. Fennell 1965. Runway performance by two strains of rats. *Q. J. Fla Acad. Sci.* **28**, 289–96.

Joynson, R. B. 1958. An experimental synthesis of the Association and Gestalt accounts of the perception of size. *Q. J. Exp. Psychol.* **10**, 65–76 and 124–54.

Joynson, R. B. 1970. The breakdown of modern psychology. *Bull. Br. Psychol Soc.* **23**, 261–9.

Joynson, R. B. 1972. The return of mind. *Bull. Br. Psychol Soc.* **25**, 1–10.

Joynson, R. B. 1980. Models of man: 1879–1979. In *Models of man*, A. J. Chapman and D. M. Jones (eds), 1–11. Leicester: British Psychological Society.

Kant, I. 1781. *Kritik der reinen Vernunft* (transl. J. M. D. Meikeljohn). London: Dent, 1974.

Kasamatsu, A. and T. Hirai 1966. An electroencephalographic study on the zen meditation (zazen). *Folia Psychiat. Neurol. Jap.* **20**, 315–36.

Kelly, G. A. 1955. *The psychology of personal constructs*. New York: Morton.

Kelvin, R. P. 1956. Thinking: psychologists and physiology. *Acta Psychol.* **12**, 136–51.

Kendler, H. H. 1970. The unity of psychology. *Can. Psychol.* **11**, 30–47.

Kendler, H. H. and J. T. Spence 1971. *Essays in neobehaviorism: a memorial volume to Kenneth W. Spence*. Englewood Cliffs, NJ: Prentice-Hall.

Kilpatrick, F. P. and H. Cantril 1960. Self-anchoring scale: a measure of the individual's unique reality world. *J. Indiv. Psychol.* **16**, 158–70.

Kimble, G. A. 1964. Categories of learning and the problem of definition. In *Categories of human learning*, A. W. Melton (ed.), 32–45. New York: Academic Press.

Kimble, G. A. and L. C. Perlmuter 1970. The problem of volition. *Psychol Rev.* **77**, 361–84.

Kluckholn, C. M. and H. A. Murray 1953. Personality formation: its determinants. In *Personality in nature, society and culture*, C. M. Kluckholn and H. A. Murray (eds), 2nd edn, 53–67. New York: Knopf.

Koch, S. 1959. Epilogue. In *Psychology: a study of a science*, S. Koch (ed.), vol. 3, 729–88. New York: McGraw-Hill.

Koestler, A. 1964. *The act of creation*. London: Hutchinson.

Kogan, N. and M. A. Wallach 1964. *Risk taking: a study in cognition and personality*. London: Holt, Rinehart and Winston.

Köhler, W. 1918. Nachweis einfacher Strukturfunktionen beim Schimpansen und beim Haushuhn: Uber eine neue Methode zur Untersuchung des bunten Farbensystems. *Abh. Preuss. Akad. Wiss.* **2**, 1–101.

Krishnamurti, J. 1956. *Commentaries on living*, D. Rajagopal (ed.), London: Gollancz.

Kuhn, T. S. 1962. *The structure of scientific revolutions*. Chicago: University of Chicago Press.

Kuhn, T. S. 1970a. Postscript – 1969. In *The structure of scientific revolutions*, 2nd edn. Chicago: University of Chicago Press.

Kuhn, T. S. 1970b. Reflections on my critics. In *Criticism and the growth of knowledge*, I. Lakatos and A. Musgrave (eds), 231–78. Cambridge: Cambridge University Press.

Kvale, S. and C. E. Grenness 1967. Skinner and Sartre: towards a radical phenomenology of behaviour? *Rev. Exist. Psychol. Psychiat.* **7**, 128–48.

Lachman, R. 1960. The model in theory construction. *Psychol Rev.* **67**, 113–29.

Laird, J. D. 1974. Self-attribution of emotion: the effect of expressive behavior on the quality of emotional experience. *J. Pers. Soc. Psychol.* **29**, 475–86.

Lakatos, I. 1970. Falsification and the methodology of scientific research programmes. In *Criticism and the growth of knowledge*, I. Lakatos and A. Musgrave (eds), 91–196. Cambridge: Cambridge University Press.

Landauer, A. A. and R. S. Rodger 1964. The effect of 'apparent' instructions on brightness judgments. *J. Exp. Psychol.* **68**, 80–4.

Laplace, P. S. 1820. *Théorie analytique des probabilités*. Brussells: Culture Civilization, 1967.

Lashley, K. S. 1929. *Brain mechanisms and intelligence*. Chicago: University of Chicago Press.

Lashley, K. S. 1930. Basic neural mechanisms in behavior. *Psychol Rev.* **37**, 1–24.

Lashley, K. S. 1942. An examination of the 'continuity theory' as applied to discrimination learning. *J. Gen. Psychol.* **26**, 241–65.

Lashley, K. S. 1951. The problem of serial order in behavior. In *Cerebral mechanisms in behavior*, L. A. Jefress (ed.), 112–36. New York: Wiley.

Lashley, K. S., K. L. Chow and J. Semmes 1951. An examination of the electrical field theory of cerebral integration. *Psychol Rev.* **58**, 123–36.

Lassen, N. A., D. H. Ingvar and E. Skinhøj 1978. Brain function and blood flow. *Scient. Am.* **239**(4), 50–9.

Latané, B. and J. M. Darley 1970. *The unresponsive bystander: why doesn't he help?* New York: Appleton–Century–Crofts.

Laughery, K. R. and L. W. Gregg 1962. Simulation of human problem solving behaviour. *Psychometrika* **27**, 265–82.

Lawrence, D. H. 1950. Acquired distinctiveness of cues: II Selective association in a constant stimulus situation. *J. Exp. Psychol.* **40**, 175–88.

Lawrence, D. H. 1963. The nature of a stimulus: some relationships between learning and perception. In *Psychology: a study of a science*, S. Koch (ed.), Vol. 5, 179–212. New York: McGraw-Hill.

Leibniz, G. W. von 1714. *Monadologie*. (transl. R. Latta). Oxford: Oxford University Press, 1898.

Lenneberg, E. H. 1967. *Biological foundations of language*. New York: Wiley.

Lewin, K. 1951. *Field theory in social science*. New York: Harper.

Liberman, A. M., K. S. Harris, H. S. Hoffman and B. C. Griffith 1957.

The discrimination of speech sounds within and across phoneme boundaries. *J. Exp. Psychol.* **54**, 358–68.

Lorenz, K. 1950. The comparative method in studying innate behaviour patterns. *Symp. Soc. Exp. Biol.* **4**, 221–68. Cambridge: Cambridge University Press.

Lorenz, K. 1966. *The evolution and modification of behaviour.* London: Methuen.

MacCorquodale, K. and P. E. Meehl 1948. On a distinction between hypothetical constructs and intervening variables. *Psychol Rev.* **55**, 95–107.

Mackay, D. M. 1960. On the logical indeterminancy of a free choice. *Mind* **69**, 31–40.

Mackay, D. M. 1981. Neural basis of cognitive experience. In *Neural communication and control, Advances in physiological sciences,* G. Szekely, E. Labos and S. Damjanovich (eds), vol. 30, 315–32. Oxford: Pergamon.

Maier, N. R. F. 1931. The solution of a problem and its appearance in consciousness. *J. Comp. Psychol.* **12**, 181–94.

Malcolm, N. 1959. *Dreaming.* New York: Humanities Press.

Malebranche, N. 1675. *Oeuvres complètes.* Paris: Vrin, 1979.

Mandler, G. 1975. *Mind and emotion.* New York: Wiley.

Mandler, G. and W. Kessen 1974. The appearance of free will. In *Philosophy of psychology,* S. C. Brown (ed.), 305–24. London: Macmillan.

Mannheim, K. 1952. *Essays on the sociology of knowledge,* P. Kecskemeti (ed.). London: Routledge and Kegan Paul.

Marx, M. H. 1976. Formal theory. In *Theories in contemporary psychology,* M. H. Marx and F. E. Goodson (eds), 234–60. New York: Macmillan.

Maslow, A. H. 1954. *Motivation and personality.* New York: Harper and Row. 2nd edn. 1970.

Maslow, A. H. 1966. *The psychology of science.* New York: Harper and Row.

Maslow, A. H. 1969. Toward a humanistic biology. *Am. Psychol.* **24**, 724–35.

Masterman, M. 1970. The nature of a paradigm. In *Criticism and the growth of knowledge,* I. Lakatos and A. Musgrave (eds), 59–89. Cambridge: Cambridge University Press.

May, M. A. 1948. Experimentally acquired drives. *J. Exp. Psychol.* **38**, 66–77.

McClearn, G. E. 1962. *Genetic differences in the effect of alcohol upon behaviour of mice.* Proc. Third International Conf. Alcohol and Road Traffic, London.

McClintock, M. K. 1971. Menstrual synchrony and suppression. *Nature* **229**, 244–5.

McDougall, W. 1912. *Psychology: the study of behaviour.* London: Williams and Norgate.

McDougall, W. 1925. *An introduction to social psychology,* 20th edn. London: Methuen.

McDougall, W. 1932. *The energies of men: a study of the fundamentals of dynamic psychology.* London: Methuen.

McDougall, W. 1936. *An introduction to social psychology,* 23rd edn. London: Methuen.

McFie, J. 1972. Factors of the brain. *Bull. Br. Psychol Soc.* **25,** 11–14.

McGeoch, J. A. 1933. The formal criteria of a systematic psychology. *Psychol Rev.* **40,** 1–12.

McGinn, C. 1979. Action and its explanation. In *Philosophical problems in psychology,* N. Bolton (ed.), 20–42. London: Methuen.

McKellar, P. 1962. The method of introspection. In *Theories of the mind,* J. M. Scher (ed.), 619–44. New York: Free Press of Glencoe.

Mednick, S. 1970. Breakdown in individuals at high risk for schizophrenia: possible predispositional and perinatal factors. *Ment. Hyg.* **54,** 50–63.

Meehl, P. E. 1954. *Clinical* vs. *statistical prediction.* Minneapolis: University of Minnesota Press.

Meehl, P. E. 1957. When shall we use our heads instead of the formula? *J. Counsel. Psychol.* **4,** 268–73.

Merleau-Ponty, M. 1942. *The structure of behavior.* Boston: Beacon, 1963.

Merleau-Ponty, M. 1945. *Phenomenology of perception.* New York: Humanities Press, 1962.

Mill, J. S. 1882. *Auguste Comte and positivism,* 3rd edn. London: Trubner.

Millenson, J. 1967. An isomorphism between S–R notation and information processing flow diagrams. *Psychol Rec.* **17,** 305–19.

Miller, G. A. 1956. The magical number seven, plus or minus two: some limits on our capacity for processing information. *Psychol Rev.* **63,** 81–97.

Miller, G. A. 1964. *Psychology: the science of mental life.* London: Hutchinson.

Miller, G. A., E. Galanter and K. Pribram 1960. *Plans and the structure of behavior.* New York: Holt, Rinehart and Winston.

Miller, N. E. 1956. Effects of drugs on motivation: the value of using a variety of measures. *Ann. NY Acad. Sci.* **65,** 318–33.

Milner, P. M. 1957. The cell assembly: Mark II. *Psychol Rev.* **64,** 242–52.

Mischel, T. 1973. Toward a cognitive social learning reconceptualization of personality. *Psychol Rev.* **80,** 252–83.

Mowrer, O. H. 1954. The psychologist looks at language. *Am. Psychol.* **9,** 660–94.

Munkelt, P. 1965. Persönlichkeitsmerkmale als Bedingungsfaktoren der Psychotropen Arzneimittelwirkung. *Psychol. Beitr.* **8,** 98–183.

Nagel, E. 1953. Teleological explanation and teleological systems. In *Vision and action,* S. Ratner (ed.), 192–222. New Brunswick, New Jersey: Rutgers University Press.

Nagel, E. 1961. *The structure of science.* London: Routledge and Kegan Paul.

Nagel, E. 1967. What is true and false in science: Medawar and the anatomy of research. *Encounter* **29** (3), 68–70.

Natsoulas, T. 1967. What are perceptual reports about? *Psychol Bull.* **67,** 249–72.

Natsoulas, T. 1970. Concerning introspective 'knowledge'. *Psychol Bull.* **73,** 89–111.

Natsoulas, T. 1978. Consciousness. *Am. Psychol.* **33,** 906–14.

Natsoulas, T. and E. Levy 1965. *A further study of the verbal transformation effect*. Unpubl. manuscript, University of California, Davis (cited in Natsoulas 1967).

Neisser, U. 1963. The imitation of man by machine. *Science* **139**, 193–7.

Neisser, U. 1970. Visual imagery as process and as experience. In *Cognition and affect*, J. Antrobus (ed.), 159–78. Boston: Little, Brown.

Neisser, U. 1976. *Cognition and reality*. San Francisco: W. H. Freeman.

Neumann, J. von 1958. *The computer and the brain*. New Haven, Conn.: Yale University Press.

Newell, A. 1973. You can't play 20 questions with nature and win. In *Visual information processing*, W. G. Chase (ed.), 283–308. London: Academic Press.

Newell, A. and H. A. Simon 1959. The simulation of human thought. *RAND report* P–1734.

Newell, A. and H. A. Simon 1961. Computer simulation of human thinking. *Science* **134**, 2011–7.

Newell, A. and H. A. Simon 1972. *Human problem solving*. Englewood Cliffs, NJ: Prentice-Hall.

Nisbett, R. E. and T. de C. Wilson 1977. Telling more than we can know: verbal reports on mental processes. *Psychol Rev.* **84**, 231–59.

Nunnally, J. C. 1955. An investigation of some propositions of self-conception: The case of Miss Sun. *J. Abnorm. Soc. Psychol.* **50**, 87–92.

O'Connor, D. J. 1971. *Free will*. New York: Doubleday.

Ogburn, W. F. and D. Thomas 1922. Are inventions inevitable? *Polit. Sci. Q.* **37**, 83–93.

Oliver, W. D. and A. W. Landfield 1963. Reflexivity: an unfaced issue of psychology. *J. Indiv. Psychol.* **20**, 187–201.

Orne, M. T. 1959. The nature of hypnosis: artifact and essence. *J. Abnorm. Soc. Psychol.* **58**, 277–99.

Orne, M. T. 1962. On the social psychology of the psychological experiment: with particular reference to demand characteristics and their implications. *Am. Psychol.* **17**, 776–83.

Orne, M. T. and K. E. Scheibe 1964. The contribution of non-deprivation factors in the production of sensory deprivation effects: the psychology of the 'panic button'. *J. Abnorm. Soc. Psychol.* **68**, 3–12.

Ornstein, R. 1972. *The psychology of consciousness*. San Francisco: W. H. Freeman.

Osgood, C. E. 1953. *Method and theory in experimental psychology*. New York: Oxford University Press.

Osgood, C. E. 1956. Behavior theory and the social sciences. *Behavl Sci.* **1**, 167–85.

Osgood, C. E. 1963. On understanding and creating sentences. *Am. Psychol.* **18**, 735–51.

Outhwaite, W. 1975. *Understanding social life*. London: George Allen and Unwin.

Palermo, D. S. 1971. Is a scientific revolution taking place in psychology? *Sci. Stud.* **1**, 133–55.

Paxton, R. 1976. Some criteria for choosing between explanations in psychology. *Bull. Br. Psychol Soc.* **29,** 396–9.

Pearson, K. 1892. *The grammar of science.* London: Scott.

Penfield, W. 1938. The cerebral cortex in man. *Archs Neurol. Psychiat.* **40,** 417–42.

Penfield, W. 1969. Consciousness, memory, and man's conditioned reflexes. In *On the biology of learning,* K. H. Pribram (ed.), 127–68. New York: Harcourt, Brace and World.

Perkins, M. 1953. Intersubjectivity and Gestalt psychology. *Philosophy Phenom. Res.* **13,** 437–51.

Perry, R. B. 1918. Docility and purposiveness. *Psychol Rev.* **25,** 1–21.

Peters, R. S. (ed.) 1953. *Brett's history of psychology.* London: George Allen and Unwin.

Peters, R. S. 1958. *The concept of motivation.* London: Routledge and Kegan Paul.

Pfungst, P. 1911. *Clever Hans (the horse of Mr von Osten): A contribution to experimental, animal and human psychology* (transl. C. L. Rahn). New York: Holt.

Piaget, J. 1971. *Insights and illusions of philosophy* (transl. W. Mays). New York: World (first French edition, 1965).

Pilkington, G. W. and W. D. Glasgow 1967. Towards a rehabilitation of introspection as a method in psychology. *J. Existentialism* **7,** 329–50.

Pinneo, L. R. 1966. Electrical control of behaviour by programmed stimulation of the brain. *Nature* **211,** 705–8.

Place, U. T. 1956. Is consciousness a brain process? *Br. J. Psychol.* **47,** 44–51.

Platt, J. R. 1964. Strong inference. *Science* **146,** 347–53.

Polanyi, M. 1966. *The tacit dimension.* London: Routledge and Kegan Paul.

Popper, K. R. 1950. Indeterminism in quantum physics and in classical physics. *Br. J. Phil Sci.* **1,** 117–33 and 173–95.

Popper, K. R. 1959. *The logic of scientific discovery.* London: Hutchinson.

Popper, K. R. 1963. *Conjectures and refutations.* London: Routledge and Kegan Paul.

Popper, K. R. and J. C. Eccles 1977. *The self and its brain.* Berlin: Springer-Verlag.

Postman, L. 1947. The history and present status of the law of effect. *Psychol Bull.* **44,** 489–563.

Prince, M. 1905. *The dissociation of a personality: a biographical study in abnormal psychology.* New York: Longman.

Quillian, M. R. 1968. Semantic memory. In *Semantic information processing,* M. Minsky (ed.), 227–70. Cambridge, Mass.: MIT Press.

Radford, J. 1974. Reflections on introspection. *Am. Psychol.* **29,** 245–50.

Radford, J. and A. Burton 1974. *Thinking: its nature and development.* London: Wiley.

Reeves, J. W. 1958. *Body and mind in western thought.* London: Penguin.

Reeves, J. W. 1965. *Thinking about thinking.* London: Secker and Warburg.

Reichenbach, H. 1938. *Experience and prediction*. Chicago: University of Chicago Press.

Reitman, W. R. 1965. *Cognition and thought: an information processing approach*. New York: Wiley.

Richardson, J. T. E. 1975. Concreteness and imageability. *Q. J. Exp. Psychol.* **27**, 235–49.

Riecken, H. W. 1962. A program for research on experiments in social psychology. In *Decisions, values and groups*, N. F. Washburne (ed.), Vol. 2, 25–41. New York: Pergamon.

Rochester, N., J. H. Holland, L. H. Haibt and W. L. Duda 1956. Test on a cell assembly theory of the action of the brain, using a large digital computer. *IRE Trans. Info. Theory* **IT-2** (3), 80–93.

Roe, A. 1953. A psychological study of eminent psychologists and anthropologists, and a comparison with biological and physical scientists. *Psychol Monogr.* **67**, whole no. 352, 1–55.

Rogers, C. R. 1951. *Client-centred therapy*. Boston: Houghton Mifflin.

Rogers, C.R. 1956. Some issues concerning the control of human behavior. *Science* **124**, 1057–66.

Rogers, C. R. 1965. *Client-centred therapy*. New York: Houghton Mifflin.

Rosenblueth, A., N. Wiener and J. Bigelow 1943. Behavior, purpose and teleology. *Phil. Sci.* **10**, 18–24.

Rosenthal, R. 1965. The volunteer subject. *Hum. Relat.* **18**, 389–406.

Rosenthal, R. 1966. *Experimenter effects in behavioral research*. New York: Appleton–Century–Crofts.

Rosenthal, R. 1967. Covert communication in the psychological experiment. *Psychol Bull.* **67**, 356–67.

Rosenthal, R. and K. L. Fode 1963. The effect of experimenter bias on the performance of the albino rat. *Behavl Sci.* **8**, 183–9.

Rosenthal, R. and L. Jacobson 1966. Teachers' expectancies: determinants of pupils' I.Q. gains. *Psychol Rep.* **19**, 115–8.

Rosenthal, R., P. Kohn, P. M. Greenfield and N. Carota 1965. Experimenters' hypothesis confirmation and mood as determinants of experimental results. *Percept. Mot. Skills* **20**, 1237–52.

Rosenthal, R. and R. L. Rosnow (eds), 1969. *Artifact in behavioral research*. New York: Academic Press.

Russell, B. 1913. On the notion of cause. *Proc. Aristotelian Soc.* 1912–13, 1–26.

Russell, B. 1921. *The analysis of mind*. London: George Allen and Unwin.

Russell, B. 1927. *The analysis of matter*. London: George Allen and Unwin.

Russell, E. S. 1945. *The directiveness of organic activities*. Cambridge: Cambridge University Press.

Rychlak, J. F. 1977. *The psychology of rigorous humanism*. New York: Wiley.

Rycroft, C. 1966. Causes and meaning. In *Psychoanalysis observed*, C. Rycroft (ed.), 7–22. London: Constable.

Ryle, G. 1949. *The concept of mind*. London: Hutchinson.

Samuel, A. L. 1959. Some studies in machine learning using the game of checkers. In *Computers and thought,* E. A. Feigenbaum and J. Feldman (eds), 71–105. New York: McGraw-Hill, 1963.

Sarason, I. G. 1965. The human reinforcer in verbal behavior research. In *Research in behavior modifications: new developments and implications,* L. Krasner and L. P. Ullman (eds), 231–43. New York: Holt, Rinehart and Winston.

Schachter, S. and J. E. Singer 1962. Cognitive, social and physiological determinants of emotional state. *Psychol Rev.* **69,** 379–99.

Schelting, A. von 1934. *Max Weber's Wissenschafteslehre.* Tübingen: Mohr.

Schlick, M. 1925. *Philosophy of nature* (transl. A. von Zeppelin). London: Greenwood Press, 1949.

Schoenfeld, W. N. and W. W. Cumming 1963. Behavior and perception. In *Psychology: a study of a science,* S. Koch (ed.), Vol. 5, 213–352. New York: McGraw-Hill.

Schrödinger, E. 1958. *Mind and matter.* Cambridge: Cambridge University Press.

Schultz, D. P. 1969. The human subject in psychological research. *Psychol Bull.* **72,** 214–28.

Schutz, A. 1932. *Der sinnhafte Aufbau der Sozialen Welt Eine Einfurhrung in die verstehende Soziologie.* Transl. as *The phenomenology of the social world.* London: Heinemann, 1972.

Scriven, M. 1960. The compleat robot: a prolegomena to androidology. In *Dimensions of mind,* S. Hook (ed.), 113–33. New York: New York University Press.

Seaborn Jones, G. 1968. *Treatment or torture.* London: Tavistock.

Sechenov, I. M. 1935. *Collected works.* Moscow: State Publishing House.

Selfridge, O. G. and U. Neisser 1963. Pattern recognition by machine. *Scient. Am.* **203** (2), 60–8.

Seligman, M. E. P. 1970. On the generality of the laws of learning. *Psychol Rev.* **77,** 406–18.

Shaffer, J. A. 1965. Recent work on the mind–body problem. *Am. Phil Q.* **2,** 81–104.

Shallice, T. 1972. Dual functions of consciousness. *Psychol Rev.* **79,** 383–93.

Shallice, T. 1978. The dominant action system: an information processing approach to consciousness. In *The stream of consciousness,* K. S. Pope and J. L. Singer (eds), 117–57. New York: Plenum Press.

Shallice, T. and E. K. Warrington 1970. Independent functioning of verbal memory stores: a neuropsychological study. *Q. J. Exp. Psychol.* **22,** 261–73.

Shapere, D. 1971. The paradigm concept. *Science* **172,** 706–9.

Shapiro, D. 1976. The effects of therapeutic conditions: positive results revisited. *Br. J. Med. Psychol.* **49,** 315–23.

Shapiro, M. B. 1961. The single case in fundamental clinical psychological research. *Br. J. Med. Psychol.* **34,** 255–62.

Sheehan, P. W. 1967. A shortened form of Betts' questionnaire upon mental imagery. *J. Clin. Psychol.* **23,** 386–9.

Sheehan, P. W. and U. Neisser 1969. Some variables affecting the vividness of imagery in recall. *Br. J. Psychol.* **60,** 71–80.

Shweder, R. A. 1977. Likeness and likelihood in everyday thought: magical thinking and everyday judgments about personality. *Curr. Anthrop.* **18,** 637–58.

Simon, H. A. 1952. A formal theory of interaction in social groups. *Am. Sociol Rev.* **17,** 202–11.

Simon, H. A. and K. Kotovsky 1963. Human acquisition of concepts for sequential patterns. *Psychol Rev.* **70,** 534–46.

Simon, H. A. and A. Newell 1956. Models: their uses and limitations. In *The state of the social sciences,* L. D. White (ed.), 66–83. Chicago: University of Chicago Press.

Skinner, B. F. 1938. *The behavior of organisms: an experimental analysis.* New York: Appleton–Century–Crofts.

Skinner, B. F. 1948. *Walden two.* New York: Macmillan.

Skinner, B. F. 1950. Are theories of learning necessary? *Psychol Rev.* **57,** 193–216.

Skinner, B. F. 1953. *Science and human behavior.* New York: Macmillan.

Skinner, B. F. 1964. Behaviorism at fifty. In *Behaviorism and phenomenology,* T. W. Wann (ed.), 79–97. Chicago: Chicago University Press.

Skinner, B. F. 1971. *Beyond freedom and dignity.* New York: Knopf.

Slovic, P. and S. Lichtenstein 1971. Comparison of Bayesian and regression approaches to the study of information processing in judgment. *Organiz. Behav. Human Perform.* **6,** 649–744.

Smart, J. J. C. 1959. Sensations and brain processes. *Phil Rev.* **68,** 141–56.

Smart, J. J. C. 1968. *Between science and philosophy.* New York: Random House.

Smart, R. 1966. Subject selection bias in psychological research. *Can. Psychol.* **7,** 115–21.

Smith, M. Brewster 1969. *Social psychology and human values.* Chicago: Aldine.

Smith, R. D. 1968. Heuristic simulation of psychological decision processes. *J. Appl. Psychol.* **52,** 325–30.

Spence, K. W. 1950. Cognitive versus S–R theories of learning. *Psychol Rev.* **57,** 159–72.

Spence, K. W. 1951. Theoretical interpretations of learning. In *Handbook of experimental psychology,* S. S. Stevens (ed.), 690–729. New York: Wiley.

Sperry, R. W. 1952. Neurology and the mind–brain problem. *Am. Scient* **40,** 291–32.

Sperry, R. W. 1964. The great cerebral commissure. *Scient. Am.* **210** (1), 42–52.

Sperry, R. W. 1966. Brain bisection and mechanisms of consciousness. In *Brain and conscious experience,* J. C. Eccles (ed.), 298–313. New York: Springer-Verlag.

Sperry, R. W. 1969. A modified concept of consciousness. *Psychol Rev.* **76,** 532–6.

Sperry, R. W. 1974. Lateral specialization in the surgically separated hemispheres. In *Neurosciences: third study program,* F. O. Schmitt and F. Worden (eds), 5–19. Cambridge, Mass.: MIT Press.

Spiegelberg, H. 1971. *The phenomenological movement: a historical introduction,* 2nd edn. The Hague: Nijhoff.

Spinoza, B. de 1677. *Ethics* (transl. A. Boyle). London: Dent, 1959.

Stebbing, S. 1937. *Philosophy and the physicists.* London: Methuen.

Stephenson, W. 1953. *The study of behavior.* Chicago: University of Chicago Press.

Still, A. 1979. Perception and representation. In *Philosophical problems in psychology,* N. Bolton (ed.), 135–57. London: Methuen.

Stolorow, R. D. and G. E. Atwood 1979. *Faces in a cloud: subjectivity in personality theory.* New York: Aronson.

Storms, M. D. and R. E. Nisbett 1970. Insomnia and the attribution process. *J. Pers. Soc. Psychol.* **2,** 319–28.

Stoyva, J. and J. Kamiya 1968. Electrophysiological studies of dreaming as the prototype of a new strategy in the study of consciousness. *Psychol Rev.* **75,** 192–205.

Stretch, R. 1966. Operant conditioning in the study of animal behaviour. In *New horizons in psychology,* B. M. Foss (ed.), 287–304. London: Penguin.

Stromeyer, C. F. and J. Psotka 1970. The detailed texture of eidetic images. *Nature* **225,** 346–9.

Suppes, P. 1969. Stimulus–response theories of finite automata. *J. Math. Psychol.* **6,** 327–55.

Sussman, G. J. 1975. *A computer model of skill acquisition.* New York: American Elsevier.

Sutherland, N. S. 1959. Motives as explanations. *Mind* **68,** 145–59.

Sutherland, N. S. 1970. Is the brain a physical system? In *Explanation in the behavioural sciences,* R. Borger and F. Cioffi (eds), 97–122. Cambridge: Cambridge University Press.

Sutherland, N. S. 1974. Computer simulation of brain function. In *Philosophy of psychology,* S. C. Brown (ed.), 259–68. London: Macmillan.

Sutherland, N. S. and N. Mackintosh 1971. *Mechanisms of animal discrimination learning.* London: Academic Press.

Tart, C. T. (ed.) 1969. *Altered states of consciousness.* New York: Wiley.

Taub, E., S. J. Ellman and A. J. Berman 1966. Deafferentation in monkeys: effect on conditioned grasp response. *Science* **151,** 593–4.

Taylor, C. 1964. *The explanation of behaviour.* London: Routledge and Kegan Paul.

Taylor, C. W. and F. Barron 1963. *Scientific creativity: its recognition and development.* New York: Wiley.

Taylor, W. K. 1959. Pattern recognition by means of automatic analogue apparatus. *Proc. Inst. Elect. Engrs* **106** (Part B), 198–204.

Thigpen, C. H. and H. M. Cleckley 1957. *The three faces of Eve.* London: Secker and Warburg.

Thinès, G. 1977. *Phenomenology and the science of behaviour.* London: George Allen and Unwin.

Thomas, S. N. 1978. *The formal mechanics of mind.* Ithaca: Cornell.

Thorndike, E. L. 1911. *Animal intelligence: experimental studies.* New York: Macmillan.

Thorndike, E. L. 1935. *The psychology of wants, interests and attitudes.* New York: Appleton–Century–Crofts.

Thorndike, R. L. 1968. Review of 'Pygmalion in the Classroom'. *Am. Educ. Res. J.* **5**, 708–11.

Titchener, E. B. 1899. *An outline of psychology.* New York: Macmillan.

Tolman, E. C. 1925. Behaviorism and purpose. *J. Phil.* **22**, 36–41.

Tolman, E. C. 1932. *Purposive behavior in animals and men.* New York: Appleton–Century–Crofts.

Toulmin, S. 1970. Reasons and causes. In *Explanation in the behavioural sciences,* R. Borger and F. Cioffi (eds), 1–26. Cambridge: Cambridge University Press.

Turing, A. M. 1950. Computing machinery and intelligence. *Mind* **59**, 433–60.

Uhr, L. and C. Vossler 1961. Recognition of speech by a computer program that was written to simulate a model for human visual pattern recognition. *J. Acoust. Soc. Am.* **33**, 1426.

Uhr, L., C. Vossler and J. Uleman 1962. Pattern recognition over distortions by human subjects and a computer model of human form perception. *J. Exp. Psychol.* **63**, 227–34.

Underwood, B. J. 1963. Stimulus selection in verbal learning. In *Verbal learning and behavior,* C. N. Cofer and B. S. Musgrave (eds), 33–75. New York: McGraw-Hill.

Valentine, E. R. 1978. Perchings and flights: introspection. In *Thinking in perspective,* A. Burton and J. Radford (eds), 1–22. London: Methuen.

Valentine, J. D. 1982. Towards a physics of consciousness. *Psychoenergetics* **4**, 257–74.

Valins, S. 1966. Cognitive effects of false heart-rate feedback. *J. Pers. Soc. Psychol.* **4**, 400–8.

Vaughan, C. J. 1964. *The development and use of an operant technique to provide evidence for visual imagery in the rhesus monkey under 'sensory deprivation'.* Unpubl. doctoral dissert., University of Pittsburgh (cited in Stoyva & Kamiya 1968).

Wallach, H., D. N. O'Connell and U. Neisser 1953. The memory effect of visual perception of three-dimensional form. *J. Exp. Psychol.* **45**, 360–8.

Walter, W. Grey 1953. *The living brain.* London: Duckworth.

Wann, T. W. (ed.) 1964. *Behaviorism and phenomenology: contrasting bases for modern psychology.* Chicago: University of Chicago Press.

Warren, N. 1971. Is a scientific revolution taking place in psychology? *Sci. Stud.* **1**, 407–13.

Warren, R. B. 1948. An attempt at perspective. *Proc. Am. Phil Soc.* **92**, 271–81.

Wason, P. C. 1960. On the failure to eliminate hypotheses in a conceptual task. *Q. J. Exp. Psychol.* **12**, 129–40.

Wason, P. C. and J. St B. T. Evans 1975. Dual processes in reasoning. *Cognition* **3**, 141–54.

Wason, P. C. and P. N. Johnson-Laird 1972. *Psychology of reasoning: structure and content.* London: Batsford.

Watson, J. B. 1907. Kinaesthetic and organic sensations: their role in the reactions of the white rat to the maze. *Psychol Rev.* **8**, Monogr. Suppl., whole no. 33, 1–100.

Watson, J. B. 1914. *Behavior: an introduction to comparative psychology.* New York: Holt.

Watson, R. I. and D. T. Campbell (eds) 1963. *History, psychology and science: selected papers by Edwin G. Boring.* New York: Wiley.

Weisen, A. 1965. *Differential reinforcing effects of onset and offset of stimulation on the operant behavior of normals, neurotics and psychopaths.* Unpubl. Ph.D. thesis, University of Florida (cited in Eysenck, 1966).

Weiskrantz, L., E. K. Warrington, M. D. Sanders and J. Marshall 1974. Visual capacity in the hemianopic field following restricted occipital ablation. *Brain* **97**, 709–28.

Wertheimer, M. 1972. *Fundamental issues in psychology.* New York: Holt, Rinehart and Winston.

Whyte, L. L. 1960. *The unconscious before Freud.* New York: Basic Books.

Whytt, R. 1751. *An essay on the vital and other involuntary motions of animals.* Edinburgh: Hamilton, Balfour and Neill.

Wiener, N. 1948. *Cybernetics or control and communication in the animal and the machine.* London: Wiley.

Wiggins, J. S., K. E. Renner, G. L. Clore and R. T. Rose 1971. *The psychology of personality.* Reading, Mass.: Addison-Wesley.

Wilding, J. M. 1978. Bits and spaces: computer simulation. In *Thinking in perspective,* A. Burton and J. Radford (eds), 159–80. London: Methuen.

Winch, P. 1958. *The idea of a social science and its relation to philosophy.* London: Routledge and Kegan Paul.

Wittgenstein, L. 1953. *Philosophical investigations.* Oxford: Blackwell.

Wolpert, E. A. 1960. Studies in psychophysiology of dreams. II An electromyographic study of dreaming. *Archs Gen. Psychiat.* **2**, 231–41.

Woodworth, R. S. 1906. Imageless thought. *J. Phil Psychol. Scient. Meth.* **3**, 701–8.

Woodworth, R. S. 1918. *Dynamic psychology.* New York: Columbia University Press.

Woodworth, R. S. and H. Schlosberg 1954. *Experimental psychology,* 3rd edn. London: Methuen.

Wooldridge, D. E. 1963. *The machinery of the brain.* New York: McGraw-Hill.

Wundt, W. 1862. *Beiträge zur Theorie der Sinneswahrnemung.* Leipzig.

Wyckoff, L. B. Jr. 1952. The role of observing responses in discrimination learning. *Psychol Rev.* **59**, 431–42.

Young, J. Z. 1951. *Doubt and certainty in science: a biologist's reflections on the brain.* Oxford: Clarendon Press.

Ziehen, T. 1898. *Leitfaden der physiologischen psychologie,* 4th edn. Jena: Fischer.

Zobrist, A. and F. Carlson 1973. An advice-taking chess computer. *Scient. Am.* **228** (6), 92–105.

Index